Antitrust and the Formation of the Postwar World

COLUMBIA STUDIES IN CONTEMPORARY AMERICAN HISTORY

COLUMBIA STUDIES IN CONTEMPORARY AMERICAN HISTORY
Alan Brinkley, General Editor

Lawrence S. Wittner, *Rebels Against War: The American Peace Movement, 1941–1960*   1969
Davis R. B. Ross, *Preparing for Ulysses: Politics and Veterans During World War II*   1969
John Lewis Gaddis, *The United States and the Origins of the Cold War, 1941–1947*   1972
George C. Herring, Jr., *Aid to Russia, 1941–1946: Strategy, Diplomacy, the Origins of the Cold War*   1973
Alonzo L. Hamby, *Beyond the New Deal: Harry S. Truman and American Liberalism*   1973
Richard M. Fried, *Men Against McCarthy*   1976
Steven F. Lawson, *Black Ballots: Voting Rights in the South, 1944–1969*   1976
Carl M. Brauer, *John F. Kennedy and the Second Reconstruction*   1977
Maeva Marcus, *Truman and the Steel Seizure Case: The Limits of Presidential Power*   1977
Morton Sosna, *In Search of the Silent South: Southern Liberals and the Race Issue*   1977
Robert M. Collins, *The Business Response to Keynes, 1929–1964*   1981
Robert M. Hathaway, *Ambiguous Partnership: Britain and America, 1944–1947*   1981
Leonard Dinnerstein, *America and the Survivors of the Holocaust*   1982
Lawrence S. Wittner, *American Intervention in Greece, 1943–1949*   1982
Nancy Bernkopf Tucker, *Patterns in the Dust: Chinese-American Relations and the Recognition Controversy, 1949–1950*   1983
Catherine A. Barnes, *Journey from Jim Crow: The Desegregation of Southern Transit*   1983
Steven F. Lawson, *In Pursuit of Power: Southern Blacks and Electoral Politics, 1965–1982*   1985
David R. Colburn, *Racial Change and Community Crisis: St. Augustine, Florida, 1877–1980*   1985
Henry William Brands, *Cold Warriors: Eisenhower's Generation and the Making of American Foreign Policy*   1988
Marc S. Gallicchio, *The Cold War Begins in Asia: American East Asian Policy and the Fall of the Japanese Empire.* 1988
Melanie Billings-Yun, *Decision Against War: Eisenhower and Dien Bien Phu*   1988
Walter L. Hixson, *George F. Kennan: Cold War Iconoclast*   1989
Robert D. Schulzinger, *Henry Kissinger: Doctor of Diplomacy*   1989
Henry William Brands, *The Specter of Neutralism: The United States and the Emergence of the Third World, 1947–1960*   1989
Mitchell K. Hall, *Because of Their Faith: CALCAV and Religious Opposition to the Vietnam War*   1990
David L. Anderson, *Trapped By Success: The Eisenhower Administration and Vietnam, 1953–1961*   1991
Steven M. Gillon, *The Democrats' Dilemma: Walter F. Mondale and the Liberal Legacy* 1992
Wyatt C. Wells, *Economist in an Uncertain World: Arthur F. Burns and the Federal Reserve, 1970–1978*   1994
Stuart Svonkin, *Jews Against Prejudice: American Jews and the Fight for Civil Liberties*   1997
Doug Rossinow, *The Politics of Authenticity: Liberalism, Christianity, and the New Left in America*   1998
Campbell Craig, *Destroying the Village: Eisenhower and Thermonuclear War*   1998
Brett Gary, *The Nervous Liberals: Propaganda Anxieties from World War I to the Cold War*   1999
Andrea Friedman, *Prurient Interests: Gender, Democracy, and Obscenity in New York City: 1909–1945*   2000
Eric Rauchway, *The Refuge of Affections: Family and American Reform Politics, 1900–1920*   2000
Robert C. Cottrell, *Roger Nash Baldwin and the American Civil Liberties Union*   2000

Antitrust and the Formation of the Postwar World

Wyatt Wells

COLUMBIA UNIVERSITY PRESS   NEW YORK

COLUMBIA UNIVERSITY PRESS
Publishers Since 1893
New York   Chichester, West Sussex
Copyright © 2002 Columbia University Press

Library of Congress Cataloging-in-Publication Data

Wells, Wyatt C.
   Antitrust and the formation of the postwar world /
Wyatt Wells.
       p. cm.—(Columbia studies in contemporary
American history series)
   Includes bibliographical references (p.) and index.
   ISBN 0–231–12398–1 (acid-free paper)
   1. Antitrust law—United States—History. 2. Conflict
of laws—Antitrust law—History. 3. Competition,
Unfair—History. 4. Cartels—History.   I. Title.
II. Columbia studies in contemporary American
history.
   KF1652 .W45 2001
   343.73'0721—dc21
                                        2001032520

⊗

Columbia University Press books are printed
on permanent and durable acid-free paper.
Printed in the United States of America

c   10 9 8 7 6 5 4 3 2 1

For my parents, Charles and Ann,
and for my wife, Barbara

Contents

Preface

The inspiration for this book came from W. J. Reader's *Imperial Chemical Industries: A History*, which I first read in graduate school. Among other matters, these volumes chronicle the U.S. government's antitrust suit against Imperial Chemical Industries and DuPont in 1944, at the height of World War II. The strangeness of the case struck me. DuPont and ICI were two of the Allies' chief munitions suppliers; ICI did no business in the United States; and the arrangements in question involved not war production but contracts about which Washington had known for years. Several years later, while teaching a course on World War II, I took up the matter again. I thought to produce an article on this intriguing episode, but it soon became clear that the issues went well beyond one antitrust case and, indeed, involved the basic shape of the world economy after 1945. Seven years of work and countless revisions and reappraisals later, the result is *Antitrust and the Formation of the Postwar World*.

Many people and institutions contributed to this book. At different times I have received valuable advice from Paul Conkin, Otis Graham, Dewey Grantham, David Hoth, William Leuchtenburg, Thomas McCraw, David Moss, Huw Pill, Bruce Scott, Debora Spar, Richard Vietor, Ann Wells, Harwell Wells, and Louis Wells. The staff of Columbia University Press and its readers also made many wise suggestions. Liza and Nathaniel Chapman and Ellen and Swift Martin were sources of bottomless hospitality while I conducted research. The Franklin D. Roosevelt Library, the Harry S. Truman Presidential Library, the Hagley Museum and Library, the American Heritage Center at the University of Wyoming, and Auburn University Montgomery's Grant-in-Aid program all helped finance my research. I wrote much of this book while the Newcomen Fellow at the Harvard Business School in 1996 and 1997. The staffs of the Hagley Library, the American Heritage Center, and the Truman and Roosevelt Libraries, as well as of the National Archives, the Library of Congress, and the Public Records Office, all skillfully guided me through their collections. Finally, I would like to thank my family, friends, and colleagues who have tolerated my obsession with cartels, antitrust, and related matters over the past seven years.

Wyatt Wells
Montgomery, Alabama

Antitrust and the Formation of the Postwar World

Introduction

In the wake of World War II, the United States sought to impose its antitrust tradition on the rest of the world. Before the war, businesses operating across national borders had lived with a basic contradiction: the laws of most industrial countries tolerated and even encouraged cartels, whereas the statutes of the United States, the world's largest economy, banned them. Most cartels finessed the issue, making arrangements with U.S. companies that ventured abroad, agreements that exploited loopholes in the American antitrust statutes. Still, the potential for conflict always existed.

Antitrust, which Supreme Court Justice Abe Fortas once described as a "social religion," had a hallowed place in American economic and political life.[1] The antitrust laws were a reaction to the growth of big business in the late nineteenth century, a development that most Americans viewed ambiguously. They respected the efficiency of these organizations but feared their economic and political power. The antitrust laws, as they evolved in the early twentieth century, sought to preserve the advantages of big business while eliminating the abuses. They banned collusion among competing firms—cartels—and other "unfair" business tactics that large firms used to gouge consumers and destroy competitors. But these laws imposed no limits on the growth of companies that exploited economies of scale and scope to deliver products more efficiently than rivals.[2]

Business developed differently in other industrial countries. European firms often cooperated in cartels that set prices and allocated markets, and governments frequently supported these efforts. In time, many cartels reached across national borders. By setting minimum prices, they protected small firms against larger competitors, and by stabilizing markets, they kept the overall economy stable. More broadly, their supporters contended that cartels, by replacing "every man for himself" competition with cooperation for the common good, raised economic life to a higher moral plane.

Until World War II, Americans paid relatively little attention to foreign cartels. The conflict, however, focused attention on conditions abroad even as it catapulted the United States into a position of unprecedented power. A relatively small group associated with the Antitrust Division of the Justice Department took advantage of the country's new interest in foreign affairs and its enhanced position in the world to attack foreign cartels. This group had an almost mystical faith in the virtues of antitrust and often attributed Europe's political failures—the world wars, Nazism—to the continent's lack of such a tradition. Self-interest played a part as well. The war had marginalized antitrust enforcement, and the successful pursuit of antitrust abroad offered its advocates a way back to power in Washington.

The attack on cartels proceeded without reference to conditions abroad. American firms enjoyed a huge domestic market, a stable currency, and a political system conditioned by democracy and the rule of law. They could afford to compete, and by competing became more efficient. The situation in most other industrial countries was quite different. Domestic markets were small, currencies unstable, exports limited by a host of trade restrictions, and the political future uncertain. Firms, worried about survival, had good reason to cling together in cartels.

The successful export of antitrust depended on economic developments abroad. After 1945, the nations of western Europe integrated their markets, stabilized their currencies, and built or reinforced democratic governments. In this context, companies could afford the dangers of competition, and most European governments heeded urging from Washington and enacted antitrust statutes roughly comparable to American law. Yet in the absence of favorable conditions—for example in Japan—antitrust foundered.

The story of the export of antitrust still resonates. As a brief filed in the spring of 2000 in the Microsoft antitrust case noted, "International prohibitions against anti-competitive commercial activity have become so prevalent that they must be deemed to have risen to the level of the laws of nations."[3] Today antitrust law shapes the policy of almost every large company, no matter where headquartered. In the first half of 2000, authorities in Europe blocked the mergers of MCI/WorldCom and Sprint, American telecommunication firms; General Electric and Honeywell, U.S. aerospace companies; and aluminum producers Alcan of Canada, Pechiney of France, and Alusuisse of Switzerland. American software producer Microsoft found itself the object not only of an antitrust suit by the U.S. government but also of investigations for monopolistic practices by other countries. This was not the result of impersonal economic or political forces but a consequence of the efforts of a relatively small group of Americans working in the 1940s and early 1950s. Yet this group's success ultimately depended on general economic and political conditions, conditions that in the twenty-first century still dictate the possibilities and limits of antitrust.

1   The Cartel Ideal

In the fifty years before World War II, the world backed away from the idea that economic competition necessarily promoted the common good. The retreat, although gradual at first, became headlong with the outbreak of World War I in 1914. Among the chief manifestations of this trend was the expansion of cartels, which played an ever-growing role in domestic and international trade and by 1939 had become a major factor in the world economy.

Cartels in Theory

Between the world wars, business executives, government officials, and intellectuals increasingly argued that competing firms ought to work together in cartels, cooperating to stabilize markets and plan for the future. These organizations would ideally replace the "every man for himself" ethos of competition with cooperation for the common good and would cover not only national but international markets.

Cartels, strictly defined, are formal agreements among independent firms to restrict competition. Cartels usually set prices, allocate markets, and provide for ongoing consultation among signatories. These organizations are commonly the product of hard times, created when industries face excess capacity or falling demand; however, cartels created during economic downturns often survive after the return of prosperity either out of habit or as insurance against future difficulties.

Although collusion among businesses is no doubt as old as trade itself,[1] cartels did not appear in their modern form until the last quarter of the nineteenth century. At that time, prices for almost all goods were falling sharply throughout the world, and firms in many countries organized cartels to resist the drop.[2] The tendency was perhaps strongest in Germany, where, as one historian put it, "there was no Smithian belief in an invisible hand, guiding individual economic actions so that their total sum coincides with the best national interest. The optimal allocation of resources was a moral matter as much as a technical one."[3] In 1897, the German Imperial Court ruled, "If prices continue to remain so low that economic ruin threatens entrepreneurs, their union [in cartels] appears not merely as a rightful exercise of self-preservation, but rather as a measure of serving the interests of the whole as well."[4] Germans had no monopoly on enthusiasm for cartels, however, and before 1914, every industrial country had at least a few.

Some cases of these organizations spanned national borders. Many scholars have argued that, at least initially, nationalism held cartels together—firms cooperated at home to compete more effectively abroad.[5] Yet the logic that drove competitors within a national market to organize cartels also applied to companies operating internationally. When strong firms confronted one another across national boundaries, they often decided to cooperate rather than engage in costly and, quite likely, inconclusive economic warfare. Before 1914, effective international cartels existed in the steel rail (for railways), explosive, and synthetic alkali industries, among other sectors.[6]

Between the world wars, economic and political conditions pushed an unprecedented number of firms into international cartels.[7] In the early 1920s, all the industrial countries suffered from some combination of high inflation and severe recession, and the 1930s were remarkable chiefly for the Great Depression, which crippled the world economy. Even the prosperity of the late 1920s was uneven. The rapid growth of firms making new products like automobiles, radios, and rayon buoyed most economies, but older industries such as railroads, shipbuilding, textiles, and coal mining were depressed, as was agriculture as a whole; workers and companies in those fields did not share in the general abundance. In Britain, for instance, unemployment never fell much below 10 percent during the late 1920s, largely because of depressed conditions in older sectors.[8]

Many of these difficulties originated during World War I, which had wrecked the economic equilibrium of the early twentieth century. During that conflict, many industries, responding to military demand, had expanded capacity far beyond what peacetime markets could absorb. This problem was particularly severe in "heavy industries" such as metals, machinery, and chemicals. The war had also choked off foreign trade and disrupted established channels of exchange. The British blockade had isolated German firms producing chemicals, electrical machinery, and steel from their overseas export markets, and during the four years of fighting, new firms located in Allied or neutral countries had filled the void. With peace, the Germans were determined to recapture lost markets. The interlopers, often backed by their governments, were determined to hold on—a situation that promised savage competition. Nor was the German experience unique. Because of shortages of shipping, raw materials, and manpower, Britain's huge textile industry lost many of its foreign markets during the war, mainly to Japanese and Indian producers. After 1918, British firms tried to regain lost sales, but they generally failed, leaving idle the textile mills that had stopped work during the war. These distortions all entailed overproduction, which cartels could address by restricting output and allocating markets.

The Great War also destabilized currencies. Before 1914, international finance revolved around the gold standard. In the industrial countries, governments stood ready to redeem their currency in gold on demand at a fixed rate, which allowed for easy conversion of the money of one nation into that of another. With the uncertainties of foreign exchange eliminated, international trade and investment were much simpler. The exigencies of military finance quickly wrecked the system. Unable to pay the staggering expense of war either by raising taxes or by conventional borrowing, governments began to print money, unleashing inflation that soon forced them to sever the link between their currencies and gold. After 1918, the heavy reparations bill imposed on Germany and the tangle of war debts among the victorious Allies put a strain on financial exchanges that made resumption of the gold standard difficult at best. A concerted effort to stabilize currencies did provide a few years of order in the late 1920s, but the Depression soon sabotaged the effort. Severe deflation and financial panics forced governments to abandon fixed exchange rates. Instead, they began to manipulate their currencies to further recovery, usually at the expense of their trading partners. The most common tactic was devaluation, which, by cheapening exports and raising the price of imports, improved a country's competitive position. Some governments went further. In the midst of crisis, authorities in several nations, particularly in central Europe, imposed currency controls that, when the panic was over, they retained and managed shamelessly for their own ends. The Nazi regime in Germany was particularly notorious for not allowing foreign firms to repatriate profits, forcing them to reinvest the money in Germany.[9]

The situation vastly increased the risks associated with foreign trade. Even if customers paid their bills on time and in full, no firm could be sure exactly what the money it received abroad might be worth at home, or if it could repatriate its earnings at all. A devaluation could suddenly change a profitable export market into an unremunerative one and ruin the work of years. The very possibility of financial instability made planning difficult. Such uncertainty inclined firms to attempt to reduce risks in other areas, something effective cartels might accomplish.

The treaties ending the Great War added other difficulties. The Treaty of Versailles transferred Alsace-Lorraine from Germany to France, and with it much of Germany's pig iron capacity. Previously the output of Alsace-Lorraine's blast furnaces had gone to rolling mills in the Ruhr Valley, but after 1919 an international border stood in the way. Logically, some sort of cooperative arrangement between France and Germany would have been in order, but war-inspired bitterness and economic chaos in Germany after 1918 made such a solution impossible. Instead, the Germans built new blast furnaces and the French new rolling mills, further exacerbating the over-supply of steel.[10] Conditions in eastern Europe were worse. There a group of small states emerged in what had been the Austro-Hungarian Empire and the western reaches of the Russian Empire, and each of these countries was intent on building up its own industry, preferably at the expense of its neighbors. In Russia itself, the Bolshevik regime tightly controlled foreign trade. Producers who before 1918 had sold throughout the old empires found themselves excluded from their traditional markets by prohibitive tariffs and other restrictions.

Almost every nation raised protective barriers during the 1920s and 1930s, putting further strain on a system of international trade already severely damaged by war. Even Britain abandoned its long-standing policy of free trade and imposed a protective tariff. To a large degree, this reflected hard times. Many governments had traditionally increased tariffs during downturns to insulate domestic producers from foreign competition; the unprecedented difficulties of the interwar years encouraged nations to raise barriers to new highs. The experience of the Great War had also strengthened the protective impulse. The conflict had demonstrated unambiguously the importance of manufacturing to national defense; military considerations led government after government to protect "strategic" industries, a tendency that became

particularly strong in the 1930s, as the ambitions of Germany, Italy, and
Japan made war seem ever more likely. One example of the consequences
was the glut in synthetic nitrates throughout the 1930s. Though used chiefly
in fertilizers, nitrates were an indispensable ingredient for military explosives,
a fact that led almost every European country to use tariffs and subsidies to
protect its own suppliers regardless of overall market conditions.[11]

The contraction of foreign markets encouraged exporters from different
countries to join together. In part, they hoped to avoid destructive competition for shrinking opportunities. Perhaps even more important, they wanted
to negotiate market-sharing arrangements with domestic producers in importing countries, thereby forestalling protectionist measures that might shut
out foreign sellers altogether. The steel cartel negotiated agreements with
producers in importing countries to apportion local markets, and the nitrates
cartel not only fashioned such accords but actually established a fund to pay
national competitors to adhere to them.[12]

The world's governments adopted no common program to stabilize currencies, reduce protection, or otherwise revive the international economy.
To a degree, the failure reflected the distrust carried over from World War
I and was exacerbated in the 1930s by the rise of fascist regimes bent on
national aggrandizement. Perhaps even more important, however, leadership was lacking. Though Britain had traditionally coordinated efforts to
keep international trade and finance stable and growing, the war had weakened the United Kingdom. The effort to reestablish the value of sterling and
pay off war debts to the United States absorbed British attention and wealth
throughout the 1920s, and the Depression forced the abandonment of even
these limited goals in 1931.

Only the United States had the resources to take Britain's place, but its
people were reluctant. Unlike subjects of the United Kingdom, who for
centuries had seen international trade as the avenue to prosperity, Americans
had traditionally looked inward to the development of their own vast nation.
Many Americans believed that their country could effectively isolate itself
from economic turmoil abroad. Such opinions were not universal: American
agriculture depended heavily on foreign markets, and many industrial firms
and banks had substantial interests in other countries. Nevertheless, isola-
tionist sentiments conditioned Washington's forays abroad. It consistently
refused to write off debts that its Allies had incurred during World War I. In
1924, the U.S. government brokered an agreement that stabilized German
finances. Subsequently, American bankers extended credits to European

governments and businesses to facilitate reconstruction. But the United States also raised tariffs in 1921 and 1922, despite a large trade surplus, making it difficult for the rest of the world to earn the dollars needed to service debts to the United States.[13] In 1931, as the Depression deepened, President Herbert Hoover placed a moratorium on the payment of inter-governmental obligations, effectively suspending the problems of German reparations and Allied war debts. Yet at the same time, Hoover signed the notorious Hawley-Smoot tariff, which raised duties still higher, often to pro-hibitive levels.

The first administration of Franklin Roosevelt did no better. Its only major initiative in the international sphere was to wreck the London Economic Conference, which had convened to stabilize the world's currencies. The president feared that it might conflict with his plans for domestic reform, which included devaluation and inflation. The series of bilateral trade agreements subsequently negotiated by Secretary of State Cordell Hull, though useful, did not constitute a general solution to the problems of the inter-national economy. Although not unmindful of problems abroad, the United States refused to make substantial sacrifices—tariff reductions or financial aid—to revive foreign economies.[14]

International cartels filled part of the vacuum left by government inac-tion. The world's economic problems were beyond the power of any indi-vidual firm or even most national cartels. Yet before 1914, international cartels had operated successfully in several lines of business—steel rails, synthetic alkali, explosives—setting prices and allocating markets. In the 1920s and 1930s, many businessmen seized on this proven technique to impose order on their industries and to insulate themselves, as much as possible, from the risks of operating in a disturbed world.

The enthusiasm for cartels reflected more than the desire of business to protect itself from hard times, however. Many in academia and government believed that cartels were a "higher" form of economic organization that replaced the brutal ethos of competition with a system of cooperation. This sentiment gained strength from the vogue for economic planning between the world wars. As one historian of the New Deal noted, "That humanity could and must manipulate its social as well as its natural environment, and do so rationally and collectively, had been the central message of leading social theorists since the late nineteenth century."[15] Still, fears of centralized regimentation tempered much of the enthusiasm for planning. The words of one commentator on the American business scene in 1931 applied throughout the industrial world: "Moderate and liberal opinion . . . believes in a *decentralized* method of voluntary agreement for cooperation using an absolute minimum of regulation, politics, or coercion."[16]

Cartels met these criteria. As one expert put it, they promised to be "efficient instruments for superseding the 'anarchical' state of competition within the limits of the capitalist economy, and for safeguarding small and middle-sized enterprises against being overwhelmed by the competitive power of large concerns. They are, moreover, regarded by some of their supporters as important means of smoothing out the ups and downs of general business conditions."[17] In a speech before the House of Lords in 1944, Lord Harry McGowan, the chairman of Imperial Chemical Industries (ICI) of Britain, stated, "Such agreements [cartels] can lead to a more ordered organization of production and can check wasteful and excessive competition. They can help to stabilize prices at a reasonable level. . . . They can lead to a rapid improvement in techniques and a reduction in cost, which in turn, with enlightened administration of industry, can provide a basis of lower prices to consumers. They can spread the benefits of inventions from one country to another by exchanging research results, by the cross-licensing of patents, and by the provision of important 'know-how' in the working of these patents."[18] Many government officials hoped that cartels would coordinate the modernization of chaotic and often antiquated industries. Stanley Baldwin, the prime minister of Great Britain, commented soon after his country's none-too-efficient steel makers joined the international steel cartel in 1935, "I make bold to say that in four or five years the [British] steel industry will be second to no steel industry in the whole world."[19]

Some observers even saw international cartels as the basis for a new world order, offering an institutional framework for cooperation that bypassed governments, which were often hamstrung by ancient rivalries and petty squabbling. In the 1920s, a German economist wrote that international cartels "are expected to help to bridge over the enmities created or inflamed by the War or at least to mitigate their disastrous influence upon the economy of the different nations and on the world economic order."[20] French premier Edouard Herriot argued in his book *The United States of Europe*, "The [international] cartel is a sign of progress, uniting national economies which were previously hostile."[21]

The League of Nations, though more cautious than Herriot, also endorsed cartels. The authors of the final report of the league's World Economic Conference of 1927 noted that "in certain branches of production they [cartels] can—subject to certain conditions and reservations—on the one hand, secure a more methodical organization of production and a reduction in costs by means of a better utilization of existing equipment, the development on more suitable lines of new plant, and a more rational grouping of undertakings, and, on the other hand, act as a check on economic competition and the evils resulting from the fluctuation in industrial activity." The report did, however, warn that cartels might exploit consumers. It went on: "They cannot be regarded as a form of organization which could by itself alone remove the causes of the troubles from which the economic life of the world and particularly of Europe is suffering."[22]

Between the world wars, most governments encouraged the growth of cartels. In some countries these organizations had always enjoyed support, but in other nations this attitude represented a substantial change. Before 1914, British courts had refused to enforce cartel accords, permitting companies both to sign agreements and to break them at will. Starting in the 1920s, the courts began to enforce the "reasonable" provisions of cartel accords—and in practice, judges found few provisions unreasonable. The new approach brought British law close to that of Germany, where cartel agreements had the force of contracts. Elected authorities in Britain also abandoned laissez-faire and encouraged depressed industries like textiles and steel to organize "rationalization" cartels to shut obsolete plants and coordinate pricing and sales.[23] Governments around the world actually organized some international cartels themselves, most notably for sugar, rubber, and wheat.[24] As one historian wrote, "In the interwar period general acceptance of cartels was very high; such views were shared throughout the world."[25]

The Düsseldorf Agreement of 1939 exemplified the hopes invested in international cartels as well as their limits. The accord, signed on March 16 in Düsseldorf by the German Reichsgruppe Industrie and the Federation of British Industry, declared, "It is essential to replace destructive competition wherever it may be found by constructive cooperation, designed to foster the expansion of world trade." To this end, "the two organizations have agreed to use their best endeavors to promote and foster negotiations between individual industries in their respective countries." The agreement called for the creation of a joint standing committee to encourage and mediate cartel talks.[26] The participants no doubt hoped to lay the foundation for a system of international economic cooperation. Unfortunately, the German government had no interest in such plans. On March 16, Adolf Hitler sent the German Army to occupy what remained of Czechoslovakia, heightening international tensions and leading the British to renounce the Düsseldorf accord. Six months, later Britain and Germany were at war.[27]

Nevertheless, an air of inevitability surrounded the growth of cartels. Alfred Mond, Lord Melchert, the first chairman of Imperial Chemical, spoke for many when he said, "The trend of all modern industries is towards greater units, greater coordination for more effective use of resources. . . . One of the main consequences is the creation of inter-relations among industries which most seriously affect the economic policies of nations."[28]

International Cartels in Practice

Between the world wars, many industries organized effective international cartels. The process was rarely easy. Each industry had unique requirements, and perhaps more important, leading participants had to develop mutual trust. Nevertheless, by 1939, international cartels were a major force in the world economy.

International cartels represented one of the most ambitious undertakings in economic history. Because cartels seek to establish cooperation among traditional rivals, their enthusiasts often liken them to treaties between nations. Certainly the difficulty of negotiating and implementing cartel accords equals that of the most complex government agreements. Bringing commercial rivals together in a system of cooperation demands great diplomatic talent. Though cartels hold out sizable advantages to participants, they also entail significant short-run costs. Cartels seek first and foremost to stabilize prices, which forces them to limit sales during downturns either by idling production or by stockpiling output. Under these conditions, member firms have a strong incentive to cheat. A company that cuts prices and expands sales while other firms restrict output and keep charges up will gain market share and earn substantial profits at the expense of its cartel partners. To be sure, this will eventually wreck the cartel, as sooner or later the other members will find out what is going on and retaliate. But firms often tolerate this. They may be under financial pressure (falling sales) and not have the luxury of planning for the long term; their managers may not trust their cartel partners and decide to strike the first blow; or firms may simply decide to seize quick profits rather than wait for incalculable benefits at some future date.[29] Yet even if a cartel does prevent cheating and stabilize the market, its success may induce outsiders to enter the business, undermining the organization.

Many economists consider cartels inherently unstable. As one textbook put it, "Collusive agreements tend to break down," largely because of the incentive to cheat.[30] The author of a scholarly article on cartels observed, "If one member cheats, the other is better off cheating than observing the quota. Since the other is better off cheating even when the one observes the quota, it appears that cheating dominates observing the quota."[31] In other words, dishonesty is the safest and therefore most likely course.

This argument ignores the success of many cartels over extended periods. The steel rail cartel lasted from the 1880s to World War II; some chemical cartels survived almost as long. Several factors explain this success. Before 1945, in Germany and several other countries, cartel agreements had the status of contracts, which meant that cheaters faced legal sanctions. Firms were also adept at cloaking domestic and even international cartels in the guise of patent agreements, the violation of which also entailed considerable legal risks. Governments often organized cartels themselves, or at least endorsed them, and few companies were willing to flaunt the desires of political authorities.

Yet cartels can endure even without the support of law. Cheating on a cartel agreement yields profit only if it proceeds undetected, because once the other cartel members learn what is going on they will retaliate. Accords often contain provisions for careful market monitoring, usually through an autonomous agency, to detect violations and permit quick action against cheaters. Such provisions encourage members to abide by their promises. As one economist put it, "Once detected, the deviations [cheating] will tend to disappear because they are no longer secret and will be matched by fellow conspirators [cartel members]."[32] Even if a firm gets away with cheating for a while, the inevitable retaliation may discourage such action in the future. The resurgence of competition will hurt everyone and re-create the situation that encouraged the formation of a cartel in the first place, which in turn may lead to the creation of a new cartel. This time, however, with the example of retaliation fresh in their minds, participants are less likely to cheat. As one economist argued, "If a market situation is repeated for an infinite number of periods, it is possible that an industry will settle at a cartel price, and the reason why each firm does not defect from the implicit cartel agreement is the future losses that it will incur when competitors retaliate."[33]

Nor do cartels inevitably attract outside challengers. Significant barriers to entry exist in many industries. Efficient production often involves economies of scale that require large capital investment, and sometimes patents cover vital technology. Such obstacles are rarely insurmountable, but they substantially increase the risks of challenging a cartel. Much depends on the cartel's policy. As one expert noted, "The more the cartel exploits its monopolistic position to exact higher prices—and thus giving a strong stimulus to new enterprises—the greater prospect there is of the latent competition becoming reality." But "they [cartels] may be used not to increase the profits of their members but to keep them from falling below a certain level—a thing which may easily happen in open competition."[34] In the latter circumstance, the incentives for outsiders to enter the industry are much weaker, often insufficient to compensate for the risk of doing so. As one economist put it, "To recognize that a cartel might collapse because it cannot control external production or detect cheating is quite different from believing that all are necessarily doomed. . . . No general prediction about the durability of cartels is justified."[35]

Effective cartels did not develop in every industry. Some industries, like textiles, contained too many producers to organize. In consumer goods industries like cigarettes, soap, and candy, firms defended themselves against the vagaries of the market by using advertising and other promotional techniques to build up brand loyalty among consumers. International cartels between the world wars generally fell into one of three broad categories: market-sharing agreements in industries dominated by a few large firms producing undifferentiated commodities; accords organized around the exchange of technology; and government-sponsored cartels.

The international steel organization, an example of the first of these three types, enjoyed perhaps greater influence and notoriety than any other cartel.[36] The largest of the heavy industries in terms of capital and labor employed as well as the value of output, steel was particularly suited to cartelization. Its products differed little from producer to producer, and all manufacturers had ready access to the most advanced technology. The efficient production of steel required substantial investment, which limited the number of firms in the business to a level where negotiations were manageable. At the same time, their substantial capitalization made steel makers particularly eager for stable prices that would allow them to pay the interest on their debts and dividends to stockholders.

Steel producers organized their first comprehensive international cartel in the 1920s. Even before 1914, national cartels such as Germany's had established themselves as leading factors in the business, and international cartels had governed specific areas like steel rails. Postwar conditions, however, involved difficulties beyond the power of these organizations. The over-

supply of steel after World War I affected all of Europe, depressing employment and prices and squeezing the profits of steel makers. In 1926, producers
in Germany, France, Belgium, Luxembourg, and the Saar organized a cartel
that consisted not of individual firms but of each country's national steel
makers' organization.[37] The cartel claimed only about one-third of world
steel capacity but accounted for approximately two-thirds of the world's steel
exports and covered many of the most efficient firms competing in international markets. Ostensibly intended to govern only exports, the cartel in
fact set output quotas for each member, levying fines on national organizations that exceeded their quotas and providing rebates to countries that
fell short. An office in Luxembourg overseen by representatives of the various
national cartels kept track of the market for steel, administering the system
of fines and rebates.

This organization did not survive the Depression. The cartel had a program beyond its capabilities. Though it aimed to control total output, the
cartel lacked the resources to monitor the activities of dozens of companies
in member countries. Moreover, it was supposed to operate through the
national bodies, but the French and Belgian steel makers' organizations
could not control their members, which violated the accord at will. The
advent of the Depression and the consequent drop in demand for steel
required the cartel to reduce output sharply to maintain prices, which it
failed to do. Instead, producers cut prices and poached customers from one
another to try and keep their works operating at capacity. By 1931, steel
makers had abandoned the cartel.

The steel cartel re-formed in 1933. Business was absolutely terrible, and
steel makers had reason to think that an effective cartel might help. The
prices of products traded in the world markets had declined precipitously:
merchant bars went from £6 a ton in 1929 to £2 in 1933, and structural
shapes and billets both dropped from £5 a ton to £2. By comparison, steel
rails, a part of the business governed by a cartel established in the 1880s,
had fallen hardly at all: from a high of £6 10s a ton in 1929, to £5 10s in
1933. Because the British government had devalued sterling by about 15
percent over this period and traders continued to calculate prices in gold
(pre-devaluation) pounds, the cash actually earned from sales had barely
changed at all.[38] The materials for constructing a cartel were also stronger.
The Belgian and French steel makers' associations now enjoyed greater control over members, thanks largely to the support of their governments and
bankers. The former desired stability in this central industry, whereas the

latter, who financed the growing deficits of steel makers, feared that without a plan for cooperation steel firms would never repay their debts. Together they forced firms to follow the dictates of the cartel.[39]

The new cartel included the same members as the old—Germany, France, Belgium, the Saar, and Luxembourg—but it combined more limited objectives with a much stronger organization. The cartel gave each group of producers exclusive rights to its home market as well as an export quota enforced by the familiar system of fines and rebates. Once again, a small staff in Luxembourg kept track of sales and administered the fines and rebates. But the general export quotas merely represented a stopgap measure. Plans called for the creation of "comptoirs," sub-cartels for each steel product such as wire rods and galvanized sheets. These would not simply set quotas for sales but, ideally, organize the export trade. The new steel organization quickly brought under its umbrella older, product-specific organizations such as that for steel rails and had by 1939 erected thirteen new comptoirs, which together dominated the world trade in steel. All the comptoirs had staffs that operated like the main organization, keeping track of sales and assessing fines and rebates. In some cases, such as the venerable steel rail cartel, the comptoir itself managed sales, taking orders and allocating them among members. Ideally, all the comptoirs would develop such capabilities, which would reduce costs by merging and rationalizing marketing networks, as well as make it very difficult for members, now shorn of their foreign outlets, to cheat. Only a few comptoirs had reached this level by 1939, however.

The steel organization expanded rapidly. British producers joined in 1935. Originally the United Kingdom had remained outside the cartel both because its national steel makers' organization was quite weak and because continental producers considered its firms inefficient and hence little threat to their plans. To the extent that the British did export, their steel went to Commonwealth markets, where it did not compete with European products. British steel makers developed a strong organization in the 1930s, however, largely because of pressure from the government and the Bank of England. By this time, the United Kingdom had become a major importer of steel, a development London used to its advantage. In early 1935, Whitehall imposed a prohibitive tariff on imported steel, designed to force the cartel to come to terms with British producers. The tactic worked. British steel makers soon signed an accord with the cartel limiting imports to Britain and granting them export quotas, after which Whitehall immediately scaled back the tariff. By this time, the cartel had already signed agreements with Polish, Czech, and Austrian producers, bringing continental Europe's major steel exporters into its fold.[40] In cases such as South Africa, where strong domestic producers existed within a major import market, the cartel negotiated accords to divide local business with these firms. Such arrangements guaranteed stable prices and market share for all while eliminating both the dangers of foreign dumping (sales at below market prices) and the threat of prohibitive tariffs imposed by national governments to defend the home industry.

Next the cartel sought the cooperation of American steel makers. Although the United States was both the largest producer and the largest consumer of steel, its market was insulated from the rest of the world. Imports and exports accounted for only 1.6 and 3.6 percent, respectively, of total U.S. output in 1936, a fairly typical year.[41] American steel makers were technically quite efficient, but high labor and transportation costs made it difficult for them to compete in world markets. They concentrated on sales at home, where in the 1920s, strong demand and a high tariff guaranteed good prices.

The Depression changed matters. Unable to run their large works at anywhere near capacity, American producers saw their unit costs escalate.[42] This both left them more vulnerable to foreign competition and led them to look to export markets as a way to occupy at least part of their idle plants. Producers on both sides of the Atlantic had good reason to negotiate. First, however, the U.S. companies had to get around the American antitrust laws, which banned cartels. They did this by working through a Webb-Pomerene company, a type of organization authorized by Congress in the Webb-Pomerene Act of 1918 that allowed U.S. firms to cooperate in export markets. According to prevailing interpretations of the law, Webb-Pomerene companies could participate in cartel accords as long as they dealt only with markets abroad.[43] American steel makers united under the aegis of a Webb-Pomerene company and began negotiations. The talks took quite a while, in part because the cartel gave priority to discussions with European producers. The two sides finally signed an agreement in 1938, granting the Americans export quotas and—though the written accord said nothing of this—limiting shipments to the United States.[44]

As far as members were concerned, the steel cartel worked well. In 1933, prices on the international market quickly rose and then stabilized for the next three years. Merchant bars and structural shapes increased from £2 a ton to £3 (50 percent), and billets went from £2 a ton to £2 16s (40 percent). Steel prices briefly went up in the world boom of 1936 and 1937 and gave back some of their gains in the subsequent recession, although they remained above their 1933 to 1936 level for the rest of the decade.[45] Moreover, as the world economy gradually improved and producers were able to use their facilities more fully, profits increased substantially.

Consumers had a more ambiguous experience. The cartel raised prices, but its partisans insisted that the organization moderated both upward and downward swings in the market. Ideally cartels were supposed to keep prices from rising too high—as well as from sinking too low—because high prices and the inordinate profits they brought attracted outside competitors who destabilized markets. The extraordinary stability of steel prices from 1934 to 1936 suggests that the steel organization did indeed pursue such a policy. As Ervin Hexner, the historian of the cartel, remarked, "It did not abuse economic power, concentrated in private hands, by creating general artificial scarcity in steel supplies, nor did it use concerted business strategy to increase its returns substantially over returns from domestic sales in steel-exporting countries."[46]

This conclusion ignored the cartel's impact on prices within members countries. Except for Belgium and Luxembourg, all the steel-making nations consumed far more steel at home than they exported. Many producers viewed foreign sales chiefly as a way to keep their plants operating at capacity and so reduce unit costs, not as a source of profits. By granting members sole rights to their home markets, the cartel allowed producers freedom to set prices for their most important customers. In some countries such as Britain, domestic prices more or less matched international ones, but in other nations, most notably Germany, they were substantially higher.

Still, partisans of cartels usually held up the steel organization as a paragon. Certainly it brought a measure of stability to the market for steel without exploiting consumers in too crass a fashion, and by 1939 it dominated most aspects of the international steel trade, effectively replacing the free market with a system of agreements. Only the outbreak of war disrupted its operations. In one area, however, the cartel fell short of the hopes of its more optimistic partisans—it failed to execute a concerted program of modernization. Some firms took advantage of the stability offered by the cartel to update their facilities and streamline their organizations, but others apparently considered the security it guaranteed an excuse for inertia. Efficiency (or the lack thereof) continued to reflect the efforts of management.

Many other industries that like steel used capital-intensive technology to turn out undifferentiated commodities organized cartels. The producers of copper, lead, aluminum, petroleum, and "heavy" chemicals such as synthetic alkali and nitrates faced chronic overcapacity that threatened ruinous competition.[47] To avoid this danger, they formed organizations that set prices and allocated markets among members, cartels that held together largely because the companies involved firmly believed that unrestrained competition would be a disaster for all.

The electric lamp cartel stood in sharp contrast to the steel organization. It regulated competition in part by restricting access to proprietary technology. One company, the American giant General Electric (GE), dominated it, bending the organization to its own purposes. The cartel was also able to coordinate policies on production and design among its members.[48]

From its formation in the 1890s, General Electric had controlled the production and sale of electric lamps in the United States. Patents provided the foundation of its authority. The antitrust laws had never applied to the technological monopolies granted by patents. In 1926, the Supreme Court had decided in a case involving GE's lightbulb cartel: "A patentee, in licensing another person to make, use, and vend [the patented article], may lawfully impose the condition that sales by the licensee shall be at prices fixed by the licensor and subject to change at his discretion."[49] At first General Electric held Thomas Edison's basic patent on the lightbulb, and although this expired in the 1890s, by 1909, the firm had acquired the rights to the tungsten filament bulb, which represented a revolutionary improvement over earlier lamps.[50]

Though it allowed other producers to make lightbulbs, General Electric put strict limits on their operations. In a 1927 agreement with its most formidable competitor, Westinghouse, General Electric imposed a system of discriminatory royalties, charging only 1 to 2 percent on sales up to 25.4421 percent of the combined sales of the two companies, but 30 percent on sales above that level,[51] making such sales unprofitable to Westinghouse. The agreement also required Westinghouse to license back to GE, free of charge or condition, any improvements it developed in electric lamps—a provision that effectively eliminated Westinghouse's incentive for research, as it could not profit from innovations.

To maintain its position, General Electric invested heavily in research, hoping to expand its technological lead. It failed to develop any great breakthroughs but did obtain patents on useful improvements like tipless bulbs, nosag filaments, and frosted bulbs, as well as on various automated machines for making lamps. General Electric hoped that these rights would allow it to maintain control of the American market even after its patent on the tungsten filament expired in the early 1930s. To further discourage potential challengers GE passed much of the savings from improved productivity on to consumers, reducing prices for bulbs about 70 percent between 1922 and 1942.[52]

World War I turned General Electric's attention abroad. Before 1914, German firms had dominated the market for lamps in Europe, and GE and Westinghouse each had broad-ranging patent agreements with the largest of these, Algemeine Elektrizitäts Gesellschaft (AEG) and Siemens, which had kept trans-Atlantic competition to a minimum. The war cut the Germans off from foreign markets and led to the rise of new competitors, strong British and French companies and, most important, the Dutch firm Philips. With the return of peace in 1918, Siemens and AEG merged their electric lamp operations into an independent company called Osram, absorbed several small German producers, and launched an export drive to recapture lost markets. This program sparked a series of fierce price wars punctuated by unsuccessful attempts to organize a cartel.

The situation alarmed General Electric. The United States absorbed about half the lightbulbs produced in the world, and GE feared that as competition on the European continent became more savage, firms there (which had their own patents) would be tempted to invade the rich American market or to license their technology to GE's competitors. At the same time, confusion in Europe offered General Electric the opportunity to re-shape the industry to its own liking. The company resorted to industrial diplomacy. As a first step it set up under the leadership of Gerard Swope a subsidiary, International General Electric (IGE), which took responsibility for all the company's foreign dealings and assumed all its holdings abroad. This put GE's foreign affairs in the hands of a group of executives assigned solely to the subject.

In 1924, IGE negotiated what became known as the Phoebus cartel for electric lamps. The agreement, which counted IGE but not its parent company as a party, reserved for each producer its home market and set quotas for exports enforced by a system of fines levied on those who exceeded the limits. It set up an independent Swiss company, Phoebus, to oversee operations, keeping track of sales and levying fines on those who oversold their quota. Financial arrangements cemented the organization. At this time GE was immensely profitable, so much so that it was able to dispense completely with bank loans.[53] In contrast, the war and subsequent inflation had deranged the finances of most of the European firms. GE already had stakes in several foreign companies; in the 1920s, it expanded the size and number of these investments. By 1930, it owned 20 percent of Osram, 10 percent of Tungsram of Hungary, 46 percent of Associated Electrical Industries of Britain, 44 percent of Compagnie des Lampes of France, 40 percent of Tokyo Electric, 17 percent of Philips, and 25 percent of AEG. It also purchased $11 million in debentures from Siemens, which after GE was probably the world's most formidable producer of electrical machinery.[54] The management of these firms welcomed General Electric's investment, and the companies retained their legal and practical independence. Yet in most cases IGE was the largest stockholder and as such enjoyed a very strong voice in the formation of overall policy.

The Phoebus cartel had an ambitious agenda. First, it stabilized prices at a fairly high level. The demand for lightbulbs was inelastic—that is, it changed little with the price of the object. Because as a rule consumers spent far more on electricity to power bulbs than on bulbs themselves, the price of electricity was the chief factor determining the demand for lamps. European producers reasoned that higher prices on bulbs would not depress sales while boosting profit margins per unit sold. General Electric particularly liked this policy, which allowed it to keep prices in the United States lower than European ones and so discourage challengers from the continent. In addition, the cartel provided for licensing technology among members, a system that earned GE substantial royalties. Finally, Phoebus pursued a far-reaching program of technical standardization. European firms had been producing electric lamps with a dizzying variety of voltage, longevity, brightness, and socket size. The cartel sought to regularize bulbs, setting up a central laboratory in Switzerland to which all members had to submit their goods. Few objected to the policy, as standardization lowered production costs as well as confusion among consumers. Another initiative, however, did not earn such universal praise. Phoebus (and in the United States, GE) systematically changed bulbs to allow them to produce more light per unit of electricity. This also cut the average life span of bulbs by about 20 percent, forcing consumers to purchase more of them. The cartel did not advertise the change, but when called to account, managers pointed out that the new bulbs provided more light per unit of power and so benefited customers. It was not clear, however, why consumers could not have chosen for themselves between the new, brighter bulbs and the old, longer-lasting ones.

In the early 1930s, competitors challenged the Phoebus cartel. The basic patent governing tungsten filaments expired, robbing GE of its most powerful weapon against rivals. The American firm still had rights to high-quality bulbs and filaments as well as automated machines for producing lamps, but new competitors circumvented these advantages. Small Japanese companies using labor-intensive methods and low-wage workers began to export bulbs throughout the world at prices well below those of the cartel. As a rule, the Japanese products were inferior, but many consumers were willing to take the chance to save money. Negotiation was not an option. The Japanese firms, which were generally quite small, numbered in the dozens— far too many to bring into the cartel. Nor was there any organization in Japan capable of speaking for lamp producers as a whole. In the United States, GE responded aggressively. It enjoyed a stronger position than Phoebus because its prices were lower, a difference that reflected in part the relative cheapness of electricity in the United States, which made electric lamps more of a mass market item than in Europe, and in part GE's desire to discourage potential challengers. As the Japanese began to make inroads, GE introduced a new, cheaper bulb in direct competition with their products that, coupled with a moderate tariff (20 percent), confined Japanese imports to less than 10 percent of the American market. The cartel did less well. Perhaps because it lacked GE's central management, Phoebus never developed a coordinated response to the Japanese challenge, and by 1939, the cartel's share of the market outside the United States had declined from almost 90 percent to 60 percent. Japan had become the world's second largest producer of lightbulbs, behind only the United States.

On the surface, the Phoebus cartel seemed a mixed success. Producers commanded high prices for well over a decade, and the cartel also imposed a measure of standardization, reducing the costs of production. Yet it attracted competition from Japanese firms that it failed to neutralize. On a deeper level, however, the cartel achieved the objectives of its organizer, General Electric, which looked to the Phoebus cartel to protect its immense American market. Throughout the interwar years, GE and its licensees produced approximately 90 percent of electric lamps sold in the United States. During this period, General Electric never made less than 20 percent on its capital invested in electric lamps, even during the worst years of the Great Depression. Viewed in this light, Phoebus was quite a success.

The Phoebus cartel provides an example of how and why firms in "high-tech" fields—electrical machinery, "fine" chemicals like dyes and drugs,[55] and optical instruments—organized cartels. Technology drove these industries, and each company wanted access to the discoveries of its competitors. The cost of inventing and bringing to market a new product could be huge.

For instance, DuPont spent $27 million to develop nylon before selling so much as a pound of it.[56] Firms sought to spread the cost of such ventures. Finally, the disruption of World War I had left some of these industries, such as dyestuffs and lightbulbs, with considerable excess capacity. Companies in these fields responded by devising complex webs of agreements that exchanged patent rights and other technical know-how and limited competition. Though rarely as lopsided as Phoebus, these accords did not treat all signatories equally. Firms with choice patents and superior research establishments usually imposed their wills on their weaker brethren. A company might force a better deal. In 1932, the German chemical giant IG Farben accorded Imperial Chemical a more prominent place in the dyestuffs cartel largely because ICI had demonstrated its ability to make important innovations in the field.[57] Such promotion did not come easily, however.

The production of raw rubber differed immensely from that of high-tech goods such as lightbulbs.[58] In the 1920s and 1930s, the makers of tires and other rubber goods used natural latex tapped from rubber trees grown largely on hundreds of plantations scattered throughout Southeast Asia. Though the automobile boom provided an expanding market for tires and, therefore, rubber, planters suffered from severe cycles of boom and bust. Rubber trees only begin to produce latex about six years after first planted, which prevented producers from rapidly adjusting supply to demand. A sudden surge in purchases always fell on a fixed number of trees, and when new output finally did become available, there was no guarantee of buyers. As a result, prices gyrated wildly.

Falling prices after World War I inspired the first rubber cartel. The maturation of trees planted during the initial advance in wartime demand combined with the postwar recession to drive rubber prices down from $.487 a pound in 1919 to $.163 in 1921.[59] This situation alarmed not only planters but also the British government, whose colonies produced about 72 percent of the world's rubber, whose subjects (250,000 of them) had investments in rubber plantations, and whose empire depended on the sale of rubber abroad to pay for imports. A cartel seemed the obvious solution, but there were far too many planters for them to negotiate an accord among themselves. In 1922, London imposed a cartel on producers in Malaya, who grew most of the Empire's rubber. Whitehall had tried to secure the acquiescence of producers in the Dutch East Indies, who accounted for 25 percent of world rubber output, but the Dutch government refused. It feared antagonizing the United States, the chief consumer. Nevertheless, London believed that unilateral action could retrieve the situation. The British program assigned each of its producers a quota based on 1920 output, allowing planters to export a certain percentage of that quota based on a formula tied to the price of raw rubber in London commodities markets. If the price fell short of a certain target, authorities would reduce production, but if the price surpassed this benchmark they would allow more exports.

This scheme exacerbated rather than mitigated the bust–boom cycle of the rubber industry. The restrictions on output coincided with a surge of growth in the automobile industry in the United States and an accompanying increase in the demand for tires. The cartel's mechanism for expanding output proved clumsy, and its chief response to higher demand was not to increase production but to raise the target price. By 1925, rubber was fetching $.730 a pound. Soon, however, prices began to fall as the growth of demand slowed and the Dutch East Indies began to exploit the reduction in British output by exporting more rubber. By 1927, the Dutch colony was producing 37 percent of the world's rubber, whereas the British Empire's share had slipped to 54 percent. Meanwhile, prices had fallen to $.223 a pound. Realizing as one English analyst put it, that "the British restriction scheme was benefiting Malay not at all, but her chief competitor [the Dutch East Indies] very much," London abandoned the program in 1928.[60]

The Depression led rubber producers to organize a new cartel. The downturn drove the price of natural latex to $.034 a pound in 1932, the lowest ever, creating desperation among producers. Governments led the way to restructuring. In 1934, after almost a year of negotiation, all the major producers—the British Empire, the Dutch East Indies, Siam (Thailand), and French Indochina—announced an agreement to stabilize the market. The accord apportioned market share among participants, strictly limited the planting of new rubber trees, and established the International Rubber Regulation Committee (IRRC) to determine total production and otherwise run the cartel. Member governments promised to enforce the IRRC's decisions in their territories. The agreement also contained an unusual feature designed to reconcile consumers, who had not fared well under the first cartel, to the new arrangement. It created an advisory committee of firms making tires and other rubber goods from Britain, the United States, and Germany. Though this body had no formal authority over policy, the IRRC regularly consulted with it.

The IRRC avoided the worst mistakes of its predecessor. It included all major producers, reducing the risk that outsiders would undermine its program, and it pursued a moderate pricing policy that eschewed any specific target but instead sought to keep demand and output in balance. When the cartel began operation in 1934, prices had already rebounded from their Depression low to $.12 a pound. Initially the cartel labored to reinforce the trend by restricting production, but as rubber demand increased during 1936, it allowed output to expand. Prices peaked at $.25 a pound in 1936, retreating during the subsequent recession, during which the IRRC reversed course and limited production. Prices bottomed out at $.146 in 1937 and rebounded to $.20 in 1940, which found the cartel again expanding output to meet wartime demand. Although the rubber market was still volatile, the IRRC had provided a measure of stability.

Perhaps nothing better demonstrates the vogue for cartels than the willingness of governments to create bodies like the IRRC to regulate trade in businesses too fragmented to organize themselves. Authorities usually acted for industries on which their national economies were particularly dependent or whose producers enjoyed special political influence. Cuba, whose sugar crop provided most of its exports, led in organizing the international sugar cartel, to which it required native producers adhere. The United States participated in the sugar cartel, in large part to help Cuba, which was in some ways an American protectorate and in whose sugar plantations U.S. citizens had heavy investments. Washington was also a party to an international agreement covering the sale of wheat, of which it was a leading exporter. Chile, whose export earnings came largely from the sale of natural nitrates, conducted talks on behalf of its many producers with the large foreign firms selling synthetic nitrates, and it made sure that producers within its borders kept these agreements. Like the IRRC, some of these cartels gave consumers a voice in operations. The sugar and wheat accords included the governments of consumer countries, limiting any tendency by the cartels to abuse their power by setting exorbitant prices.

By 1939, international cartels dominated large parts of the world economy. They governed some of the world's most dynamic and technically sophisticated industries like chemicals and electrical machinery as well as ancient businesses such as wheat and copper. The National Association of Manufacturers (NAM) estimated that before 1939, cartels were active in industries that accounted for 42 percent of world trade.[61] This figure ignores the widely varying strength of different organizations, some of which were little more than wishful thinking on the part of their organizers, and so exaggerates cartels' power. Nevertheless, effective cartels did exist in the chemical, electrical machinery, steel, nonferrous metal, petroleum, sugar, rubber, and wheat trades, which together accounted for about a quarter of international exchange during the 1930s.[62] In the late 1920s, perhaps the foremost German expert on the subject noted, "For several decades everyone has been affected by them [cartels] in a greater or lesser degree, not merely in Germany but—we may safely say—in every corner of the globe."[63]

Strong cartels, such as those for steel, electric lamps, and rubber, changed the nature of business. Instead of struggling for a better position vis-à-vis their competitors, firms cooperated to improve overall conditions in their industry. The most efficient companies still enjoyed larger sales and profits, but they obtained these through negotiation rather than competition. The possibility remained that companies might take aggressive steps against rivals, cutting prices or suing to invalidate key patents, but the role of such tactics was analogous to that of war in eighteenth-century European diplomacy—kept discreetly in the background and, when invoked, managed with restraint. Even when a firm did break with a cartel, its object was usually a better agreement, not the end of cooperation. Industrial diplomats came to hold important, sometimes dominant, positions in companies. One study of the heavily cartelized chemical industry noted, "Each of the major integrated chemical enterprises—I.G. Farben, I.C.I., Du Pont—developed a 'foreign policy' that encompassed a range of mutual problems, including not only market restraints but also technological exchanges, joint ventures, intercompany investments, and related matters. Each of these companies also established administrative departments to monitor negotiations and implementation of agreements."[64] Executives like Harry McGowan of Imperial Chemical and Gerard Swope of GE rose to leadership in their firms on their skills as industrial diplomats.

Of course, cartels did not abolish markets. An organization that pushed prices too high and took advantage of its customers, such as Phoebus in the 1930s or the rubber cartel in the 1920s, risked attracting outsiders that could wreck its schemes. Yet, managed conservatively, cartels could substantially reduce the risks of doing business, allowing firms to stabilize market share and command better prices.

2   The Context of Antitrust

Alone among industrial nations, the United States rejected cartels—at least in theory. Americans had been ambivalent toward big business ever since it emerged in the late nineteenth century, respecting its efficiency but fearing its economic and political power. These concerns led Washington to regulate the activities of large firms, outlawing cartels and imposing other restrictions on these companies. A few cartels did exist in the United States, but they were exceptions that participants usually justified by reference to special conditions. As a whole, Americans placed great confidence in economic competition as a check on the power of big business and looked askance at cartels.

The Antitrust Tradition

The antitrust laws, which largely banned cartels, had deep roots in the American political tradition. They evolved in the fifty years before World War II, shaped by a struggle between those who sought to break up large firms and those who believed that such companies offered economic advantages. By the 1930s, most in the United States took the antitrust laws for granted, considering them as part of an "American way" that tolerated big business but preserved a measure of competition among even the largest firms.

For most Americans, the status of cartels was part of a larger constellation of issues involving the place of big business in society. During the late nineteenth century, the U.S. economy had changed radically. Before 1850, a complex network of independent merchants, most of whom employed no more than a handful of clerks and did business only in a limited geographic area, managed the flow of goods through the economy. The largest manufacturing companies, New England's textile mills, each employed at most a few hundred workers. No firm had much control over its markets. On the whole, economic power, and the social and political power that went with it, was widely diffused. Slowly after 1850, and more rapidly after 1870, the situation changed. New technologies, particularly the development of the railroad, encouraged the growth of large, bureaucratic companies—big business. By 1900, these firms managed railways and telegraphs and dominated the production of steel, oil, copper, farm implements, electrical machinery, papers, cigarettes, soap, and more.[1]

Big business wielded unprecedented power. In most areas railroads enjoyed monopolies over transportation—farmers had to ship their crops out on a single railroad, and merchants had to bring their goods in the same way. Yet neither group had much control over the railways, which were governed by bureaucracies headquartered far away and ultimately often controlled by financiers in New York, Boston, Philadelphia, Baltimore, or even London. Managers charged shippers "what the market would bear," rates that secured maximum revenue. Railways had close ties with all levels of government, which chartered and sometimes financed them. No firm was willing to leave such important relationships to chance, and to protect their position and, ideally, improve it, railroads plunged into politics, contributing mightily to the political corruption endemic to the United States in the late nineteenth century. Large industrial firms, which often ruthlessly destroyed smaller competitors and bought the support of government officials, presented a similar aspect to the public.

Many Americans concluded that big business posed a dual threat. On one hand, it gouged consumers and destroyed smaller competitors, distorting economic life. On the other, it corrupted government and robbed communities of their autonomy, eroding political democracy. Historian Matthew Josephson summed up these concerns in his classic 1934 study of the rise of big business in the late nineteenth century, *The Robber Barons*: "Under the new dispensation . . . the strong, as in the Dark Ages of Europe, and like the military captains of old, having preempted more than others, having been [possessed] . . . of land and highways and strong places, would own because they owned. Chieftains would arise, in the time-honored way, to whom the crowd would look for leadership, for protection, finally for their very existence. They would be the nobles of a new feudal system."[2]

Yet big business also generated immense wealth that it spread widely, if not evenly. Companies like Standard Oil, Swift, Heinz, Pillsbury, and Procter & Gamble made and distributed high-quality consumer goods far more cheaply than the old independent merchants. Railroads opened up for economic development parts of the country previously isolated, most notably the Great Plains and the Rocky Mountains. Innovative firms like General Electric and Westinghouse brought to market entirely new products, such as electric lights and streetcars, that made life easier. However uncomfortable with big business, most Americans also understood that it contributed substantially to their high standard of living. Writing in the 1930s, journalist Dorothy Thompson observed, "Two souls dwell . . . in the bosom of the American people. The one loves the abundant life, as expressed in the cheap and plentiful products of large-scale mass production and distribution. . . . The other soul yearns for former simplicities, for decentralization, for the interests of the 'little man,' . . . denounces 'monopoly' and 'economic empires,' and seeks means of breaking them up."[3]

Progressive Era reformers reflected this ambivalence. After 1900, activists labeled Progressives, touting a wide variety of programs, seized the political stage. Chief among the issues with which they wrestled was the place of big business in society. Many rejected large companies in toto. They contended that only government favoritism and sharp dealings like predatory pricing, concessionary railroad rates, and preferential financing had allowed large firms to triumph over smaller rivals.[4] Louis Brandeis, one of the leading lights of the Progressive Era, stated, "I am so firmly convinced that the large unit is not as efficient—I mean the very large unit—is not as efficient as the smaller unit, that I believe that if it were possible today to make corporations act in accordance with what doubtless all of us would agree should be the rules of trade no huge corporations would be created, or if created, would be successful."[5]

The rejection of big business rested as much on social and political concerns as on economic ones. The power of these companies threatened to corrupt government, regiment national life, and destroy political democracy. Woodrow Wilson spoke for many when he warned in 1912 that in big firms, "individuality is swallowed up in the individuality and purpose of a great organization. While most men are thus submerged in the corporation, a few, a very few, are exalted to a power which as individuals they could never have wielded. . . . A few are enabled to play a part unprecedented by anything in history . . . in the determination of the happiness of great numbers of people."[6] Brandeis and Wilson advocated "trust-busting," breaking up large firms.

Yet other Progressive reformers saw big business as a blessing, albeit a decidedly mixed one. They realized that large companies enjoyed economies of scale and scope that allowed them to produce and deliver goods far more cheaply than their smaller competitors. Theodore Roosevelt insisted, "Combinations in industry are the result of an imperative economic law which cannot be repealed by political legislation."[7] Still, although considering big business economically valuable, he too worried about its political power and its impact on democracy, warning, "Now the great special business interests too often control and corrupt the men and methods of government."[8] Herbert Croly's influential *The Promise of American Life*, which described alluringly the opportunities afforded by large-scale economic organization, contended, "The rich men and the big corporations have become too wealthy and powerful for their official standing in American life. They have not obeyed the laws. They have attempted to control the official makers, administrators, and expounders of the law. They have done little to allay and much to excite . . . resentment and suspicion. In short, while their work has been constructive from an economic and industrial standpoint, it has made for political corruption and social disintegration."[9] The government needed to regulate big business, preventing it from abusing its power and guaranteeing that its activities benefited society as a whole.

The thinking of Progressives like Roosevelt and Croly illustrates a key difference between the United States and other industrial countries that probably had great impact on attitudes toward big business. Most European nations (as well as Japan) had strong government institutions that could easily regulate large firms. Before the twentieth century, the U.S. government had few such capabilities, which made the power of big business seem particularly alarming.

Cartels occupied an unusual place in the American debate over big business. Businessmen in the United States, like their counterparts in other countries, had organized cartels in the late nineteenth century, most notably railroad pools. Yet they enjoyed little success, in part because of the intensely competitive culture of American business. The key development, however, came in 1890, when Congress enacted the first measure directed against big business, the Sherman Act. It banned "restraint of trade," a common-law term on which legal experts often disagreed. The courts initially interpreted the measure very narrowly, striking down only agreements among independent firms that set prices and production—that is, cartels. Individual companies, no matter how large, were exempt. This doctrine encouraged a wave of mergers around the turn of the century that brought competing firms together, circumventing the prohibition against cartels.[10] Thus in the United States, large unitary companies emerged in sectors where in Europe (particularly Germany) cartels predominated. As a result, few Americans made much of a distinction between cartels and big business, as both seemed to have the same objective—controlling markets.

During the Progressive Era, the courts reinterpreted the Sherman Act, greatly extending its reach. Decisions in the first decade of the twentieth century started the process of bringing individual companies under the law's purview, and the Supreme Court set down a comprehensive doctrine on the subject in 1911. In that year's *Standard Oil* decision, the court distinguished between companies engaged in "reasonable" and in "unreasonable" restraint of trade. Firms that grew large because of superior efficiencies were examples of the former and within the law. Those that prospered because of underhanded tactics like predatory pricing and railroad rebates represented an unreasonable restraint of trade and faced dissolution, which was the fate of Standard Oil.[11] The Clayton and Federal Trade Commission Acts, enacted in 1914 during the Wilson administration, expanded on this approach, explicitly banning "unfair" competitive practices.[12] As a practical matter, these measures did little to halt the growth of large companies, which, contrary to Brandeis's assertion, usually did enjoy economies of scale and scope. This legislation did, however, restrict some of the most objectionable practices of big business.

The *Standard Oil* decision summed up, as much as anything, the implicit compromise on big business that emerged from the Progressive Era. The country would accept large companies as long as they were efficient and stopped short of monopoly. Accordingly, many industries developed into oligopolies, dominated by a handful of very big enterprises that competed, albeit cautiously. Some dissented from this compromise. Many businessmen wanted to cooperate to stabilize markets, and they sometimes developed sub rosa ways of doing so. Many reformers continued to draw inspiration from Brandeis and to distrust all large companies. Experts also disagreed on how strictly Washington needed to enforce the antitrust laws to preserve competition. Nevertheless, the antitrust compromise proved remarkably durable.

The dissidents largely balanced out, blocking each other's schemes for radical change. The debates over enforcement, no matter how heated, did not challenge the objectives of policy. The principle that big business was acceptable as long as it was efficient and faced competition persisted.[13]

The antitrust compromise precluded cartels. These organizations sought to regulate markets, and most Americans wanted to retain at least a measure of competition. Nor did cartels meet the standard of efficiency. Whereas mergers among competing companies could secure efficiencies by combining and rationalizing operations, cartels could not because members retained their independence.

Most U.S. firms did not really need cartels. The country enjoyed a huge domestic market, a fairly stable currency, and the rule of law, advantages that more than compensated for the risks of competition. In this context, industrial rivalry probably strengthened the economy by encouraging efficiency and innovation. Firms in other industrial nations faced more daunting prospects. None had a domestic market even half the size of the American one, and their governments and currencies were often extremely unstable.[14] In such conditions, competition might well cripple everyone.

The 1920s saw a new approach to economic regulation, one that reflected the trend toward cartels abroad. Herbert Hoover, as commerce secretary and later president, sponsored trade associations for American industries. These organizations encouraged the standardization of products and disseminated the latest technical information to members. They also circulated data on output, sales, and prices, which presumably would lead firms to make more "rational" decisions and so promote economic stability. On accepting the Republican presidential nomination in 1928, Hoover proudly claimed, "During my term as Secretary of Commerce I have steadily endeavored to set up a system of cooperation between government and business. Under these cooperative actions all elements interested in the problems of a particular industry such as manufacturer, distributor, worker and consumer had been called into council together, not for a single occasion but for continuous work."[15] As historian Robert Himmelberg has pointed out, trade associations sometimes worked like cartels, regulating markets. Yet Hoover himself refused to endorse cartels per se, believing that price setting and market allocation hurt consumers and that centralized control over the economy threatened political democracy. As president, Hoover actually encouraged antitrust prosecution against trade associations that worked like cartels.[16] He sought not to eliminate competition but to reconcile it with planning and stabilization. Despite a few breaches, Hoover's trade associations left the antitrust compromise intact.

Policy toward international cartels at this time demonstrated considerable ambivalence. The 1918 Webb-Pomerene Act allowed American producers in the same line of business to form joint companies to manage their exports. Designed to allow American firms to present a common front to large foreign purchasers such as governments and to enable small firms to reduce the cost of selling abroad by working together, the act also had substantial utility for cartel builders. As early as 1918, American copper producers, which at that time dominated the world industry, had organized a cartel under the aegis of a Webb-Pomerene corporation. In 1924, the Federal Trade Commission (FTC), which oversaw Webb-Pomerene companies, made the act even more useful to cartel builders when it informed the Silver Producers Committee, a trade association, "There is nothing in the [Webb-Pomerene] act which prevents an association formed under it from entering into any cooperative relationship with a foreign corporation for the sole purpose of operation in a foreign market. The only test of legality in such an arrangement would be the effect upon domestic conditions within the United States."[17] Though the silver cartel never materialized, producers in other industries took the "silver letter," as it was called, as permission for Webb-Pomerene companies to sign cartel accords that apportioned foreign markets. Exactly how a cartel could influence world markets without affecting those in the United States was not entirely clear. As the head of the copper industry's Webb-Pomerene company admitted in 1940, "You had one market practically, and that was a world-wide market."[18] Yet before 1940, the FTC challenged none of the agreements signed by Webb-Pomerene companies, which tied American firms to the electrical machinery, copper, steel, and synthetic alkali cartels, among others.

At the same time, the American government did attack international cartels that, it believed, abused their power. Here again Herbert Hoover was the critical figure. As commerce secretary he vigorously opposed the international rubber and potash cartels, doing his best to develop new supplies of both materials.[19] This policy reflected national self-interest. In the 1920s, the United States imported large quantities of both rubber and potash, and the sharp price increases engineered by the two cartels hurt. Yet in these cases economic calculation accorded with Hoover's convictions. Throughout his career he opposed cartels, and in the international sphere he merely concentrated attention on those that affected his country the most.[20] Nevertheless, no one in Washington seems to have contemplated a general attack on international cartels.

The Great Depression transformed the political as well as the economic situation. The unprecedented economic collapse threw millions out of work and propelled Franklin D. Roosevelt into the White House. Roosevelt, one of the canniest politicians this country has ever produced, immediately embarked on a program of economic reform—the New Deal—which he justified in large part with references to the evils of big business. Americans had accepted large companies chiefly because they generated great wealth, and the Depression brought to the surface all the doubts the people harbored about these organizations. Roosevelt capitalized on this sentiment, a process that began early. As one historian observed, "Franklin Roosevelt drew his first notable applause during his inaugural address [in 1933] when he assailed the money-changers, and the next, and even louder applause, when he promised to end business misconduct."[21] The rift between Roosevelt and business grew during his first administration. In 1936, when accepting renomination by the Democratic Party, the president drew inspiration from Louis Brandeis's book *Other People's Money*, declaring that before he had entered the White House, "A small group had concentrated into their own hands an almost complete control over other people's property, other people's money, other people's labor—other people's lives. For too many of us life was no longer free; liberty no longer real; men could no longer follow the pursuit of happiness." He continued, "Here in America we are waging a great and successful war. It is not alone a war against want and destitution and economic demoralization. It is more than that; it is a war for the survival of democracy."[22] In 1937, Secretary of the Interior Harold Ickes, one of the most influential members of Roosevelt's cabinet, declared that the central question before the country was "a struggle for power, for the control of lives, labor, and possessions of whole peoples—a struggle between the many and the few, a struggle between those who would live and let live and those who want the thrill of the power of ruling others." "The future of America," he said, "depends upon whether big business can . . . be compelled to conform to our laws, be compelled to accept the will of the majority, be compelled to cooperate with the rest of us in trying to make democracy work."[23]

The Roosevelt administration was not firing its rhetorical barbs into a void. The president's opponents subjected him and his administration to a flood of abuse, warning that the New Deal would bankrupt the government and destroy the free enterprise system. However exaggerated these sentiments appear in retrospect, they reflected disagreement over important issues. The New Deal imposed major reforms on private enterprise that most businessmen staunchly opposed: regulating the financial system, strengthening organized labor, and sharply raising taxes on the wealthy. Despite some important exceptions, the business community came to hate FDR with a passion.

Yet Roosevelt's policies toward big business were actually more ambiguous than his white-hot rhetoric suggested. Some reforms did strike at important interests of these organizations, but others offered them substantial benefits. Some of Roosevelt's advisers drew inspiration from Louis Brandeis and urged aggressive antitrust policies, but others looked to the experience of Hoover's trade associations and forwarded schemes for economic planning in which business would have a substantial role. The division of opinion evident among Progressive Era reformers persisted during the New Deal. As historian Ellis Hawley noted, "On one hand, the Depression produced insistent demands for planning, rationalization, and the erection of market controls that could stem the forces of deflation and prevent economic ruin. On the other, it intensified antimonopoly sentiment, destroyed confidence in business leadership, and produced equally insistent demands that big business be punished and competitive ideals made good."[24] Roosevelt maneuvered between these forces, balancing them as the political situation dictated.

The New Deal actually saw the acme of cartels in the United States. As was always the case during economic downturns, the Depression made these organizations attractive to businessmen. Meanwhile, the unprecedented collapse made the public willing to consider new approaches to economic policy. In the early 1930s, several articles and books appeared on cartels, most notably one by Gerard Swope, the president of General Electric and an architect of the Phoebus cartel. In 1930, he urged, "Production and consumption should be coordinated on a broader and more intelligent basis [through cartels] thus tending to regularize employment."[25] Swope's plans required substantial revision of the antitrust laws, however, which President Hoover refused to countenance.

Roosevelt proved more receptive. Soon after taking office he secured passage of the National Recovery Act (NRA), which suspended the antitrust laws and provided for the creation of mandatory "codes of conduct" for each industry. These would regulate production and sales, as well as the conditions of labor, and business would cooperate with the government, organized labor, and consumer groups in drafting codes.[26] Unfortunately, different groups interpreted the NRA quite differently: businessmen saw it as an aegis under which to organize cartels; enthusiasts of planning wanted to erect industry-wide organizations through which the government could guide economic development; and trust-busters hoped that the codes, by banning underhanded tactics and restricting collusion, would actually reinforce competition as well as protect smaller firms against their more powerful rivals. As Hawley wrote, "The NRA was not a single program with a single objective, but rather a series of programs with a series of objectives, some of which were in direct conflict with each other."[27] The result was a mess that contributed mightily to the deterioration of relations between the business community and the Roosevelt administration. As Hawley put it, the NRA led to "the conviction of one side [business] that cooperation would lead to bureaucratic socialism, of the other [New Dealers] that it would lead to fascism or economic oppression."[28] Most seemed relieved when, in 1935, the Supreme Court struck down the NRA as unconstitutional.

Despite this fiasco, the Roosevelt administration continued to sponsor cartels for favored sectors of the economy. Agricultural programs instituted price supports and limited planting. Government regulation of trucking, airlines, and railways restricted capacity and propped up prices; legislation governing coal and petroleum did the same. Although cartels remained the exception in the American economy, the exceptions were significant.

Still, cartels lost ground intellectually under the New Deal. In 1933, the country appeared on the verge of embracing these organizations. Desperate to halt the downward spiral of the economy, Americans seemed willing to abandon the antitrust tradition. The NRA, however, soured many people on cartels, including businessmen who had been among their foremost advocates. The fierce hostility that developed between business and government under the New Deal increased the presumption against cartels. Businessmen were extremely reluctant to submit their arrangements to federal oversight, whereas New Dealers refused to tolerate cartels in whose operations Washington did not have a leading voice.

Many opposed to cartels in principle tolerated the organizations in practice, particularly when they themselves benefited. Yet in these cases the advocates of a cartel usually insisted that market "imperfections" made deviations from the ideal of competition necessary. Sometimes serious imbalances did exist, although in other cases talk of "imperfections" was largely an exercise in hypocrisy.[29] Regardless, even the advocates of specific cartels portrayed these organizations as exceptions to the norms of economic life.

The first Roosevelt administration generally left international cartels alone. Trying to organize a domestic system of cartels, the NRA, the president could hardly have launched a campaign against similar organizations abroad. In fact, the Department of Agriculture actually participated in the international sugar and wheat cartels. Moreover, Roosevelt evinced little interest in foreign affairs during his first term in office, concentrating instead on domestic reform. As one student of antitrust policy has written, "There is little evidence of United States government opposition to notorious foreign cartels or the open participation in them by American firms during the interwar period."[30]

The Antitrust Drive

In Roosevelt's second term, his administration launched perhaps the most ambitious antitrust drive in the nation's history. It developed unexpectedly, propelled by political expediency and the enthusiasm of middle-level officials, yet it drew on the established antitrust tradition and would have lasting implications at home and abroad.

The antitrust drive had its origins in the sharp recession of 1937 and 1938. The downturn, probably triggered by large cuts in government spending and the Federal Reserve's tightening of monetary policy, surprised the administration and encouraged enemies of the New Deal, who saw the recession as a harbinger of the president's political demise. His administration was already in trouble. Roosevelt's notorious "Court-packing" plan, which sought to remake the high bench in the image of the New Deal, had alienated many of the president's supporters and had galvanized his opponents. Controversial "sit-down" strikes had further sapped his support, as had Roosevelt's ill-considered attempts to "purge" conservatives from the Democratic Party. In 1938, the Republicans scored large gains in the off-year elections, and starting in 1939, they worked effectively in Congress with conservative Democrats to stymie Roosevelt's plans for further domestic reform.

Beset by difficulties, the administration intensified its attacks on Roosevelt's favorite political foil, big business. In late 1937, Harold Ickes and Robert Jackson, two of the president's closest advisers, delivered perhaps the most savage attacks on the business community yet by prominent New Dealers. Among other things, they blamed the recession on a "capital strike," a conspiracy of the wealthy to discredit the New Deal.[31] Others advanced a more measured explanation for the recession that nevertheless placed the onus for the nation's economic ills on large companies. They blamed the recession and, indeed, the Depression itself on the power of big business to control prices and restrict output. Thurman Arnold, who took over the Justice Department's Antitrust Division in 1938, wrote, "When industry becomes highly organized, it gains the power to control prices which the people must pay. The exchange of raw materials and services by unorganized groups for the products of organized industry becomes more and more a one-sided bargain. When this happens a farm problem always arises because the farmer cannot buy. Then an unemployment problem becomes acute because the manufacturer cannot sell its goods." According to Arnold, this situation explained the 1937 recession. "With the expanding market [in 1936]," he wrote, "most industries attempted, by raising their prices, not to distribute the most goods but to obtain the largest share of that expanding purchasing power. The result was that we became choked with our own wealth."[32]

In 1938, President Roosevelt sent a message on antitrust policy to Congress stating, "One of the primary causes for our present difficulties lies in the disappearance of price competition in many industrial fields, particularly in basic manufacture where concentrated economic power is most evident."[33] "Private enterprise," the president warned ominously, "is ceasing to be free enterprise and is becoming a cluster of private collectivism: masking itself as a system of free enterprise after the American model, it is in fact becoming a concealed cartel system after the European model."[34]

Roosevelt embraced antitrust out of desperation. Heretofore he had displayed little interest in the subject, yet earlier reforms had failed to bring economic recovery, and political reverses made it nearly impossible to get major new programs from Congress. Antitrust prosecution was all that remained. Whatever doubts the president himself may have harbored, however, those who designed and carried out his program were sincere. As far as they were concerned, the antitrust drive was not a political ploy or a second-best policy but a radical effort to restore economic competition.

The drive against monopoly followed two different avenues: the investigation by the Temporary National Economic Committee (TNEC) and prosecutions by Justice Department's expanded and reenergized Antitrust Division. At first, both focused on the domestic scene, but the TNEC did not ignore conditions abroad, and the Antitrust Division would eventually make international cartels one of its prime targets.

The TNEC, which drew members from both Congress and the administration, launched an exhaustive investigation of economic power that, its supporters believed, would suggest reforms. By the time it had finished its work, however, the outbreak of war in Europe had diverted public attention from the question of monopoly. Moreover, the very thoroughness with which the TNEC pursued its job retarded its effectiveness. Its reports were generally of high quality, but their complexity put off the public, not to mention politicians looking for easy solutions.

The TNEC examined the two chief ways in which American firms participated in international cartels: Webb-Pomerene companies and patent agreements. It evinced skepticism about the utility of the former, questioning whether participation in cartel agreements dividing up foreign markets was the best way to expand exports. The committee also noted, "Doubt has been expressed, too, that firms can assign quotas and fix prices in foreign markets without influencing prices in the domestic market."[35] Nevertheless, the committee concluded, "On the whole, foreign cartels and foreign corporations exerted only a minor influence on production in this country."[36]

The TNEC devoted more time to patents. The use of patents as a basis for monopolies and cartels infuriated critics of economic concentration. To their minds the government had created the patent system to allow inventors to enjoy the benefits of their discoveries. Corporations, artificial legal constructs, could not actually invent anything, and their ownership of patents seemed perverse. Particularly galling, the patent laws allowed companies to enlist the government in enforcing monopolies. The TNEC report on patents argued that corporate manipulation had "lifted the patent out of the province in which it is supposed to operate, separates it from the objective it is supposed to serve. . . . It sets the grant down in a universe of business, makes it a counter in the acquisitive game." This report, which among other things discussed GE's lightbulb cartel, did not neglect the international application of patent agreements. "In peace or war," it noted, "the international cartel poses its problems. A corporation barricades its monopoly by securing grants [patents] in all dominant nations. If concerns here and abroad lay claim to rival technologies, the conflict is usually resolved by private understanding. Like countries engaged in power politics, an international cartel marks out spheres of influence. . . . An agreement between gentlemen which vaults over frontiers becomes the actual regulation of commence with foreign nations."[37]

The TNEC recommended important changes in the patent laws. Some were of a technical nature, such as procedures to speed up applications and to prevent companies from using various legal devices to extend the life of a patent beyond its seventeen-year limit.[38] But the TNEC went further. It recommended "legislation which will require that any future patent is to be available for use by anyone who may desire its use and who is willing to pay a fair price for the privilege. Machinery . . . should be set up to determine whether the royalty demanded by the patentee may be fairly be said to represent reasonable compensation."[39] Congress did not pass this broader suggestion into law.

The brunt of the effort against monopoly fell, somewhat surprisingly, on the Antitrust Division of the Justice Department. Long a stagnant bureaucracy, this agency suddenly became a focus of activity in the late 1930s under the leadership of Thurman Arnold. His predecessor, Robert Jackson, had launched several important cases, but Arnold massively expanded the activities of the bureau. He increased its staff of lawyers from fifty-eight when he took over in 1938 to two hundred by 1940, and during the same period the number of cases filed annually grew from eleven to ninety-two. These prosecutions were particularly aggressive. The Antitrust Division would file several cases, each with dozens of defendants, to break up anticompetitive practices that infected entire industries. For instance, the government launched a series of actions against contractors and construction unions whose arrangements, the Antitrust Division claimed, stifled innovative building techniques and kept construction costs high. The Justice Department also began to use consent decrees more widely. Under these, the government agreed to suspend prosecution in exchange for alterations in the policies of the accused organization. Because decrees did not formally terminate prosecution but merely left the matter in limbo, Arnold could use them to exert continuing review over business.[40] Initially few of the division's cases dealt with international cartels, but in time that would change.[41]

Thurman Arnold summed up in himself reformers' contradictory attitudes toward big business. A native of Laramie, Wyoming, educated at Princeton and Harvard Law School, he was a colorful character even by the standards of New Deal Washington. He was known for an irreverent wit that occasionally, his critics said, shaded into buffoonery. As a professor at Yale Law School, Arnold had made his reputation with the publication of *The Folklore of Capitalism*, which among other things contained a scathing critique of the antitrust laws. It claimed that they "enabled men to look at a highly organized and centralized industrial organization and still believe that it was composed of individuals engaged in buying and selling in a free market." "They [antitrust measures] were part of the struggle of a creed of rugged individualism to adapt itself to what was becoming a highly organized society." "The actual result[s] of the antitrust laws," Arnold insisted, "were to promote the growth of great industrial organizations by deflecting the attack on them into purely moral and ceremonial channels."[42]

These statements would seem to disqualify Arnold for leadership of the Antitrust Division, but he managed to reconcile vigorous antitrust enforcement with such views by shifting the emphasis of prosecution. Arnold argued, "Most of the books in the past on the antitrust laws have been written with the idea that they are designed to eliminate the *evil of bigness*. What ought to be emphasized is not the evils of size but the evils of industries which are not efficient or do not pass efficiency on to consumers. If the antitrust laws are simply an expression of a religion which condemns largeness as economic sin they will be regarded as an anachronism in a machine age." He concluded, "The test is efficiency and service—not size."[43] This view ranged Arnold in opposition to many labor unions, which sometimes obstructed more efficient production techniques that might reduce employment, and it elicited from him great enthusiasm for one of the largest industrial empires built during the early twentieth century, the Ford Motor Company, which had produced the first car within the reach of the masses. Arnold wanted to use antitrust laws not to restrain the growth of large companies but to clear and police the channels of trade, guaranteeing efficiency.

Yet at an instinctive level Arnold disliked and distrusted big business. In his public statements it is difficult to find positive reference to any large firm other than Ford, and although less doctrinaire than Brandeis, Arnold seems to have believed that most big companies owed their success to underhanded tactics or collusion. This attitude may have reflected his upbringing in Wyoming, where most citizens assumed that large, eastern companies exploited the state's natural resources with little regard for the well-being of the inhabitants. As the editor of his papers wrote, Arnold was, as a Westerner, "acutely aware of the impact of [economic] colonialism on his region." For him, "Brandesian economic doctrine made sense."[44]

Arnold's importance sprang as much from the people he trained and inspired as from his own achievements. His subordinates at the Antitrust Division included Tom Clark, a Texan who later became attorney general and a Supreme Court justice; Wendell Berge, a Nebraskan who had been with the Antitrust Division since 1930 and who, as its chief after 1943, would launch some of the most important prosecutions of international cartels; and Corwin Edwards, a Nevada-bred economist brought in from the Federal

Trade Commission who provided much of the economic rationale for the antimonopoly program and who later became a major figure in occupation policy toward Japan. It was probably no accident that, along with their chief, all of these men hailed from west of the Mississippi.[45]

Before the outbreak of World War II in September 1939, this group concentrated on domestic conditions. War, however, would force them to pay more attention to foreign affairs and open up new avenues for antitrust prosecution.

3   Reform versus Mobilization

The outbreak of war in Europe in 1939 created difficulties both for American firms participating in international cartels and for the antitrust drive. War automatically suspended cartel agreements between firms in the countries involved. Because the United States did not formally enter the conflict until December 1941, however, cartel accords still bound American firms, often to German ones. Because the United States was, despite its legal neutrality, supporting Germany's foes, this at best was embarrassing and at worst interfered with mobilization, which was under way well before the Japanese attack on Pearl Harbor. At the same time, the Antitrust Division of the Justice Department found that mobilization put a premium on reconciliation between the business community and government, a process that marginalized it. In response, Thurman Arnold began to focus on international cartels, arguing that they retarded mobilization and that by attacking them his bureau contributed to mobilization. These issues festered for the two and a half years that Washington remained neutral. Only American entry into the war forced the suspension of cartel accords and a decision on the proper role of antitrust in the national emergency.

Cartels in Wartime

The outbreak of war in Europe in September 1939 had grave implications for all Americans. Although technically neutral, the United States found itself playing a large role in the conflict. The Roosevelt administration strongly opposed German ambitions, but initially it believed that Britain and France could contain the Nazis on their own. During the first nine months of war, the United States pursued a policy of benevolent neutrality toward the Allies, allowing them to purchase what they needed in this country and tolerating the British blockade that cut off trade with Germany. The fall of France to the Nazis in June 1940 radically changed the situation, however, making a German victory seem likely. Washington increasingly channeled support to Britain, selling it weapons on favorable terms and, after March 1941, providing military aid through the Lend-Lease program. The United States also built up its own defenses, initiating construction of a two-ocean navy, imposing conscription, and laying plans for an air force of thousands of planes. Although most Americans still hoped to avoid conflict, by the fall of 1941, war with Germany seemed probable.

At the same time the war initiated economic recovery. Defense orders, first from Britain and France and then from the American government itself, reactivated factories long idle. For the first time in a decade firms were able to sell all they could produce, and millions of unemployed workers found jobs. Yet prosperity brought its own problems, most notably inflation and shortages.

Some firms, however, had special difficulties: cartel ties with German firms that remained in force despite the slide toward war. The problem ran deepest in the chemical industry. Before 1914, German companies had dominated the production of the industry's most sophisticated products, fine chemicals like dyestuffs, pharmaceuticals, and photographic chemicals. They sold approximately 80 percent of the world's dyes; pioneered drugs like aspirin, novocaine, and salvarsan (the first effective treatment for syphilis); and sold to Kodak ingredients critical for its film. Between 1914 and 1918, however, the British blockade cut the Germans off from their chief export markets. Allied governments seized the patents and local facilities of German companies, selling them to domestic firms on good terms. These companies quickly replaced the Germans, doing well as long as the war continued. Peace, however, brought renewed German competition for which the newcomers were not equipped. The German firms had superior research establishments and unsurpassed experience in developing and bringing to market new products. Moreover, they possessed know-how in the production and sale of chemicals that their challengers could not gain simply by purchasing seized patents. Fierce competition loomed as German firms sought to reestablish themselves while the newer companies, generally supported by their governments, tried to hold on to recent gains.

Eventually a series of mergers and a network of cartel agreements worked out in the 1920s brought order to the chemical industry. In the United States, several leading companies joined to form Allied Chemical. Allied took its place as the nation's second largest chemical firm after DuPont, which had itself expanded in part by acquisitions. The two strongest British firms, Nobel and Brunner-Mond, merged with several smaller competitors to form Imperial Chemical Industries (ICI), which became not only the leading chemical producer in Britain but also that nation's largest industrial firm. The most important merger occurred in Germany, where in 1925 all the leading dyemakers and several other firms joined to form IG Farbenindustrie. These firms already participated in a cartel known as IG Farbenindustrie, but they had concluded that their situation required even closer coordination. After the merger they retained the name, which translates roughly as "dye industry cartel," because of the good will attached to it. The IG, as it was known, was the world's largest chemical company and by most measures the biggest firm of any sort in Europe. It had unmatched research capabilities perhaps best symbolized by the position of Carl Bosch, a Nobel laureate chemist, at the company's head.

A complex network of international cartels supplemented these mergers. Such accords had been common before 1914 in specific fields like explosives and synthetic alkali, and they reemerged on a broader scale after the war. Leading firms such as the IG, ICI, DuPont, Allied, and Union Carbide were party to literally dozens of agreements—the historian of ICI estimates that it signed eight hundred[1]—whereas smaller companies almost always adhered to at least a few accords. Most of these cartels rested on patent rights, though a few, such as those for synthetic nitrates and alkali, involved more conventional market sharing and price fixing agreements. The average cartel covered only one product or process, but on occasion firms formed broader compacts. Imperial Chemical Industries and DuPont had an alliance under which they shared their patents, with each getting exclusive rights in its home market (the United States for DuPont and the British Empire for ICI). In third markets of mutual interest, the two companies operated through jointly owned subsidiaries.[2] Standard Oil of New Jersey (Exxon), the world's largest oil company, had an agreement with IG Farben covering the entire petrochemical field.

These agreements became suspect during the national emergency. The chemical industry produced a host of vital war materials, most obviously explosives and ammunition, but also goods like plastics and specialty rubber. No nation threatened by war could permit international cartels to govern the production of such materials. Moreover, IG Farben, the ultimate symbol of German industrial prowess, was a party to most chemical cartels—often the dominant party.

No American firm had more stake in its cartel ties than Standard Oil of New Jersey. During the 1920s, IG Farben had invested heavily in hydrogenation, a process to produce oil from coal, perfecting it by 1929. Yet the Germans despaired of ever making the process commercially viable because recent discoveries in Texas and Oklahoma had driven oil prices well below the cost at which Farben could make petroleum from coal. Hydrogenation, however, interested Standard, which thought the process could increase the amount of gasoline its refineries could get from a barrel of oil. Moreover, Standard believed that some governments, desiring self-sufficiency in oil, might subsidize hydrogenation, in which case Standard would have to provide the technology or lose business. In 1929, the two firms struck a deal. In exchange for a block of Standard stock worth about $35 million, Farben transferred the rights to the hydrogenation process outside Germany to the Standard/IG company. Standard owned 80 percent of the firm; the IG, 20 percent. The agreement also declared that Standard would stay out of the chemical business and Farben would avoid the oil industry, save in Germany, where the IG hoped that government subsidies might yet make oil from coal profitable.[3] The deal worked out well for Standard Oil. Though hydrogenation never produced much oil outside Germany, the process substantially increased the efficiency of Standard's refining operations and allowed it to develop new products like high octane gasoline and synthetic toluol, a basic ingredient of the explosive TNT. As a historian of the oil industry put it, "A good deal of technical knowledge was flowing to Standard [from IG Farben]."[4] Standard also licensed the technology to other oil companies and even to ICI. Meanwhile, the acquisition of Standard's stock allowed Farben to cover about half of the cost of developing hydrogenation.

The 1929 agreement had one significant flaw. It neglected the growing field of petrochemicals, an area between the petroleum and chemical industries that interested both Standard Oil and IG Farben. The two companies solved the problem with a 1930 accord that set up the Joint American Study Company (Jasco) to exploit any developments by the two companies in petrochemicals. The agreement had one exception—Farben retained rights to its discoveries in the German market. The two firms agreed to treat each technology separately, with the originator receiving five-eighths financial interest and enjoying control. Because the IG contributed all the initial patents to Jasco, it effectively controlled the firm.[5] This aspect of the agreement particularly appealed to Farben. Its attempts to negotiate broad alliances with firms like ICI, Allied, and DuPont had always foundered on Farben's demand for control, which the others refused to grant. These companies had no intention of returning to 1914, when the Germans had dominated their industry. But Standard, which considered chemicals a sideline, had no such reservations. By 1939, Jasco owned the rights to several valuable technologies, including the buna process for making artificial rubber.[6]

The German invasion of Poland in September 1939 put Standard Oil in an uncomfortable position. It anticipated doing substantial business with the Allies, which needed oil, while the British blockade prevented Standard from supplying its German operations with petroleum, effectively suspending its business in the Reich for the duration. Yet France and Britain might be reluctant to deal with IG Farben's partner. Moreover, if the United States eventually joined the Allies, Standard would find its ties with the IG even more embarrassing. Fortunately for the American company, Farben had its own reasons to terminate the alliance. The firms that had merged in the 1920s to form the IG had suffered heavily during World War I from the confiscation of their foreign holdings, particularly patents, and the IG believed that it could structure a divorce in such a way that it would help defend the German company's property, at least in part.

Officers of the two firms met in September 1939 in The Hague, in the Netherlands, which was then still neutral territory. They quickly reached an agreement. The IG sold its interest in the Standard/IG company to Standard Oil and put its Jasco stock in trust for the American firm. Jasco transferred to Farben all its patent rights outside the French and British empires and the United States. Though ostensibly a divorce, The Hague memorandum, as it was called, contained provisions for future cooperation. Jasco and Farben were supposed to compare their financial results on a regular basis and, should the profits of the two firms differ from what would have been the case under the old agreement, arrange compensation. Thus Farben retained a financial interest of sorts in Jasco, even though as a practical matter the company became a subsidiary of Standard. In all, the agreement covered 2,000 patents.[7] The State Department knew of the meeting in The Hague, having received an invitation from Standard to send an observer from its embassy in the Netherlands. It did not avail itself of the opportunity, however, and it seems unlikely that Washington knew the details of the arrangement.[8]

Though no other American firm was as tightly tied to IG Farben as Standard Oil, other important links did exist and often caused substantial trouble. Even DuPont, the strongest chemical firm in the United States, encountered problems. The first of these involved not ties with the German firm but DuPont's alliance with ICI of Britain. In the summer of 1939, Duperial of Argentina, the joint ICI/DuPont subsidiary in that country, signed an agreement with the IG to form an enterprise, Electroclor, to operate in fields of mutual interest. The signatories had not put the arrangement into operation before the Nazis invaded Poland, however, and once Britain was at war with Germany, ICI concluded, "The proposed partnership relation is not permissible and that as a 50 percent stockholder in Duperial they cannot sanction the completion of the agreement."[9] DuPont, as a neutral, took upon itself the thankless task of breaking off the arrangement. It offered to return Farben its money with interest, but the IG proved stubborn. It suggested that the deal go forward but that, for the duration, DuPont represent it on the board of Electroclor. DuPont refused. It told Farben, "ICI could not agree to have done indirectly what they could not do directly. Moreover, DuPont's only interest in Argentina is through Duperial in which we are equal partners with ICI. We have no men of our own in that country to represent us."[10] In the end, DuPont simply returned Farben's money and declared the matter closed, saying that it "can now only hope that the present sad and unfortunate condition of affairs may not long continue and that eventually effective and pleasant cooperation in this field can be established in Argentina."[11]

These events did not sever DuPont's relations with the IG, however. The two firms had several agreements covering specific products, including one on DuPont's great discovery, nylon, which Farben wanted to exploit in Germany. These accords continued in force despite the war in Europe, with DuPont and Farben exchanging technical information and paying each other royalties. Finally, on April 18, 1941, DuPont wrote to the IG that, considering "the nature of government restrictions on the export of technical information, . . . [w]e suggest that it be mutually agreed between us that until the present emergency has passed we discontinue our exchange of technical information, patent applications, etc."[12] Farben, realizing that the two firms had little choice, agreed.[13] Yet some agreements still bound DuPont.

In the 1930s, one of its subsidiaries, Remington Arms, had obtained rights from the IG to a superior primer for ammunition, tetrazene. The contract between the two companies banned Remington from exporting ammunition made with this product. As a result, Remington could not sell tetrazene-primed ammunition to the British, despite London's interest.[14] The prohibition apparently remained in force until the attack on Pearl Harbor.

Though DuPont's dealings with IG Farben escaped publicity, Rohm & Haas, a much smaller firm, encountered sharp criticism because of its agreement with a German enterprise. This firm's history made it particularly vulnerable. Formed in the United States before 1914 by Otto Haas, a German immigrant, the company had intimate ties to the German firm of the same name, Rohm & Haas of Darmstadt. Otto Rohm ran that company, and he had a substantial interest in the American firm, just as Haas had in the German one. American entry into World War I disrupted ties temporarily, but with peace the two quickly resumed their close relationship, again exchanging stock and licensing technology from each other for various products.

In June 1941, *Click* magazine, an imitator of *Life*, published an exposé, charging, "The Nazi bombs that pulverized Coventry and Birmingham, the German tanks that had rolled into the Low Countries and France, might well have been labeled 'Made in U.S.A.' because American dollars helped pay for them." The article quickly focused on Rohm & Haas, noting its German ties and then observing that Plexiglas, its most important product, had come from the laboratories of the German Rohm & Haas and that the American firm paid royalties to its German twin on the product. The magazine concluded, "Plexiglas is still one of the steadiest sources of revenue the Nazi war chest has in America." Finally, *Click* observed, "Today, the great bulk of Plexiglas royalties come from American defense orders." Not only was the American government indirectly subsidizing Germany, but information included in royalty reports might yield useful intelligence to the Nazis.[15]

These revelations caused an uproar and sparked talk of a congressional investigation. Yet on closer examination, the facts in the case took on a different aspect. Plexiglas had important military applications, particularly in warplanes, where it replaced regular glass because it was lighter and shatterproof, and because it better withstood the rapid changes in temperature encountered at high altitudes. Yet as one of Rohm & Haas's officials stated, "Plexiglas was a German development. We got it from Germany, and if we hadn't secured from German concerns both the patents and the technical information there wouldn't be an inch of Plexiglas in an American bomber or pursuit plane."[16] To obtain the technology, Rohm & Haas had paid royalties to its German partner. The payments, however, were based on dollar sales and contained no information on military consumption, and the company had stopped them completely at the end of 1940. One member of Congress who had had the *Click* article read into the *Congressional Record* subsequently declared himself, after a more careful study of all the evidence, "satisfied . . . that the charges contained in the article were not founded on fact."[17]

Though the Plexiglas agreement seems to have served in the interests of the United States, other accords yielded more questionable results. Right after World War I, Sterling Products Company had bought from the American government patents to many German-developed pharmaceuticals, most notably aspirin, which Washington had seized during the war. Yet Sterling had rights only in the United States, and even at home it needed German expertise to exploit fully the patents it had obtained. It soon reached an agreement with IG Farben that gave Sterling technical assistance and guarantees against IG competition in the United States and Canada in exchange for half the profits from its pharmaceutical division, Winthrop Chemicals, and a promise to abstain from exports. Farben subsequently purchased half of Winthrop.

With the outbreak of war in 1939, the British blockade cut off the IG from its lucrative Latin American markets. Determined to retain this business, Farben started supplying its Latin sales network from North America, relying on its U.S. subsidiary, General Aniline & Film, for dyestuffs and photographic chemicals. For pharmaceuticals, however, the IG turned to Winthrop. It purchased Winthrop's products unlabeled and then sent them to South America, where the IG's sales network marketed them under Farben's brand names. Winthrop and, through it, Sterling enjoyed sales that they would not have made otherwise, but the IG got the better of the deal, keeping its Latin American network supplied and maintaining its presence there. Moreover, the foreign exchange that Farben earned often ended up financing Nazi espionage and propaganda in Latin America, whereas the IG's offices sometimes provided cover for German spies.[18]

Although Sterling's experience reflected bad judgment on the part of its management, which as half owner of Winthrop simply could have refused to supply the IG, the case of Bausch & Lomb demonstrated how the terms of a cartel accord themselves could threaten national security. The history of optics resembled that of chemicals, though on a smaller scale. Before 1914, the German firm Zeiss dominated the production of optical instruments throughout the world, including military goods like rangefinders. The war cut Zeiss off from Western markets while vastly expanding the demand for military optics. Bausch & Lomb capitalized on this opportunity, but like American chemical companies it could not, in four years, match the expertise that the Germans had developed over decades. In 1921, fearing renewed competition from Zeiss, Bausch & Lomb signed a cartel accord with the German firm. Zeiss agreed to give Bausch & Lomb patent rights to all its discoveries in the military field, past and future. The American company promised to pay the Germans royalties on all military sales and to abstain from exporting. The Navy Department, which wanted access to Zeiss's technology, supported the agreement, though it is not clear it knew the details.[19]

European rearmament in the mid-1930s created problems for the accord. Britain and France placed orders with Bausch & Lomb that the company had to refuse because of its agreement with Zeiss. The American firm disingenuously announced that it would not sell its products abroad "because they might conceivably be used against the United States or its interests in another War." One of the firm's officers stated, "They are not prepared for war over there [Europe], . . . and if we refuse to help them prepare, it puts it off just that much."[20] These statements would earn Bausch & Lomb a reputation for hypocrisy when the facts came out in 1940. Rearmament in the United States led to further trouble because the cartel agreement required Bausch & Lomb to provide Zeiss with detailed information on all its sales to the U.S. military, information that German intelligence might find quite useful. Yet despite these serious problems, the United States benefited from the accord. Bausch & Lomb obtained valuable technology from Zeiss that, it claimed, "resulted in great improvement of optical fire-control equipment for our armed forces."[21] In 1940, when its cartel dealings became public, Secretary of War Henry Stimson wrote in a public letter to Bausch & Lomb, "The War Department has complete confidence in your company, for the excellence of workmanship, productive ability, and patriotic cooperation."[22] Secretary of the Navy Frank Knox provided a similar testimonial.[23]

By 1940 and 1941, cartel accords with German firms had clearly outlived their usefulness. Agreements based on common interests or, at least, a live-and-let-live attitude made little sense when the signatories' governments were in conflict. True, the United States and Germany were not technically at war, but they were definitely hostile. In the past, cartel agreements had given American firms access to valuable technology, but as long as the war continued Germany was unlikely to let such information out of the country. Yet in May 1940, the Antitrust Division reported that it was investigating ongoing foreign cartel ties in "military optical equipment, non-ferrous metals (such as magnesium, beryllium, chromium, tungsten carbide, etc.), steel alloys, various chemicals and a variety of other commodities."[24]

Why did firms maintain these agreements? First and probably most important, they were not easy to evade. Most rested on legal contracts involving patents. Second, the accords often provided American firms with valuable technology, and a company could not challenge an agreement without challenging its right to that knowledge. Finally, patent rights obtained through these accords sometimes gave American companies powerful weapons against competitors in the United States. Though Congress probably could have passed a law suspending cartel agreements for the duration of the European conflict, it never explored the possibility.[25] Such a step would have required the legislative branch to admit that war with Germany was likely, and this it refused to do. Although the vast majority of Americans hoped for an Allied victory, most still wanted to avoid direct military involvement. The failure of business to sever its cartel ties with Germany, and the failure of the government to force it to do so, represented another example of the half-hearted American response to Nazi aggression.

Antitrust and the Politics of Readiness

The outbreak of war in Europe put New Deal reformers in an uncomfortable position. Next to the question of American participation in the war, issues such as labor relations and antitrust law seemed insignificant. Rearmament, which enjoyed fairly strong support, dictated a rapprochement between business and government because it required cooperation between the two to produce weapons on a large scale. World War I had marked the end of the Progressive Era, and many Americans feared (or hoped) that World War II would do the same to the New Deal. Such concerns led Thurman Arnold and the Antitrust Division to latch on to international cartels as a way to relate their activities to mobilization.

During this time Franklin Roosevelt's attention shifted from domestic to foreign affairs, a process that had started in the late 1930s because of the president's frustration with political deadlock at home and, more important, his concern about German and Japanese aggression. By 1940, the transformation was complete. Roosevelt was devoting almost all his time to helping the British hold off the Nazis, containing the Japanese threat in East Asia, and winning an unprecedented third term as president.

The president's new focus led to some confusion in Washington. Administratively, Roosevelt's style is best described as "freewheeling." He rarely set clear lines of authority, resisted delegation, and actually encouraged infighting among subordinates by giving them overlapping responsibility. Every program seemed to require a new bureaucracy. This system kept would-be empire builders off balance, circumvented bureaucrats who might obstruct Roosevelt's plans, and allowed the president to hold open his options. It worked fairly well as long as Roosevelt maintained a close watch on developments.[26] Yet even the limited military buildup initiated in 1940 and 1941 revealed the weaknesses of this approach.

The president did not have the time to oversee the details of the military buildup himself, but he refused to let anyone else do so. In 1939, Roosevelt created the War Resources Board (WRB) to plan for possible mobilization, yet when the WRB recommended that Roosevelt lodge authority for war production in a centralized agency staffed largely by businessmen, he promptly disbanded it. With the collapse of France in 1940, FDR tried again. He established the Advisory Commission for National Defense (ACND), which had neither a leader nor a clear mandate and functioned largely as a debating forum for top officials. By January 1941, the clear failure of the ACND led Roosevelt to create the Office of Production Management (OPM). Although an improvement over the ACND, the OPM had two chief executives and limited authority. Not only did it lack power over such important agencies as the Office of Price Administration (OPA), which the president created in the spring of 1941 to combat inflation, but the OPM did not even control its own public-relations staff. To sort out the bureaucratic snarl, FDR established the Supplies Priorities and Allocations Board in the summer of 1941 to draft directives for the OPM. This innovation did not help much.[27] Arms production did increase sharply during 1940 and 1941, but it came largely from industrial capacity idled by the Depression.

Roosevelt believed that the national emergency required political unity. In the summer of 1940, he appointed two prominent Republicans, Henry Stimson and Frank Knox, to the key posts of secretary of war and secretary of the navy, respectively.[28] Though talented public servants, neither Stimson nor Knox supported the New Deal, and as the leaders of the military in a crisis they had immense influence over policy. The president also sought to make peace, or at least negotiate a truce, with the business community. As journalist and historian Bruce Catton wrote, the government had "to bring into the defense effort, as active cooperators, the proprietors of the nation's chief physical assets. The job couldn't be done without them, but their fears and suspicions—which, when Franklin Roosevelt was concerned, were deep and beyond number—had to be allayed. . . . The game had to be played their way."[29]

Antitrust seemed likely to be an early casualty of mobilization. Many assumed that firms would have to cooperate closely to deal with shortages and to fill huge military contracts. During World War I, Washington had suspended the antitrust laws. No one proposed such a drastic step in 1940 or 1941, but a climate of accommodation did exist. Jacob K. Javits, a young New York attorney who subsequently became a noted U.S. congressman and senator, urged amendment of the Sherman Act so that it would not "prevent the integration and coordination of business efforts, without which American industry cannot make its maximum contribution to national defense."[30] Thurman Arnold himself wrote, "The antitrust division will go as far as anyone likes in accepting the finding of fact of the National Defense Commission when any particular combination is necessary for national defense." Yet at the same time, he claimed, "It is difficult to imagine any case where the actual needs of defense can possibly conflict with the antitrust laws since both are aimed at efficiency in production and distribution."[31] Contrary to this assertion, however, even antitrust cases that did not deal directly with government procurement could slow mobilization. Suits required extensive attention from the top executives of the targeted firms, and even the partial mobilization of 1940 and 1941 severely taxed the nation's limited cadre of experienced managers. Every hour an executive spent dealing with the Antitrust Division was time away from organizing production. Though the situation did not justify dropping cases, it was a good reason to delay proceedings until the emergency had passed. Administrative questions aside, political realities demanded accommodation. As Business Week put it in 1941, "The Defense Commission would like to keep the industries essential to its procurement program happy and cooperative."[32] Antitrust suits rarely made their targets "happy and cooperative."

Thurman Arnold resisted this retreat from antitrust. Privately, he argued that Washington should "operate under the drastic powers of the act passed in 1916 which allows the government to compel business to furnish goods at fair prices."[33] Publicly, he continued to attack monopoly. Arnold warned, "During the last war the monopolistic combinations of war industries levied a tribute on the American consumer so wasteful that it led to proposals to draft capital in the next war. The same kind of thing can happen again today. Basic war materials are still dominated by small groups. Every combination in war industry needs constant scrutiny as to how it is using its organized power."[34] The reaction to Arnold's rhetoric was not always what he desired. As *Business Week* put it, "Arnold's own words present him in the light of baiting business and, so, raise the question of how he can expect others to accept him as sincerely trying to further the defense procurement program. It's possible consequently that Arnold himself is destroying whatever usefulness his policy may serve in that connection, even if that policy as such may be regarded as sound."[35]

Legal developments further weakened Arnold's position. In early 1941, the Supreme Court decided that the antitrust laws did not apply to labor unions. The Justice Department had invested heavily in suits targeting the anticompetitive practices of organized labor, and this decision severely hurt its prestige. At the same time, the Antitrust Division's willingness to prosecute such cases had alienated the unions, an increasingly powerful element in the Democratic Party and usually among the leading proponents of economic reform.[36]

Arnold did not stand alone, however. The war in Europe had not eliminated reformers' concerns about big business, and many of them actually blamed the conflict on the machinations of large firms. Marxists worked out the link in the greatest detail. They considered fascism to be capitalism in extremis, a last desperate attempt by the exploiting class to stave off revolution. In his book *The Spirit and Structure of German Fascism*, Robert Brady, a Marxist and a professor of economics at the University of California at Berkeley, declared Nazism "a dictatorship of monopoly capitalism. Its 'fascism' is that of business enterprise organized on a monopoly basis, and in full command of all the military, police, legal, and propaganda power of the state."[37] Harold Laski, a British Marxist whom historian Arthur Schlesinger, Jr., claimed "had the greatest effect [of any Englishman] on American left-wing thought in the thirties," wrote the foreword to this book, noting ominously, "Professor Brady shows how profound are Fascist tendencies in the United States."[38] Franz Neuman, a German émigré and Marxist in the social democratic mode, provided a more subtle analysis that nevertheless tied big business to Nazism. In his book *Behemoth*, he stated, "It is the aggressive, imperialistic, expansionist spirit of German big business . . . which is the motivating force of the [Nazi] economic system. Profits and more profits are the motive power." "Democracy," he argued, "would endanger the fully monopolized system. It is the essence of totalitarianism to stabilize and fortify it." Unlike Brady, Neuman did not consider big business identical to Nazism. For instance, it had little stake in Hitler's racial policies. Still he asserted that "with regard to imperialist expansion, National Socialism and big business have identical interests."[39] Neuman did not ignore cartels, which were particularly strong in Germany. He insisted that "the cartel structure is not democratic but autocratic." "They are much more than the democratic mask that industrial magnates use to disguise their autocratic power. Behind the powerful cartel movement there is a still more powerful trend of centralization, which had reached a scale never dreamed of before."[40]

This analysis found a receptive audience among the non-Marxist left in the United States. American reformers had traditionally feared the political consequences of economic concentration. Big business, they believed, had the ability to control government, distorting or even destroying political democracy. Accordingly, Brady's and Neuman's description of Nazism made sense to them. A review of Brady's book on the first page of the *New York Times Book Review* noted, "Here are laid bare all the objectives of the Big Business State and the role that the Nazi party has played and is playing in making such a state possible."[41] *The Nation* declared Brady's work "the clearest analysis of the motive power of German fascism and of the engineers who tend this political machine."[42] Book reviewers had no monopoly on such attitudes. In 1937, Robert Jackson, the head of the Justice Department's Antitrust Division and later attorney general and Supreme Court justice, claimed that large companies "are as dangerous a menace to political as they are to economic freedom."[43] At the same time, Interior Secretary Harold Ickes asserted that, should the New Deal falter, "then the America that is to be will be a big-business fascist America—an enslaved America."[44] For many reformers the struggle against big business at home and fascism abroad were merely different aspects of the same war. Their analysis was dubious—whatever the faults of the American business community, its members were not Nazi sympathizers. Nevertheless, this logic dictated the attitudes of many reformers toward mobilization. Military success abroad, purchased with concessions to big business at home, merely substituted one threat to democracy for another.

Arnold played to this sentiment, which to a degree he shared. He wrote, "Our great problem today is the undermining of American democracy by private groups in big business, little business, and labor. . . . The channels of trade in the distribution of every necessity are taxed by organizations which give no public account for the use of that power."[45] The situation had ominous parallels abroad. Ever since the late nineteenth century, Arnold claimed, German business had tended toward ever larger and more powerful economic concentrations. By the 1920s, "industrial Germany became an army with a place for everyone, and everyone was required to keep his place in a trade association or cartel. Here was arbitrary power without public control and regimentation without public leadership. That power, exercised without public responsibility, was constantly squeezing the consumer. There was only one answer. Germany was organized to such an extent that it needed a general and Hitler leaped to power. Had it not been Hitler it would have been someone else." Arnold conceded that the United States in 1940 was in less danger than Germany in 1930, but he warned, "We can observe a few disquieting symptoms of the same process in this country."[46]

Arnold contended that the country could not entrust mobilization to big business. As production increased in 1940 and 1941 and the economy experienced shortages of key materials—"bottlenecks"—Arnold warned of an "economic fifth column" that was behind the problem, though he added, somewhat paradoxically, that it was "not a malicious fifth column."[47] In late 1941, he stated, "For the first ten months our defense effort was hampered by the fear of expansion of the production of basic materials. Businessmen, indulging in wishful thinking, concealed shortages by over-optimistic predictions of supply. I would still insist that the general attitude of dominant American business, fearing overproduction after the war, was responsible for this lag in production."[48] Arnold attributed this attitude to "powerful groups who fear expansion may destroy their domination of industry."[49]

His analysis contained much truth. A decade of economic stagnation and memories of overcapacity following the last war had left most businessmen wary of constructing new plants, and ultimately Washington itself had to finance much of the new capacity built to supply the war effort. Yet Arnold went too far when he attributed the situation to monopoly. Skittishness about expansion affected almost every sort of business, whether it enjoyed monopoly power or not.[50] Alcoa, which enjoyed a monopoly over the production of raw aluminum, proved much readier to expand capacity than the steel industry, which was substantially more competitive. The difference largely reflected calculations of postwar demand, not the level of concentration within the two industries.[51]

Arnold focused on international cartels as a cause of problems with mobilization. These organizations, which linked large firms from around the world, including Germany, confirmed the worst fears of reformers about big business. Many even went so far as to describe them as a "fascist international." Arnold wrote to a friend soon after the war began in 1939, complaining "about the complete betrayal of England by British industrial interests. Up to the time of the outbreak of war they were furnishing Germany with the oil, the coal, and many of the other materials without which she could not have been in a position to carry on war against England."[52] In public Arnold claimed that "Hitler assisted the monopolists in democratic countries to restrict their own production while he was expanding his, playing on their fear of surplus output." "His technique was to make deals between German firms and American firms whereby, to avoid competition at home, American manufacturers would leave foreign markets to Germany. This meant, of course, the restriction of production here. Now in various important industries we find ourselves without the plant capacity to turn out essentials for defense."[53]

Even before the war started, the Justice Department had displayed a willingness to challenge the American operations of international cartels. In the summer and fall of 1939, it filed a series of suits against the fertilizer industry that targeted the international nitrates cartel. The Antitrust Division acted to protect farmers, the chief consumers of fertilizers and, according to Arnold, the foremost victims of monopoly. Nitrates, in addition to being a vital ingredient of fertilizer, were critical to other chemical products, particularly explosives. Many European governments subsidized the production of nitrates, despite worldwide overcapacity, because they wanted domestic supplies in case of war. This, coupled with the impoverishment of farmers during the Depression, had created a glut that led to the formation of an international cartel in the 1930s that allotted half the sizable U.S. nitrates market to Chilean miners of natural nitrates and the other half to domestic manufacturers. Only two American firms, DuPont and Allied Chemical, produced synthetic nitrates on a large scale.[54] DuPont used its output in-house for explosives or sold it to other firms that used it in a similar fashion. Allied made almost all the synthetic nitrates that went into fertilizer and, through a subsidiary, controlled the sale of nitrates produced as a by-product in other industries, particularly steel making. Companies in such fields produced substantial quantities of nitrates but did not want to go into the fertilizer business, which would have distracted them from their main operations. They were happy to sign long-term contracts with Allied to dispose of their nitrates. Allied itself marketed through a system of exclusive dealers with clearly defined territories that agreed to sell at prices set by the company. This not only prevented them from competing with one another but also kept them out of the way of Chile's agents. Allied further reduced the risk of competition with the South Americans by basing its prices on transportation costs from the ports where Chilean nitrates landed, even though its products originated elsewhere. At the behest of the international cartel, other foreign producers avoided the U.S. market and refused to license their technology to firms here.[55]

The Justice Department filed charges against the New York offices of the Chilean nitrates agency and the international cartel, as well as Allied Chemical and DuPont. Though the suit did not challenge practices abroad, it represented an audacious step. The Chilean cartel operated with the support of that country's government. The international cartel, which revolved around Europe's three largest and most efficient producers—IG Farben, ICI, and the Norwegian firm Norske Hydro—had ties to governments throughout Europe.

DuPont and Allied settled in May 1941. They agreed to sever all contacts with the Chilean and European cartels, and Allied promised to reduce its presence in the marketing of nitrates produced as by-products in other industries, limiting itself to 35 percent of a business that it had heretofore dominated. It also agreed to base prices on transportation costs from its own plants, not from the ports used by the Chileans.[56] The Justice Department never settled with the international cartel because the war led the organization to suspend operations, which never resumed.

Though the fertilizer case received little publicity, the suit against the Aluminum Company of America (Alcoa) claimed headlines for months. Filed under the tenure of Robert Jackson in 1937, the Alcoa trial dragged on from mid-1939 to mid-1940, producing approximately 70,000 pages of transcripts. Alcoa was a rare company, one that enjoyed a complete monopoly in the United States over the production of an important commodity, raw aluminum. The Justice Department attributed this situation to Alcoa's underhanded tactics: the purchase of all likely sources of bauxite (the raw material of aluminum) within the United States, the engrossment of the hydroelectric power vital to aluminum production through long-term contracts with utilities, a willingness to buy out competitors at inflated values, and predatory pricing to discourage rivals. The government also claimed that Alcoa relied on the international aluminum cartel to keep foreign competitors from exporting to the United States or building plants here, and that in exchange for this protection the American firm abstained from exports.

Alcoa had a second-hand relationship with the international aluminum cartel that nevertheless probably gave the American company a significant voice in its operations. Organized in 1931, the cartel allocated markets for aluminum outside the United States, and it included all the world's major producers save Alcoa. The Justice Department, however, argued that the American firm had a "back door" into this organization. In 1928, Alcoa had spun off all its foreign holdings to a Canadian subsidiary, Aluminum Limited (later Alcan), and then had distributed all the shares of this enterprise to its own stockholders, legally separating the two firms. This maneuver put Alcoa's valuable foreign assets, which had often suffered from neglect, under a single leadership devoted solely to them. But Alcoa and Aluminum Limited remained very close. Stockholding in the two firms remained concentrated, with six shareholders, one of whom was Alcoa's president, owning most of the firms' equity. The presidents of the two companies were brothers. Though Alcoa did not participate directly in the international cartel, Aluminum Limited was a leading member. The Antitrust Division assumed, probably correctly, that Aluminum Limited represented its American counterpart in the cartel, making sure that members avoided the U.S. market. Proving this in court, however, was another matter. The agreement to reserve the American market for Alcoa was informal, not contained in any official document. Indeed, it is possible that cartel members never actually discussed it, relying instead on an implicit understanding. This weakness is ironic because, from an economic point of view, the cartel charges were the strongest part of the government's case. Alcoa lacked domestic competition largely because no one could duplicate its highly efficient, tightly integrated facilities without prohibitive expense. Foreign producers already had such facilities, but they avoided selling in the United States because of the implicit understanding embodied in the aluminum cartel.[57]

The Alcoa case soon became entangled with mobilization. Aluminum is critical to the production of airplanes, and military demand promised to outstrip peacetime consumption by a huge margin. The country had to expand capacity, but how? Alcoa did invest in new facilities on its own, but soon observers realized that the firm could not keep pace with military needs.

The government had to act directly. Alcoa was willing to manage even more plants if Washington would pay for them, and many in the government, realizing that Alcoa was the only U.S. firm with experience making aluminum, were inclined to accept the offer. Yet the Antitrust Division and other critics of big business like Harold Ickes feared strengthening Alcoa and demanded an alternative.[58]

Mobilization authorities hoped the problem would somehow resolve itself. Edward R. Stettinius, a former president of U.S. Steel who was in charge of the industrial materials division of the Advisory Commission for National Defense, claimed in late 1940 that he saw "no serious shortages in aluminum supplies for aircraft and other military items now required for national defense."[59] Within six months, however, it became clear that a serious shortage did loom. In May 1941, *Time* magazine reported, "If the U.S. by terrific effort attains an aluminum ingot capacity of 600,000 tons (up 420,000 tons from 1940) by next year, and cuts off all aluminum for civil and indirect military uses, it *may* have barely enough to respond to defense needs."[60] Blame naturally attached to Alcoa, the nation's only producer. The *New Republic* reported in May 1941, "The testimony before the [Harry S.] Truman committee [on war procurement] proved that Alcoa had failed to respond to defense needs," and the magazine added, "These hearings are a clear and urgent warning that we can no longer afford to tolerate the restrictive control of a vital defense industry."[61]

Thurman Arnold blamed the shortage on the machinations of the international aluminum cartel. He pointed out that the cartel had originally assigned its members rights to a certain percentage of the total world market: Aluminum Limited got 29 percent; German producers, 20 percent; and so on. A Swiss firm created by the members oversaw operations of the cartel, keeping track of output and sales and maintaining a stockpile of aluminum to which it added or from which it sold to keep the market stable.

German rearmament wrecked the arrangement. The Reich planned to build a large air force that would require much aluminum, and according to the cartel agreement it would have to import a substantial portion of the metal. The German government had no intention of becoming dependent on suppliers abroad for a key war material; it also probably lacked the foreign exchange to buy large quantities of aluminum. In 1934, the German producers demanded freedom to sell in their domestic market unhampered by quotas. The other members grudgingly agreed, provided that the Germans sharply limited exports, which they did. By 1939, largely because of sales to the Luftwaffe, Germany had become the world's largest producer of aluminum, ahead of even the United States. As Arnold described it, "The democracies thus were free to pursue their restrictive policy without fear of German competition. Under this arrangement, Hitler tripled aluminum production for aircraft and war materials while the democracies stood still. . . . Now we know there is a shortage. We could have saved precious time and precious materials had we not listened to the wishful thinking of men whose financial interest lay in preventing new production in order to preserve their monopoly after the war."[62]

Alcoa denied these charges. In an official letter from one of its officers, Alcoa "categorically denies that it was in any way a member of the [international] cartel." The letter continued, "Any member of the cartel would have been as free as was Germany to produce as much aluminum as it desired provided it was consumed at home; but apparently only Germany was building a tremendous machine for war in the air. That other nations did not produce more aluminum is attributable not to self-limitation on the part of the aluminum industries, but to the failure of the nations within whose borders they operated to order the metal for military purposes, as Germany was doing." The current shortage was inevitable in light of the huge jump in military demand. "Chrysler Corporation," Alcoa's representative noted, "is not criticized for not immediately having a tank factory built and in operation the day the government needed a large quantity of medium tanks, nor are Ford or General Motors criticized for not beginning to build bomber plants on the date of the fall of France."[63] Alcoa's denial of involvement in cartels, though technically true, was probably disingenuous, but the rest of its argument had validity. The aluminum cartel had abandoned its quota system in 1936, and was inactive by 1938 because European rearmament had all the continent's facilities producing at capacity. Moreover, the market sharing agreement had never bound Alcoa, which was free to produce as much aluminum as it could sell in the United States. Germany produced more aluminum than any other nation because the Nazis were buying more than any other government.

Did Alcoa's monopoly impede American mobilization? One of the staff of the Antitrust Division wrote, "In a competitive industry there is always some excess capacity, which can be put to use when demand increases, but a monopoly does not have to provide spare capacity. The Aluminum Company, like any other monopoly, has kept its capacity so low that in 1939, before the national defense program commenced, it was already operating at its full capacity of 327,000,000 pounds. Therefore, when defense requirements began to increase demand, the nation was left without that safety margin of extra capacity which is always guaranteed by competition."[64] This analysis ignored the scale of military requirements. In 1941, even before the attack on Pearl Harbor, officials were speaking of the need to produce 1.2 billion pounds of aluminum a year, and in 1944, at the peak of wartime demand, the country produced 2.328 billion pounds of aluminum, a sevenfold increase over 1939.[65] Had the American aluminum industry been more competitive in 1939, prices might have been somewhat lower and output somewhat higher. Yet because Alcoa pursued a relatively moderate policy, regularly increasing capacity in line with demand and actually dropping its charges from $.23 a pound in 1931 to $.17 by 1941,[66] it seems unlikely that the difference would have been enough to affect mobilization in more than a marginal way. On the whole, greater problems arose because the debate over Alcoa's monopoly delayed government plans to expand capacity until the fall of 1941, months after shortages were evident.

Aside from the unfortunate publicity, Alcoa survived the Justice Department's assault fairly well. In October 1941, the judge in the antitrust case, after making his way through the huge quantity of testimony, decided in Alcoa's favor on every count.[67] Meanwhile, the government's Reconstruction Finance Corporation (RFC) signed a contract with Alcoa to finance aluminum plants to be designed and run by the company. Many—from radical columnist I. F. Stone to Interior Secretary Harold Ickes—criticized the deal as a gift to monopolists,[68] but the contract served its purpose by massively increasing aluminum capacity. Though supplies remained tight throughout the war, shortages of aluminum did not hamper the military effort.

The Antitrust Division did appeal the *Aluminum* decision, securing victory of sorts in 1945. The final decision, drafted by the noted jurist Learned Hand, concluded that regardless of how it developed, the very existence of Alcoa's monopoly violated the antitrust laws. The decision set an important precedent, substantially modifying the Supreme Court's 1911 *Standard Oil* decision, which had made the distinction between "reasonable" and "unreasonable" restraints of trade. Hand's opinion concluded that the control of a market was in itself "unreasonable" regardless of how obtained. Despite its sweeping language, however, the conclusion had limited impact on Alcoa itself. The decisive blow to the company's monopoly came right after the war when Washington sold, below cost, many of the aluminum plants that Alcoa had built and managed during the conflict to Reynolds Aluminum and the Kaiser organization. These two firms thus became, almost overnight, formidable competitors to Alcoa.[69] Subsequently, a suit decided in 1950 forced the dominant shareholders in Alcoa and Aluminum Limited to dispose of their holdings in one or the other, severing a key tie between the two companies.[70]

Though it garnered less publicity than the Alcoa case, the Justice Department's attack on patent agreements yielded greater results. The first important suit in the field dealt with conditions at home and involved DuPont, Standard Oil of New Jersey, and General Motors. They jointly owned the Ethyl Company, which produced a patented anti-knock compound added to almost all gasoline sold in the United States. Ethyl sold its product to refiners on the condition that they sell gasoline only to retail jobbers licensed by Ethyl. The company gave licenses to jobbers free of charge but retained the right to revoke them at will. Ethyl ostensibly imposed this system to ensure that its product, which in concentrated form was quite toxic, received safe handling. But it also used its power to force jobbers to stabilize gasoline prices. The Justice Department sued to overturn the arrangement, and in 1940, the Supreme Court concluded, "The record leaves no doubt that appellate [Ethyl] has made use of its dominant position in the [gasoline] trade to exercise control over prices and marketing policies of jobbers in a sufficient number of cases and with sufficient continuity to make its [hostile] attitude toward price cutting a pervasive influence in the jobbing trade."[71] The court allowed that a firm could impose such restrictions on a patented article, but Ethyl had no patent on gasoline, only an additive contained in it, and the Supreme Court concluded, "A patentee may not, by attaching a condition to his license, enlarge his monopoly and thus acquire some other which the statute and the patent together do not give."[72] Although the decision did not specifically relate to international cartels, it did have implications for them. The rules for domestic and international patent agreements were the same, and some international cartels did operate like the Ethyl arrangement. General Electric, for instance, used its patents on machines for making lightbulbs to regulate their sale.

The Antitrust Division sought to follow up this victory and establish more specific precedents against patent accords. It first targeted Bausch & Lomb. In 1940, Washington challenged the company's alliance with Zeiss, arguing that it was a cover for monopoly and citing internal documents from Bausch & Lomb indicating that the firm considered some of Zeiss's patents weak and continued to abide by them chiefly because they stifled its domestic

competitors. Bausch & Lomb tried to use its military contacts to avoid prosecution. As Arnold described it, the company "attached a letter to their bid
to the Navy Department for rangefinders on two cruisers in which they said
that because of the trial they would have to extend delivery date on range-
finder equipment about six months."[73] This threat was particularly serious
because Bausch & Lomb was the only American producer of such goods.
The Justice Department refused to back down. Arnold wrote, "We immediately called up Bausch & Lomb and stated that in our opinion their rep-
resentation as to necessary delays because of the suit were false, and informed
them that we would publish excerpts from letters in our possession indicating
their practices in the past. We stated we would add to the publication the
threat they made not to complete rangefinders on time for the navy, and
that we would ask for a Congressional investigation. We finally added that
we considered their representations to the navy proper to present to the court
in the event of conviction as a basis for imposition of jail sentences rather
than the fines which are ordinarily imposed." Not surprisingly, Bausch &
Lomb quickly settled the case on the government's terms, severing ties with
Zeiss and paying fines.[74]

The next year, Sterling Chemical settled a similar case. It received gentler
handling than Bausch & Lomb, supposedly because it was more cooperative.
Some noted that Sterling had retained Tommy Corcoran, a friend of Arnold's
and an influential New Dealer who had just embarked on a legendary career
as a Washington lobbyist, and alleged that the peaceful outcome owed
chiefly to his intervention with the Antitrust Division. In any case, Sterling
canceled its agreement with IG Farben without too much fuss.[75] For the
time being, however, Farben retained its half ownership in Sterling's pharmaceutical division, Winthrop.

Sometimes the Justice Department achieved its goals even before settling
a case. In the 1920s, General Electric had licensed from the German steel
maker Krupp a process to make tungsten carbide, an extremely hard alloy
used for the cutting edge of machine tools. Once assured of monopoly
through this patent agreement, GE raised the price of tungsten carbide in
the United States to over $200 a pound, whereas in Europe Krupp charged
about $50. The situation attracted the attention of the Justice Department,
and the Antitrust Division filed suit against GE and Krupp. General Electric's position was already eroding because in 1940, a federal court invali-
dated several of its tungsten carbide patents.[76] The antitrust suit further em-
boldened potential competitors. As was its usual practice, GE had licensed

other companies to produce tungsten carbide but had set strict conditions on their output and prices. With the antitrust suit under way, one of these firms decided that it could ignore its agreement. It cut charges sharply, forcing GE to follow suit, and the price soon fell to between $27 and $45 a pound.[77]

Another Justice Department case freed up the magnesium industry. Alcoa, Dow Chemical, and IG Farben owned key patents among themselves covering the production and fabrication of magnesium, a light metal useful in both airframes and incendiary explosives. They had joined together in the 1930s and had forged an agreement under which Dow made all the country's raw magnesium and Alcoa and the IG licensed all fabricators, a group of which Alcoa was the largest. In January 1941, the Justice Department indicted the combination, arguing "that there are inadequate facilities in the present period of national defense for the production of magnesium . . . [and] that the development and use of magnesium and magnesium products in the manufacture of airplanes and other products has been restricted, restrained, and discouraged."[78] Dow and Alcoa settled the case in April 1942, paying $140,000 in fines and agreeing to license their patents free of charge.[79]

Despite its successes, the Justice Department did not get the precedent it wanted against patent agreements. Because most companies settled out of court on terms favorable to the government, none of these cases reached a final decision before the attack on Pearl Harbor. Presumably companies settled because they considered defeat likely, but they may have also acted to avoid the negative publicity attached to cartel ties with German firms. The legitimate boundaries of patent agreements remained undefined.

Arnold's attack on cartels had yielded mixed results. On one hand, the uproar surrounding the aluminum case probably delayed the badly needed expansion of capacity. On the other, the magnesium and tungsten carbide cases made heretofore tightly held patents widely available and, with tungsten carbide, drove prices down.

The cartel issue did not generate the sort of public reaction for which Arnold had hoped. The effort did earn approval. A *New York Times* editorial claimed, "No sharp line can be drawn between manufacturing for commerce and manufacturing for national defense. . . . The Government has a right to scrutinize these international patent licenses. They are in effect private treaties which have world-wide economic effects."[80] Yet many were skeptical of Arnold's oft-repeated claim that cartel agreements had seriously hampered mobilization. With respect to the magnesium case, *Time* noted, "Collusion was not necessary to explain why the U.S. magnesium industry is so small. Its market is new and limited; it has only recently become sufficiently corrosion-proof to be widely used in U.S. Navy planes."[81]

The Antitrust Division occupied a precarious position. Prosecutions continued largely because no one in the various mobilization agencies had the authority to stop them. Should Washington centralize mobilization, as it presumably must sooner or later, the Antitrust Division would face strong pressure to desist. Unless Arnold could somehow rally overwhelming public support, he would have little choice but to comply.

War, Rubber, and the Last Stand of Thurman Arnold

American entry into the world war ended Thurman Arnold's antitrust crusade. The need to coordinate mobilization and placate the business community led to sharp restrictions on the Antitrust Division and eventually forced President Roosevelt to get rid of Arnold. Arnold resisted, however, using international cartels to relate the activities of his bureau to mobilization. The effort failed in its immediate objects but would define the cartel issue for the rest of the decade.

The Japanese attack on Pearl Harbor and Germany's declaration of war against the United States in December 1941 focused American public life, giving the nation an overriding goal—military victory. Eager to minimize domestic political division, Roosevelt announced that "Dr. Win-the-War" had replaced "Dr. New Deal."[82] Overworked and increasingly in poor health, the president devoted most of his time to foreign and military affairs. Congress also turned away from domestic reform and even scrapped several New Deal agencies.[83] The military situation lent urgency to the drive for unity at home. During the first half of 1942, the Japanese overran Southeast Asia, as well as American outposts in the western Pacific, and German submarines inflicted severe losses on Allied shipping in the Atlantic, often within sight of American shores. In Europe, the German army was advancing deep into Russia. With crises on almost every front, domestic squabbling seemed inappropriate.

The president streamlined the mobilization bureaucracy, although he did not advance as fast as he might have. In January 1942, Roosevelt created the War Production Board (WPB), merging the discredited OPM and SPAB and putting them under the leadership of one person, Donald Nelson, a Sears, Roebuck executive. But confusion persisted. The WPB lacked control over military procurement, which meant that it did not set production targets, the goals that determined all other decisions. The Office of Price Management remained outside the WPB's purview, as did the special agencies Roosevelt created to deal with specific problems like the rubber shortage. In May 1943, Roosevelt tried again, naming James Byrnes, a South Carolina politician and former Supreme Court justice, to head the newly constituted Office of War Mobilization (OWM), which would coordinate the activities of all other wartime agencies. Byrnes did a superb job, reducing infighting and generally imposing a measure of harmony on mobilization.[84] Nevertheless, his appointment came eighteen months after the attack on Pearl Harbor.

War cast business in a special role. Large companies provided ready-made organizations through which to mobilize industrial resources, and Washington relied on them both as producers and as coordinators of the activities of thousands of subcontractors. "Dollar-a-year men," executives on loan from private firms, even staffed mobilization organizations.[85] This policy yielded impressive results. Management expert Peter Drucker described the obstacles General Motors faced in building large plants to make aircraft, a business entirely new to it: "This division was built up in great haste in 1942 and 1943. It was necessary to train in the shortest possible time more than forty thousand workers and close to two thousand foremen. Many of the foremen had never before been in an industrial plant, not even as unskilled workers."[86] General Motors' experience was not unique—Alcoa's payroll increased by three and a half times during the war, and DuPont's more than tripled.[87] Despite the strain, American companies produced huge quantities of arms and material critical to defeating the Axis. The federal government's dependence on private industry, however, made it reluctant to antagonize business interests.

Government controls replaced the workings of the free market. Victory required Washington to allocate resources on military rather than economic criteria. It limited the output of consumer goods despite rising income and financed the expansion of heavy industry with little reference to the economic viability of plants. The government rationed scarce materials like steel, aluminum, and copper. It fixed prices. In this atmosphere, Arnold's crusade to restore economic competition was irrelevant, if not counterproductive.

Washington's wartime management of foreign trade in commodities demonstrates the problems the Antitrust Division faced. Here the U.S. government not only tolerated existing cartels but actually organized new ones, a process under way well before the attack on Pearl Harbor. Nazi victories during the spring of 1940 had forced the United States to focus intently on Latin America. The economies of these nations looked as much to Europe as to the United States, at least until German military success and the British blockade cut off trade. This situation threatened severe economic dislocation as European export markets vanished, and it gave the Germans, who after 1940 controlled the European continent, a way to insinuate themselves into South America. Washington, intent on securing its own hemisphere, worked to exclude the Nazis from the region. At a July 1940 meeting of the foreign ministers of the nations of the Americas, Secretary of State Cordell Hull recommended the "creation of facilities for the temporary handling and orderly marketing of accumulated surpluses of those commodities which are of primary importance to the maintenance of the economic life of the American republics, whenever such action becomes necessary." This meant the "development of commodity agreements with a view to assuring equitable terms of trade for both producers and consumers"—"commodity agreement" being a common euphemism for cartel.[88]

The coffee accord provides a good example of how these arrangements worked. Europe had absorbed about 40 percent of Latin America's coffee before the war; the loss of this market created a severe crisis. Because the United States was the only large importer remaining, it seemed likely that producers would soon be dumping coffee there, driving the price down. Washington feared the economic and political dislocation that would follow such a development, and in April 1941 put into effect an agreement with Latin American producers under which the United States took from each country a fixed amount of coffee at a fixed price.[89] This formula did not eliminate the problems caused by the disappearance of European markets, but it did keep the price from collapsing and gave producing nations a framework in which to organize their own schemes to limit output.

During the next several years, the U.S. government negotiated dozens of commodity agreements, chiefly (but not solely) with Latin American governments. Unlike the coffee accord, most were aimed at goods in short supply rather than those in surplus, and by 1943, a variety of agreements with over twenty countries covered nearly seventy commodities. In cases such as wheat and sugar, Washington worked through cartels established in the 1930s. Commodity accords usually provided for the United States to purchase a fixed amount at a set price; sometimes the agreement committed the United States to purchase a country's entire output. The accords furnished supplying countries with generous prices guaranteed over several years, which encouraged production. At the same time, they ensured supply and protected Washington from even higher prices. During the war, shortages abounded and, had the government left importation in private hands, different American firms probably would have bid against one another, driving prices to astronomical levels.[90] By 1945, much of U.S. foreign trade ran through what were in effect government-controlled cartels.

The war severely weakened Thurman Arnold and the Justice Department's Antitrust Division. The businessmen whom the government charged with running mobilization agencies had little use for antitrust prosecutions, and the civilian and uniformed personnel of the War and Navy Departments generally agreed with them. The focus of industry on war production lent private enterprise an aura of patriotism and made it more likely that antitrust prosecutions, by forcing executives to concentrate on matters other than production, would hinder the military effort. Finally, the centralization of authority over mobilization, however halting, made it more difficult for Arnold to ignore the wishes of others in the government.

American entry into the war put an end to the Antitrust Division's campaign against patent cartels linking German and American firms, in which Arnold had invested so heavily. The declaration of war automatically suspended such agreements.[91] As Wendell Berge of the Justice Department noted in 1944, "The argument that these agreements are abrogated by the war can be harmful to our cartel program. The defendants urge this abrogation in order to show that our case against them is moot." Unfortunately from the perspective of the Antitrust Division, temporary suspension did not resolve the long-term problem posed by restrictive accords. Berge argued, "It is exceedingly likely that these agreements will be resumed after the war unless there is a court decision finding them invalid."[92]

Realizing the weakness of its position, the Antitrust Division continued to try to make a place for itself in mobilization, an effort that involved heavy emphasis on international cartels. The task proved difficult, however, as the case against General Aniline & Film and General Dyestuffs demonstrated. These two companies were the chief subsidiaries of IG Farben in the United States. General Aniline produced a wide variety of goods, enjoying particular strength in dyes and photographic chemicals. General Dyestuffs marketed Aniline's products, as well as those made in Germany by the IG. Together they had a substantial presence in the American market, selling about 40 percent of dyestuffs consumed in the United States, as well as a

host of other products.[93] The two firms composed perhaps the most important German investment outside Europe, and the IG was not eager to lose
them as its predecessors had lost their American assets in World War I.
Almost from the beginning Farben had tried to conceal its interest in General Aniline and General Dyestuffs, first running them through a Swiss holding company and then, after war began in Europe, transferring nominal
ownership to Germans resident in the United States. As early as 1935, representatives of the IG told incredulous DuPont officials "repeatedly and
unequivocally that the German IG did not own directly or indirectly the
General Aniline Works."[94] Despite such assertions, however, the link between the American firms and the IG remained a secret open to anyone
who took the trouble to examine the matter.

American entry into the war forced Washington to take action against
these two companies, particularly General Aniline, a major industrial firm
in a high-tech field. A Treasury Department memo noted that the company
"has succeeded by several devices in providing access for its men—often
German aliens or German-born American citizens—to the drafting rooms
of about 3500 industrial plants, including defense installations and Government experimental laboratories, and in amassing valuable industrial information." In another instance, "a company laboratory, in charge of a German
alien assisted by two other German aliens, was found to be developing and
processing films of experimental United States Army tanks." The Treasury
Department concluded that General Aniline "provides the German Government, through IG Farben, with unusual opportunities for the concealment of German agents and expenditures for propaganda and other subver-
sive purposes."[95] Yet the company's considerable resources would make it a
valuable military contractor if the government could eliminate German influence.

On December 19, 1941, less than two weeks after the attack on Pearl
Harbor, the Antitrust Division filed suit against Farben, General Aniline &
Film, and General Dyestuffs, claiming that the three had "agreed to combine all their dyestuff properties in the United States into a single manufacturing company and not to compete otherwise in the manufacture or sale
of dyestuffs." The suit also attacked similar ties among these companies
governing photographic chemicals, an area in which Farben was the world's
leader. The government sought the end of these accords.[96]

Though at first glance plausible, the reasoning behind the suit weakened
on closer examination. The Antitrust Division wanted to sever the ties be-

tween IG Farben and its American subsidiaries. Yet if General Dyestuffs and
General Aniline were indeed subsidiaries of IG Farben, the agreements cited
by the Justice Department were simply management arrangements legal
under the antitrust laws, which did not require that different parts of a company compete against one another. The Antitrust Division had a case only
if it accepted the fictitious claims of General Aniline and General Dyestuffs
that they were independent of IG Farben. In this circumstance, the government might well secure a consent decree or court order terminating the
agreements, though the war would have already suspended such accords.
But this would not eliminate pro-German managers or spies on the payrolls
at the two firms.

In March 1942, Washington resolved the problem by seizing ownership
of General Aniline & Film and General Dyestuffs. The Alien Property Custodian, a wartime agency responsible for the assets of Axis nationals, took
over these properties—along with other IG assets like its 50 percent holding
in Winthrop Chemical and its Jasco stock, which had been in trust for
Standard Oil of New Jersey—and promptly installed new management.
Eventually, General Aniline became an important war contractor.

The Antitrust Division, however, could not bring itself to drop the matter.
Its suit dragged on for years. More important, the Antitrust Division objected
to the managers whom the Alien Property Custodian had put in charge of
General Aniline. One was an officer of an oil company, and as an Antitrust
Division memo observed, "the connection between IG Farben and all oil
concerns here is well-known." Another was the chairman of the Corn Products Refining Company, which had had German subsidiaries before the war.
"It can be assumed," the same Justice Department memo noted, "that these
subsidiaries . . . are connected by cartel agreements with other German
chemical works, especially with IG Farben."[97] These accusations were both
unfair and unwise. They cited no specific evidence concerning the individuals in question. Even had the Antitrust Division possessed such information, cartels were an accepted way of doing business in almost every country
except the United States. Within the United States, patent agreements had
traditionally served a similar function, and the Justice Department, despite
its success in negotiating consent decrees, had yet to get a definitive court
ruling against such accords. Aside from the legal and moral questions, almost
every major chemical and oil firm had at some time participated in some
sort of cartel. Washington could not mobilize these critical industries while
shunning the companies that constituted them. In any event, the Alien Prop-

erty Custodian ignored the Antitrust Division's objections, which Arnold may not have pushed very hard. Their very mention, however, could not have won the Antitrust Division friends among those responsible for mobilization.

Thurman Arnold and the Antitrust Division seized on the rubber crisis as a last chance to relate antitrust, and specifically the drive against international cartels, to mobilization. Japanese victories in the first half of 1942 had cut the United States off from Southeast Asia, by far the most important source of natural rubber, and catastrophe threatened. Americans relied heavily on cars and trucks for transportation, and Washington planned to build a vast mechanized army. Without rubber tires, the country could not keep its economy running, much less wage a victorious war. The nation had a rubber stockpile that might, if carefully husbanded, last for eighteen months, but beyond that the prospects were bleak unless the country found new supplies.

The government counted on a massive synthetic rubber program to avoid disaster. The German army already ran on synthetic tires made of a substance produced by IG Farben, buna rubber. DuPont also produced a synthetic of its own devising, neoprene, but neoprene required calcium as a feedstock, whereas buna used cheaper and more plentiful oil. Jasco, the joint Standard/IG company that had in 1939 become a de facto subsidiary of Standard Oil of New Jersey, controlled the American rights to buna rubber. In December 1941, Standard put the rights to buna into a patent pool set up by the rubber industry and covering several types of synthetics. Washington soon laid plans for a massive artificial rubber industry that it would finance and in which buna would have the leading place, composing almost three-quarters of output.[98]

At this point the Antitrust Division intervened. It had been investigating the relationship between Standard and IG Farben for at least a year, and in early 1942, the Antitrust Division informed Standard that it intended to file suit. After a considerable internal debate Standard decided to settle, even though most of its officers believed that their firm had done nothing wrong.[99] On March 25, 1942, the company signed a consent decree with the government, paying $50,000 in fines and agreeing to license all its synthetic rubber patents free of charge for the duration of the war, thereby in all likelihood forgoing several million dollars in revenue.[100] Standard's press release on the occasion no doubt reflected the thoughts of its management: "The developments made under these agreements [with IG Farben] have advanced the progress of American industry and its ability to meet the war emergency. Nevertheless the company realizes that to obtain vindication by trying the issue in the courts would involve months of time and energy of most of its officers and many of its employees. Its war work is more important than court vindication."[101]

Though Standard thought otherwise, Thurman Arnold did not consider the matter closed. The very day after signing the consent decree he appeared before the special Senate committee charged with monitoring mobilization and chaired by Harry S. Truman. Arnold announced, "We believe that the [Standard] cartel arrangements with Germany . . . are the principal cause for the present shortage of synthetic rubber." Backed by a mass of documents subpoenaed from Standard's files, the antitrust chief outlined in detail the agreements with Farben by which Standard had gained control of hydrogenation and how the American firm had ceded dominance over the petrochemical field to the Germans through the Jasco Agreement. The latter accord gave Farben the authority to refuse to license the buna patents in the United States, a power it had exercised at the behest of the German government, which did not want this technology exploited abroad. As Arnold put it, simplifying the tale somewhat, "Standard Oil delayed the use of buna rubber in this country because the Hitler government did not wish to have this rubber exploited here for military reasons." Berlin relented only at the end of 1938, but even then Arnold claimed, "Standard delayed the introduction of buna rubber even after it had received permission from IG Farben to make suitable arrangements." Jasco attached prohibitive conditions to licenses, requiring that firms use synthetic output only internally (not selling raw rubber to anyone else), pay a very high royalty of $.075 per pound, and license back to Standard any improvements in the buna process. These terms, which Standard retained even after assuming full control of Jasco, found few takers. Arnold claimed that "Standard, apparently, could not bring itself to offer terms to these rubber companies which would afford even a modicum of independence." The nation's buna capacity remained negligible until the attack on Pearl Harbor. Referring to unsuccessful attempts by Goodyear Tire and Dow Chemical to negotiate licenses for buna in 1938, Arnold mused, "I don't know what Goodyear could have done with it. I don't know what Dow could have done with it. But if we look . . . we can see what free enterprise and experimentation is capable of, and I am perfectly sure that had this thing been opened we would have developed it [synthetic rubber] as Germany did."[102]

Standard Oil's restrictive policy, Arnold claimed, extended not only to buna, the IG's discovery, but also to its own invention, butyl rubber. In the mid-1930s, at the same time that Farben was refusing to license American production of buna, Standard turned over to Jasco its newly discovered butyl process for making synthetic rubber, which Arnold claimed effectively put it under German control.[103] After 1939, the American firm gained control of Jasco, but Arnold observed "that on Standard's own development; namely, butyl, Standard refused to license all but two rubber companies, with the exception of specialty companies." This policy stifled a promising development. Arnold noted that butyl's cost, "as estimated by Standard, was between 7 and 15 cents a pound, compared with approximately 20 cents per pound for natural rubber. In addition, it apparently can be used to make an overall tire. No natural rubber is necessary for the carcass," as was the case with other synthetics.[104]

Thurman Arnold could explain Standard Oil's actions. He asserted, "There is no alliance with German interests from unpatriotic motives." Rather, the company acted "to restrict world production in order to retain . . . control." Standard's drive for a protected market reflected a broader problem. "There is essentially no difference," Arnold claimed, "between what Standard Oil of New Jersey has done in this case and what other companies did in restricting the production of magnesium, aluminum, tungsten carbide, dye stuffs, and a variety of other critical materials."[105]

Arnold's revelations caused an uproar. Senator Truman said, "Even after we were in the war, Standard Oil of New Jersey was putting forth every effort . . . to protect the control of the German government over a vital war material."[106] Senator Joseph O'Mahoney of Wyoming told a Standard executive, "Your difficulty proceeds from the fact that you are bound by two loyalties . . . loyalty to IG Farben [and] . . . loyalty to the United States."[107] TRB, the leading columnist of the *New Republic*, mused, "Standard of New Jersey was still more loyal to the business international than to the United States of America."[108] The final report of Truman's committee, though more measured than Arnold's testimony, stated, "The documentary evidence out of Standard's own files requires the conclusion that Standard, as a result of its cartel arrangements with IG Farben, and as a result of its general business philosophy, did hamper the development of synthetic rubber in the United States."[109]

Standard Oil of New Jersey vigorously denied Arnold's claims. Its president said, "Any charges that the Standard Oil Co. or any of its officers has been in the slightest respect disloyal to the United States is unwarranted and untrue. I repel all such insinuations with all the vigor at my command. I do so with indignation and resentment." He continued: "Standard has no apologies to make for the part it played and is now playing in the development of synthetic rubber. It brought to this country from Germany the IG buna rubber invention now being used in the government rubber program." Standard conceded that until 1938 the IG had, according to its rights under the Jasco agreement, blocked the licensing of buna rubber on orders from the German government. Yet Farben had developed buna, and the Jasco accord gave it no power over the process that it would not have enjoyed in any case. At the same time, however, the Germans had provided Standard with substantial technical information on buna through Jasco, withholding only the actual blueprints for the large plant that the IG was building in Germany to produce it.[110]

After gaining control of Jasco in 1939, Standard had tried to develop the buna process commercially. Unfortunately, buna production costs were high. In 1942, Standard estimated the cost at approximately $.25 to $.30 a pound, whereas natural rubber cost under $.10 a pound. This calculation reflected the impact of a much-improved method developed by Standard in 1941 for producing butadiene, the critical ingredient of buna. The old method, devised by the IG, was considerably more expensive. As the head of Standard's research operation put it, the commercialization of buna required either "general industry cooperation in which the industry itself removes competitive hazards, or else the government must step in and take control of the matter."[111]

Standard had explored both private cooperation and public support. In January 1940, it had devised a combine that would encompass the entire rubber industry. Each tire firm would agree to use buna for a certain percentage of its output, passing the extra cost on to consumers. This setup would guarantee that no one firm would gain a cost advantage over the others by forgoing the most expensive synthetic for natural rubber. Moreover—though Standard's officers did not emphasize the fact—it would have guaranteed Standard's control of the synthetic rubber business because Standard would have owned 51 percent of the combine.[112] The plan collapsed, in part because it was too complicated, and in part because of fears that it would violate the antitrust laws.[113] Standard's approach to the government fared no better. In 1940, it had recommended to the Advisory Commission on National Defense that the United States build plants capable of producing 150,000 tons of synthetic rubber per year, supplying a quarter of U.S. consumption. The government soon scaled the program back to 40,000 tons. In the end, President Roosevelt and Jesse Jones, the head of the Reconstruction Finance Corporation, which was supposed to finance the plants, decided against the investment. It would have been expensive and have absorbed scarce resources, and neither Roosevelt, Jones, nor anyone else in the government imagined that the Japanese would be able to cut off American supplies of natural rubber.[114]

Subsequently, Standard abandoned immediate plans for large-scale production and instead issued licenses only for the production of specialty rubber. In a few cases, the synthetic article was superior to natural rubber, largely because it better withstood corrosion from petroleum. Buna could, therefore, command a substantial premium for products like engine hoses and sealants. DuPont already did a good business with its synthetic, neoprene, and Standard hoped to profit as well. Because Standard anticipated that rubber companies would get a high price for specialty products, as much as $1 a pound, it charged a relatively steep royalty of $.075 a pound. Standard also anticipated making money selling the rubber companies butadiene, the critical ingredient for buna. At the same time, Standard limited the uses to which rubber firms could put buna, keeping open the possibility of initiating mass production itself if the opportunity arose. Nevertheless, specialty rubber production in the United States expanded from a rate of about 2,500 tons a year at the beginning of 1939 to a rate of 20,000 tons at the end of 1941, with buna accounting for much of the increase.[115]

Outside experts supported Standard's account. In 1942 William Balt of the War Production Board blamed the government for the failure to develop synthetic rubber.[116] P. W. Litchfield, the chairman of Goodyear Rubber, whose exclusion from synthetic production Thurman Arnold had so lamented, stated that his firm had been able to develop tires from buna rubber despite Standard's control over the process. But he added, "We never pushed so hard on the synthetic in volume until it became apparent at Pearl Harbor that we were likely to have a sudden cession of our crude rubber supply." Litchfield said, "We are looking forward, roughly, on synthetic to somewhere about twenty-five cents a pound. We know that crude rubber can be produced in the plantations, running full, probably somewhere in the neighborhood of ten cents a pound." As he explained it, "At that particular time [before the attack on Pearl Harbor] there was plenty of crude rubber coming in, and this [synthetic] cost so much more than crude that there wasn't any need to do any more than learn how to do the job in case necessity should later prove it to be necessary." The president of Goodrich Rubber, which had actually sold a few synthetic tires before the attack on Pearl Harbor, when asked point blank, "Did your failure to reach an agreement with Standard Oil impede your development of synthetic rubber . . . in any way?" replied, "No, it did not."[117]

Butyl rubber presented an equally complex picture. The product itself represented an improvement by Standard on vistanex, a polymer developed by IG Farben.[118] As required by its contracts with the IG, Standard turned over the process to Jasco. Standard nevertheless continued research on butyl during the 1930s. Unfortunately, when the Americans gained control over Jasco in 1939, the product was far from commercial exploitation. Not until 1941 did Standard perfect mass production of butyl, a development that led it to build a small plant for the specialty market.[119] The company confined itself to this niche because butyl, although relatively inexpensive, equaled neither buna nor natural rubber in quality. Rubber companies managed to produce an all-butyl tire in 1941 that would last for 10,000 miles, but it would quickly disintegrate if driven above 35 miles per hour.[120] Such a product was unlikely to compete with tires made from natural latex.[121]

The evidence indicates that Standard Oil's policies did not seriously hinder the development of synthetic rubber. Indeed, its ties to IG Farben may have given it access to technology that would otherwise have been unavailable to Americans. Although Arnold often pointed to Germany's widespread use of synthetic rubber, this reflected heavy government subsidies, which the United States did not institute until 1942. Without such subsidies, synthetic rubber was not economically viable in the early 1940s. It is hard to escape the conclusion that, in the case of rubber, Arnold either did not know what he was talking about or did not care.

In the end, synthetic rubber saved the United States. A program of gasoline rationing reduced the wear and tear on tires and allowed the United States to stretch its stocks of natural rubber until massive plants producing the synthetic article came on line. In 1944, America produced about 800,000 tons of artificial rubber,[122] approximately three-quarters of it buna. Without this material, the U.S. war effort might well have collapsed.

Whatever the facts, this episode severely damaged Standard Oil's public image. The company did have defenders. The *New York Times*, reviewing the evidence in an April 1942 editorial, claimed, "Mr. Arnold's charges that the Standard Oil is responsible for the shortage of synthetic rubber simply evaporate."[123] Yet the *Wall Street Journal* provided a better picture of the political situation when it observed, "Even if each and every one of the charges brought by the representatives of the Department of Justice should be found to be without a shred of basis, there will be many people who to the end of their days will believe—or affect to believe—that in this time of war the Standard Oil Company was giving aid and comfort to the enemy for greed or profit."[124] Since before the turn of the century, economic reformers had demonized Standard Oil, and many Americans were willing to credit almost any charge leveled against it. In September 1943, Vice President Henry Wallace asserted, "Subterfuge, concealment and double dealing, deliberately stalled some of our rubber and chemical companies in order to keep them from developing synthetic rubber. . . . Behind all this subterfuge, concealment, and double dealing was the sinister figure of the cartel of Standard Oil and IG Farbenindustrie."[125] As late as 1976, John Morton Blum's book *V Was for Victory*, one of the best and most widely read accounts of the home front during World War II, repeated Arnold's accusations uncritically.[126] Twenty years later, Alan Brinkley repeated the same exaggerated charges in *The End of Reform*, his generally superb history of liberalism during the late 1930s and the war.[127]

The Standard Oil case, as laid out by Thurman Arnold, served as the starting point for the debate over international cartels. Despite intense publicity at the time, the issue never penetrated except in the shallowest fashion to the proverbial "man on the street," who was concerned chiefly with winning the war and securing a good job when it was over. Most Americans opposed anything unfortunate enough to be labeled a "cartel," but few thought further on the subject. As one irate journalist wrote in 1945, "The American people, though temporarily aroused [against cartels] when the agencies of the government ripped open the veil of secrecy in the first days of the war, are showing signs of lapsing again into indifference and apathy."[128]

The cartel issue did penetrate the consciousness of a large group of academics, journalists, and middle-level government officials who thought in the same terms as Thurman Arnold and who, in the hectic atmosphere of wartime Washington, shaped policy toward cartels. Of equal importance, the rubber case discouraged corporate executives who might otherwise have defended international cartels. As the history of Standard Oil put it, "The effect [of Arnold's accusations] on the personnel of parent company and domestic affiliates was traumatic."[129] Once it had regained its collective balance, Standard tried to dissociate itself from cartels, sacrificing the truth if necessary. In 1943, the company's president actually stated at a stockholder's meeting, "We never had *any* cartel agreement with I.G. Farbenindustrie. What we *did* do was to *buy* from IG Farben some patent rights and part interest in inventions."[130] Most other firms, eager to avoid Standard's public humiliation, followed suit. If the companies that had negotiated cartels were unwilling to defend them, few others were likely to do so.

Thurman Arnold's public-relations coup in the Standard Oil case did not salvage his position within the government, however. Mobilization agencies and the military remained under the control of businessmen or officials sympathetic to them, and if anything, Arnold's handling of the Standard Oil case further alienated these people. Henry Stimson, perhaps the most important member of the cabinet at the time, no doubt summed up their opinion when he said of Arnold, "He had frightened business . . . making a very great deterrent effect upon our munitions production." At another point, the secretary of war described the antitrust chief as a "self-seeking fanatic."[131]

Soon the service departments gained the power to halt antitrust suits for the duration. A March 20, 1942, memo signed by Stimson, Navy Secretary Frank Knox, Arnold, and Attorney General Francis Biddle stated, "Such [antitrust] court investigations, suits, and prosecutions unavoidably consume the time of executives and employees of those corporations which are engaged in war work. In these cases we believe that continuing such prosecutions at this time will be contrary to the national interest and security." The memo provided for consultation among the signatories, but "if after study and examination they disagree, then, upon receipt of a letter from the Secretary of War or the Secretary of the Navy stating that in his opinion the investigation, suit, or prosecution will seriously interfere with the war effort, the Attorney General will abide by that decision."[132]

The military used its power aggressively. By early 1943, the army had forced the Antitrust Division to halt cases against GE involving lightbulbs and tungsten carbide and against various chemical companies involving heavy chemicals, dyestuffs, and plastics.[133] These and similar actions, according to one historian, reduced Arnold's job to a "sinecure."[134]

In addition, the Antitrust Division found itself in conflict with the War Production Board. The desire of Donald Nelson, the head of the WPB, to hire as his deputy Charles Wilson, the president of General Electric, played a part in the rupture. Arnold strongly opposed the appointment, noting, "Mr. Wilson has been trained in the cartel school of industrial combination, international alliances with other businesses, to the exclusion of nationals and the elimination of independent enterprise."[135] Most disturbing, Owen D. Young, the chairman of GE, insisted that Wilson could not take the WPB job until after the resolution of antitrust charges involving Wilson personally—a demand that the Justice Department and President Roosevelt himself feared might set a bad precedent, allowing companies to dictate their relationship with the government.[136] It was one thing to treat companies generously, another to let them set the terms of cooperation. Wilson eventually got the WPB position, but Washington only suspended prosecutions against GE. As with cases against other firms, the Justice Department reserved the authority to take them up again after the war.

Arnold's intervention in the Wilson case occurred in the context of an already bad relationship with Nelson. The Antitrust Division had taken upon itself the task of reviewing WPB operations to keep monopoly at bay, and apparently the board's personnel were tired of the meddling. In September 1942, Nelson complained to Attorney General Biddle of "unremitting interference by the Antitrust Division with the work, organization and personnel of the War Production Board by unwarranted acts, thoughtless and unjustifiable disparagement of motives, and incessant nagging." "As a direct result," Nelson concluded, "the War Production Board is finding it increasingly difficult to obtain the services of able and seasoned industrial personnel, whose participation is essential to the successful accomplishment of its job."[137]

Arnold contemptuously dismissed this communication. Privately he stated, "The incoherent rambling letter of Donald Nelson is a pathetic confession of weakness."[138] For Nelson's consumption he replied, "We believe that there is monopoly domination in most of our great industries involving war production. That monopoly domination has been and is now the principal reason for our shortages in basic materials and our failure to convert independent industry to war production. We have a real function to perform in exposing undercover dealings of monopoly groups in this country." Arnold concluded, "I assume Mr. Nelson did not personally write this letter, and therefore it is no disrespect to him to say that its writer apparently does not believe in actually curbing the evils of monopoly."[139]

This reply did little to calm Nelson. It does seem that Attorney General Francis Biddle managed with some careful diplomacy to prevent a public break. In a final communication, however, Nelson complained of "a widespread and growing impression in American industry that Mr. Arnold has

made it his special, extrajurisdictional purpose to 'drive the businessmen out
of Washington.' " As for the claim that the WPB was unconcerned about
monopoly, Nelson wrote, "This charge is a typical example of the groundless
and irresponsible accusations [by Arnold]. . . . The charge is nonsense, and
I feel that Mr. Arnold must know that it is nonsense."[140]

The president got rid of Arnold in January 1943, by appointing him to
the District of Columbia Court of Appeals. Roosevelt had little choice. If
Arnold had incensed Nelson, who was by most accounts an accommodating,
low-key individual, he had almost certainly alienated everyone associated
with the military and mobilization. The administration wanted to conciliate
business, whose help it believed it needed to win the war, and the president
simply could not allow Arnold to ignore that policy.

The appeals court represented a comfortable perch, but everyone, including Arnold, realized that he had received the appointment to get him
out of the Antitrust Division. In public, Arnold took the change philosophi-
cally. "I guess I'm like the Marx brothers," he said, "they can be awfully
funny for a long while, but finally people get tired of them."[141] Privately,
Arnold was more bitter. Several years after the war, he wrote, "FDR, recognizing that he could have only one war at a time, was content to declare
a truce in the fight against monopoly. He was to have his foreign war; monopoly was to give him patriotic support—on its own terms. And so more
than 90 percent of all war contracts went to a handful of giant empires,
many of them formerly linked by strong ties with the corporations of the
Reich."[142] As it turned out, Arnold found the judiciary dull and left the bench
after only two years.

However unhappy the end of his tenure, Thurman Arnold had accomplished much as head of the Antitrust Division. Despite the rhetorical importance attached to the antitrust laws since the Progressive Era, enforcement had been uneven at best before the late 1930s. Arnold increased both
the Antitrust Division's staff and its concept of its responsibilities, and despite
a temporary retreat during the war, these changes endured. After 1945, com-
pliance with the antitrust statutes became for the first time a regular concern
of most large companies. Though not solely Arnold's accomplishment, he
deserves more credit than anyone else. Arnold also did more than anyone
else to bring the issue of international cartels to the fore and to shape the
nature of the debate on them. The process started in 1940 and 1941, cul-
minating with the Standard Oil hearings in 1942. By the time Arnold left
the Antitrust Division, the momentum was strong enough to survive his
political demise.

Yet the factors that accounted for Arnold's successes ultimately led to his downfall. He fervently believed that collusive practices pervaded American industry and made rooting them out a personal crusade. In 1938 and 1939, his enthusiasm energized the Antitrust Division and helped win important court victories. Yet Arnold's crusading spirit came at the expense of his sense of perspective. Contrary to his belief, antitrust could not solve all of the country's problems. In particular, it had little to contribute to mobilization, which suspended the normal workings of the free market and required close cooperation between business and government. Prosecutions merely distracted hard-pressed executives from military production and poisoned relations between industry and government. Whereas in peacetime Arnold had been a constructive if narrowly focused figure, in war he became a destructive one.

Congress and Cartels

Congressional policy toward cartels demonstrates the odd political dynamics of the issue. The subject did not penetrate the popular consciousness except in a shallow way, creating a prejudice against anything unfortunate enough to be labeled a "cartel," but no widespread demand for any specific set of reforms. Up to a point this was sufficient for the opponents of cartels, as almost no one was defending these organizations per se. When anticartel measures challenged powerful interests, however, the lack of deep public support proved crippling. Yet at the same time, the popular prejudice against cartels was strong enough to block any measure that might benefit these organizations.

In 1943, Senator Joseph O'Mahoney of Wyoming introduced a modest bill requiring American companies to provide the Justice Department with copies of agreements with foreign concerns, documents that would be open to public inspection.[143] Though hardly revolutionary, the measure would have increased knowledge of cartels and exposed them to greater public scrutiny. Business groups accorded O'Mahoney's bill a mixed reception. Though few voiced any objection to it in principle, many saw practical difficulties. The president of Standard Oil of New Jersey, Ralph Gallagher, warned, "The definition of 'foreign contract' as it now stands in the bill is so broad . . . that it can be interpreted as requiring the registration of all contracts which involve directly or indirectly total or partial performance outside the United States. . . . This would burden thousands of business enterprises, large and small, with the necessity of registering hundreds of thousands of routine contracts. It would overwhelm government departments with a mountain of paper." Standard's chief also feared that "the provisions of the bill making foreign contracts open to public inspection could lead to severe handicapping of American industries in their competition for foreign business."[144] Still, more careful drafting could presumably resolve these problems. Surprisingly, the Executive Branch seemed hardly more enthusiastic about the measure. Attorney General Francis Biddle wrote to O'Mahoney, "I find no objection to the enactment of the bill"—hardly a ringing endorsement. He also seconded concerns that O'Mahoney's proposal might create serious administrative problems.[145] A State Department memo stated, "We should, I think, be careful not to enthuse over it [the O'Mahoney bill]."[146] Registration might be useful, but the benefits were not worth putting heavy burdens on business or government officials.

A few businessmen hoped that a measure similar to O'Mahoney's might clarify the status of international cartels. The courts had issued no definitive ruling on the role that U.S. firms could legitimately play in these organizations, and companies wanted to know exactly what was and was not legal. Some executives, including Gallagher of Standard Oil, suggested that firms be able to submit international agreements to the government for review with the provision that approval would protect a company from antitrust prosecution.[147] In early 1945, these ideas coalesced into a proposal by the National Foreign Trade Council (NFTC), a group consisting of about seven hundred American firms involved in foreign trade.[148] The council urged Congress to "recognize that Americans may enter into international business agreements valid under foreign laws provided they result in no unreasonable restraint of trade within the United States." The council recommended a bill requiring that all companies register foreign cartel agreements with the State Department, which would then approve or disapprove of them. The State Department could subsequently rescind an affirmative ruling, but until that time, the signatories would enjoy immunity from antitrust prosecution.[149]

The NFTC program enjoyed little support. The foes of cartels naturally opposed it—the measure would give cartels legal recognition and reduce the Justice Department's authority over them by lodging the power of review with the State Department. State also opposed deviation from the antitrust principle. One memo noted, "As to 'advance clearance' and immunity from the Sherman Act, we should take a firm, negative position."[150] The business community did not lend much support either. The National Foreign Trade Council was a relatively narrow organization, representing chiefly large companies with extensive interests abroad. The more broadly constituted National Association of Manufacturers refused to endorse the bill.[151] Although individual firms did have substantial interests in international cartels, the American business community as a whole did not.

The NFTC measure raised serious legal questions as well. The courts had not yet decided exactly what sort of foreign agreements might constitute "unreasonable restraint of trade within the United States." As a State Department committee noted, "Until pending cases have been adjudicated, government officials will be as uncertain as anyone else."[152] Once the courts had ruled, the need for review would diminish. DuPont, which with its extensive cartel ties might be expected to favor the NFTC proposal, rejected it on practical grounds. "As presently written," a company official noted, "the [National Foreign Trade Council] resolution involves much of the blank check idea. One might vote favorably on it without having any adequate comprehension of what he was voting for."[153]

Congress enacted neither O'Mahoney's nor the National Foreign Trade Council's proposals. Despite Senator O'Mahoney's persistence—he introduced his bill every year from 1943 to 1945—the measure failed every time. It aroused neither strong opposition nor support and died of indifference. Why impose new administrative burdens on business and government that would change little? The National Foreign Trade Council's proposal fared even worse. Support for it was never broad, and the more people reflected on it the more doubts they developed. Although the press discussed the recommendation, it received almost no notice in Congress. The only measure enacted was an amendment to the Reciprocal Trade Act requiring that diplomats take into account "the operations of international cartels" when negotiating bilateral trade accords—an interesting statement of concern but hardly revolutionary legislation.[154]

No doubt the press of war-related business diverted attention from these measures, but lawmakers who wanted to deal with international cartels confronted broader difficulties. Congress could intervene decisively on the issue only by revising the antitrust laws, explicitly exempting international cartels from the Sherman Act or expanding that law so that it unambiguously banned American participation in them. Yet support for loosening the antitrust laws did not exist—they were too popular and international cartels too controversial. As for strengthening the law, opponents of cartels insisted that as written, the Sherman Act prohibited American participation in international accords. If Congress moved specifically to outlaw international cartels, it would be implying that as the law stood they were legal. The principals would have to fight out the issue in court without help from the legislative branch.

The possibility of legislative action did remain in one important area—the patent laws. Thurman Arnold spoke for many when he wrote in 1942, "The principal smoke screens under which domestic and international cartels have cloaked their activities are patent laws—which, like lost sheep, have gone astray."[155] Certainly firms extracted every advantage they could from patents. General Electric based its lightbulb cartel on patent agreements, and patents formed the foundation of the arrangement between Standard Oil and IG Farben, as well as countless other accords. Wendell Berge of the Justice Department warned, "In many branches of industrial production vast monopolies exercised a dominating influence over research. It is the abuse and misuse of patents by such concentrated groups wielding tremendous economic power which have brought patents into conflict with the fundamental purpose of the patent law and the Sherman Act."[156]

According to Berge, patents actually allowed large companies to choke off research. He claimed, "The power which modern monopoly wields over research, by virtue of patents, often perverts the spirit of discovery." He continued: "What incentive is there to inventors to develop new products or processes when they may be, in effect, inventing their way into a patent infringement suit?"[157] Thurman Arnold believed "that the patent law has no place in the protection of any dominating concern, that the patent laws do not encourage research by such concerns. Indeed, it is so used as to prevent the research of others from becoming effective." He added, with his usual rhetorical flair, "The use of the patent law by a struggling company is an entirely different phenomenon than if used by General Electric. If you discuss them both at the same time it is like discussing tree trunks and travelers' trunks under the same classification."[158]

Various schemes existed for changing the patent laws. The Temporary National Economic Committee had recommended the licensing of all patents for a "reasonable" fee. Thurman Arnold went a step further, writing that the holders of patents "should be prosecuted if, instead of using the patent to get the most royalties, he uses it to prevent a necessity from being produced in the greatest possible quantity. If he tries to do that, we believe the law should cancel his patent."[159]

In December 1941, a few days after the attack on Pearl Harbor, President Roosevelt appointed the National Patent Planning Commission to investigate and recommend improvements in the patent laws. Charles F. Kettering, the head of research for General Motors, chaired the group, which also included Owen D. Young, the chief of General Electric. As Senator O'Mahoney aptly observed, "This commission . . . is clearly representative of industry."[160] The commission's final report, delivered in the spring of 1943, contained proposals to streamline the granting of patents and to prevent the extension of their life beyond the usual seventeen-year limit. It also recommended mandatory licensing of patents for national defense programs and the registration with the government of patent agreements between American companies and foreign firms. Nevertheless, the commission's report concluded that "the American system [of patents] is the best in the world." It continued, "The patent system is the foundation of American enterprise and has demonstrated its value over a period coextensive with the life of our government. The principle of recognizing a property right in intellectual creation is sound and should be continued as contemplated in the constitution."[161]

The report failed to satisfy critics of the patent laws. Already in 1942, Senators O'Mahoney, Homer Bone of Washington, and Robert LaFollette, Jr., of Wisconsin had introduced a measure for radical reform. They proposed to invalidate automatically any patent that was not, within three years of its issue, actively worked, as well as to ban licensing agreements that restricted sale price or output, voiding the patents on which such accords rested. Companies would have to submit all patent agreements to the Federal Trade Commission for approval.[162] The first part of their proposal, at least, had precedent, because several other countries, including Britain, premised the validity of patents on their being utilized. Measures comparable to that suggested by O'Mahoney, Bone, and LaFollette surfaced in every session of Congress through the end of the war. A bill introduced in 1943 made "illegal any use or non-use of a patent which has the effect of unreasonably limiting the supply of any article in commerce."[163] Another variant permitted the Justice Department to involve itself in any patent case.[164]

The business community and researchers vociferously opposed such reforms. Lawrence Langner, a patent attorney, wrote in a response to Thurman Arnold, "The patent or copyright is not a monopoly in the sense that large corporations or labor unions may be monopolies, for the inventor or author, in exchange for the patent or copyright, gives the public something which did not exist before: a new invention or a new work of art. . . . The enormous sum of over $300,000,000 in capital is invested annually by research departments of American corporations and by individual independent inventors. The patents obtained upon the resulting inventions represent insurance policies for the return of this capital to the progressive industrialists or inventor who expends it." Langner concluded, "Emasculation of the American patent system will mean the decline of American invention, and this in turn will be followed by the decline of industrial civilization as we know it."[165]

The often-expressed objection to corporate ownership of patents was, businessmen argued, foolish. Hugh Sanford, a Knoxville, Tennessee, inventor whose views Thurman Arnold elicited, wrote, "The corporation pays these men [scientists] to devise improved methods in this field. It supplies the engineers or research men with the tools and equipment to make various and sundry experiments and tests and bears the expense of keeping the department and making the tests. Therefore, when the inventions are made, it would seem that the corporation is entitled to own them, and I believe that if the corporations did not put up money for research, etc., these inventions would not be made."[166] As for the claim that large companies suppressed inventions, one scientist asserted, "There is no authenticated example of the actual suppression of a major industrial development which was patented and then monopolistically withheld in order to protect obsolete practices."[167] Weakening patent protection might actually slow the transmission of knowledge. One scientist feared that "rather than disclose technological advances by applying for patents, industry in self defense would degenerate into the mere seeking to analyze and copy the other fellow's products."[168] With respect to hardships allegedly imposed by the patent laws on smaller firms, the National Association of Manufacturers claimed that in fact many small companies "could not continue without the protection afforded by the exclusive rights granted by their patents, and . . . would have had difficulty in raising funds for getting started except for such protection."[169]

Patent law presented the enemies of monopoly with a basic contradiction. As Hugh Sanford wrote, "The object of a patent is to give a monopoly, and the legitimate use of a patent to obtain a higher than average profit during the life of the patent seems to me to be entirely proper. If this could not be done by means of a monopoly, the patenting of new ideas would cease."[170] Senator O'Mahoney himself said, "It [a patent] is a justifiable monopoly. It is a monopoly which the Congress intended to grant to the individual person. However, the antitrust law is directed against the use of any device, whether patent or otherwise, to restrain trade or monopolize any industry."[171] Try as it might, the government could not abolish this contradiction but instead had to strike a balance between the goals of encouraging invention and maintaining competition.

Most lawmakers seemed unwilling to rewrite the patent laws. Although Congress approved some of the more modest recommendations of the National Patent Planning Commission, it showed no enthusiasm for a system of compulsory licensing such as that advocated by the TNEC and other critics of patent system.[172] The legislative branch apparently agreed with the lawyer who stated, "It is both impossible and impracticable to legislate against every fancied and remote possibility of the misuse of property [patents] by its owners."[173] The solution advanced by NAM seemed more reasonable. "Patents of course may become a cloak for illegal cartels," the organization noted, "but in such event redress is obtainable in this country under our antitrust laws. Those desiring to make a legitimate use of their patents should not be deprived of their rightful opportunity to do so merely because such property rights may, in some cases, have been used to cloak illegal cartels."[174] NAM clearly hoped that the courts would treat patent monopolies generously, but its argument was nevertheless strong. The complexity and contradictions inherent in patent and antitrust laws made flexibility imperative, and the courts could provide it more readily than Congress. In this area, as in others, the judiciary would decide policy toward cartels.

4   Making the World Safe for Competition

Despite the retreat from antitrust prosecution during the war, the U.S. government did not abandon the fight against international cartels. Once Allied victories in 1942 and 1943 made total victory seem probable, Washington began to think seriously about the shape of the peace settlement, a process that involved economic as well as political issues. Among other matters, Washington sought to prohibit or at least limit international cartels, negotiating with other governments for restrictions on these organizations even while petitioning American courts to outlaw them unilaterally.

A Divided Consensus

Although the cartel issue failed to excite the public as a whole, vigorous debate on the matter did proceed within a more limited circle. Interest centered among New Dealers who hoped that the subject would revive their political fortunes and business groups that presumed to speak for private industry as a whole. All claimed to oppose cartels, but they justified their positions in very different ways.

After Arnold's departure from the Antitrust Division, his staff continued their missionary work against international cartels, an activity facilitated by the suspension of many of the bureau's other labors for the duration of the war. Wendell Berge published *Cartels: Challenge to a Free World*; Corwin Edwards drafted a broadly circulated Senate report on the subject; and Joseph Borkin and Charles Welsh wrote *Germany's Master Plan*, perhaps the most-cited book on international cartels.[1] The division also provided many of the witnesses for two sets of widely publicized Senate hearings on international cartels.[2] Although the emphasis differed from person to person, all members of the Antitrust Division would have agreed with Borkin and Welsh that "during the past twenty years, this cartel device has been the first line of German assault. Not all cartels were controlled by German concerns. Yet, because restrictions in other countries served the interests of Germany, every Dutch, English, or American monopolist who signed a contract or instituted a policy limiting his output added to German power."[3]

New Dealers seized on the issue. Most disapproved of Roosevelt's wartime rapprochement with business and disliked the way large companies had identified themselves with mobilization. Cartels offered a way to tie the American business community to the fascist enemy and to identify economic reform with the Allied cause. In 1942, the *New Republic* reported, "While the American people were moving toward an alliance with the democracies, great sectors of American industry were strengthening their ties with fascist Germany" through cartel agreements. These accords, the magazine argued, meant that "American industry believes that either the Axis will triumph or there will be a negotiated peace." The situation was particularly disturbing because "sooner or later businessmen who ally themselves with fascism become fascists; and once fascism captures economic control, then a fascist coup must follow to seize political power."[4] Two years later, when Allied victory seemed more certain, the *New Republic* commented, "We are at war with the fascist international. But when we have finally achieved victory, we shall still have to face the big Corporate International of cartels."[5] Vice President Henry Wallace declared, "The international monopolists should be conspicuous by their absence at the peace table."[6] Columnist I. F. Stone of *The Nation* described the domestic implications that he saw in the spread of cartels: "The cartel at home means the limitation of production. Limitations on production means limitations of jobs, and without full employment there will be rich soil for fascism after the war. No doubt these same big producers will cultivate it."[7]

Comparable sentiments echoed in liberal papers in the provinces. The *Boston Globe* asserted that "the cartel is neither more nor less than economic totalitarianism."[8] Josephus Daniels—an old Progressive Era reformer, editor of the *News and Observer* of Raleigh, North Carolina, and a friend of the president—wrote to Roosevelt, "I think unless we can destroy monopoly,

monopoly will destroy democracy. The first thing to do is to destroy the power of the German trusts."[9] The *Capital Times*, published in Madison, Wisconsin, asserted, "There is no longer any serious disagreement about the nature of the cartel system, how, in order to preserve its power and control over world resources, it found itself in open partnership with Hitler's totalitarianism; how it backed him in his rise to power; how it helped him prepare Germany for war and paralyze the industrial capacity of potential enemies such as the United States."[10]

Next to these shrill attacks on the political implications on cartels stood indictments of their economic effects. Corwin Edwards was perhaps the most diligent critic in this field. He wrote, "The typical purpose and effect of cartelization is to set prices higher than would prevail under competition, to reduce them as seldom as possible, and to raise them further wherever opportunity permits."[11] Cartels inevitably gouged consumers, limiting overall consumption, output, and employment. By keeping prices high and guaranteeing market share, they reduced incentives for efficiency and permitted high-cost producers to survive. Overall, cartels kept society from fully developing its economic resources.

Business groups not only failed to rebut attacks on international cartels but in many cases seconded them. The National Association of Manufacturers, a relentless critic of the New Deal, declared that it "stands squarely against cartels of every description, both private and governmental." This statement did contain an important reservation, urging, "Until the government of the United States is able to make such anti-cartel agreements [with other countries], United States foreign traders should be encouraged by government to operate in other countries in accordance with the internal laws and business practices of such countries, and thus to participate in world trade on the same basis as nationals of other countries, without harassment from their own government."[12] Because most other governments condoned cartels, this was a major loophole. The National Association of Manufacturers' attack on cartels represented, in part, a public-relations ploy. The association's 1945 annual report crowed, "At a time when professional business baiters in and out of government were using the world 'cartel' as a shibboleth, NAM's announcement of its opposition to cartels won for industrial management wide public approval."[13] Because most American firms did little business abroad and had no dealings with international cartels, denunciations of these organizations cost little while generating good publicity and blunting a line of attack against industry.

Yet most American businessmen did have genuine objections to cartels. These organizations, they believed, provided avenues through which government could interfere in the affairs of private firms. Certainly that was the lesson they took from the National Recovery Act of 1933. Although businessmen wanted stable markets and prices, they refused to subordinate themselves to Washington to achieve these ends—at least not as long as Franklin Roosevelt was president. Businessmen reserved their particular ire for government-sponsored cartels. Jasper Crane, a vice president at DuPont, a firm deeply involved in international cartels, declared, "The worst type of cartel is a government cartel because private cartels in time destroy themselves, but there is no means for eradicating the government variety. Its manifestations, too, are much worse than private arrangements, for they often involve manipulated exchanges, subsidies, embargoes, excessive tariffs."[14] A 1944 convention of businessmen devoted to foreign trade and sponsored in part by NAM resolved, "Intergovernmental commodity agreements in our foreign trade [cartels] would require a degree of internal control and regimentation which would threaten the preservation of our competitive system even in domestic commerce."[15]

In contrast, New Dealers believed that government-sponsored cartels could serve useful purposes. Thurman Arnold himself wrote, "The market must be free from the *private* seizure of power. *Public* seizure of power over the market by various groups will always be a matter for debate in particular cases. Responsible economists will point out that this or that organization needs special protection. Other economists will heatedly contest. However, no one contends that private persons, without running the gamut of our system of checks and balances, should seize power over the market in a *sub rosa* manner."[16]

Distinguishing between government and private cartels was easier in theory than in practice, however. Ostensibly private cartels, such as that for steel, operated with the implicit support of many governments. Strictly private groups could manipulate government programs for their own ends. Cartels tended to create tight relationships between business and government. Public officials naturally wanted to know what major cartels were doing, and cartelists desired government support for their plans. The situation encouraged each to take the other's concerns into account when setting policy. In the aftermath of the New Deal, however, the American business community and government lacked the mutual confidence on which such cooperation must rest.

The presumption against cartels demonstrates how dissenters from the antitrust compromise balanced out each other. A lot of businessmen were at least willing to overlook private cartels, and in many circumstances reformers would tolerate the government-sponsored variety. Reformers, however, opposed private cartels and could utilize the broad public suspicion of these organizations to block them, whereas business groups could do the same against government cartels.

A few Americans resisted the anticartel clamor, but they were the proverbial "exceptions that prove the rule." Ervin Hexner, who taught economics at the University of North Carolina at Chapel Hill, wrote two books on the subject: a study of the steel cartel and a general survey of international cartels. In both he concluded that cartels, although open to abuse, could work to the benefit of society as well as members.[17] A professor at the Harvard Business School, Anton de Haas, issued a pamphlet defending cartels in the terms used by Europeans before the war, asserting that they promoted economic stability and offered a mechanism for industry-wide planning.[18] Gilbert Montague, one of the country's leading corporate lawyers, contended that attacks on cartels ignored the realities of international commerce, as well as the practices of the United States itself, which tolerated many deviations from the ideal of competition. He asked whether Washington was going "to coerce Great Britain, Soviet Russia, China and all the rest of the world to adopt the competitive system of the United States, with all the refinements added by successive [antitrust] decisions of the Supreme Court?"[19] Hexner was a Czech émigré who had represented his country's steel producers in cartel talks before fleeing the Nazis; de Haas was a Dutchman who had extensive experience with international shipping cartels; and Montague had devoted his professional life to defending companies from antitrust prosecutions and had helped draft the NRA and several of its codes. Little in these men's experience spoke to the average American, or even to the average government official or corporate executive.

Broad-based enthusiasm for cartels did exist abroad. Britain, the chief ally of the United States, was the main conduit through which Americans received these sentiments. A State Department analysis noted in 1943, "Most British governments in the 'twenties and 'thirties actively encouraged the formation of private monopolistic combinations and associations." "Competition," the report continued, "no longer serves as the supreme regulatory economic force in the United Kingdom, for monopoly shares a condominium with it."[20] This had occurred chiefly under Conservative governments, but the opposition Labour Party thought not in terms of antitrust but of nationalization and government planning. In conversations with British officials, Americans "found little interest or concern over the cartel problem. In fact [John Maynard] Keynes stated that such firms as Imperial Chemicals had worked to increase volume at lower cost and that the most backward industries were those in which they had hundreds of small and independent operators, as in the textile and mining fields."[21] At another meeting, a British official told his American counterpart, "He believed a certain number of cartels to be inevitable and that the United States would be forced to accept them as our economy ceased expanding."[22] Privately, some in London dismissed U.S. attacks on international cartels as a "general witch-hunt."[23]

British industrialists aggressively defended cartels as a positive good. A paper entitled "A National Policy of Industry," signed by 120 leading businessmen, concluded, "Where similar products are manufactured in different countries, these international agreements [cartels] . . . are essential to keep production equitably allocated between countries and companies, in tune with the maximum world demand attainable. They exercise a stabilizing influence against violent fluctuations and dislocating shifts of the currents of trade, and thus have an essential part to play in postwar reconstruction."[24] The strongest support for cartels came from Imperial Chemical, a firm deeply involved in them. Lord McGowan, its chairman, wrote in 1943, "The era of unrestricted competition was one of strife. It meant certainly the survival of the fittest, but there were too many weak who went to the wall. The element of competition must be present in every healthy economy, but there are few today who would recommend a return to unrestricted competition as a *basis* for our economy." He continued, "If the principle of agreement is desirable at home, it is essential in a world market where all the ordinary problems of supply and demand, prices and raw materials, are complicated by national jealousies, currency fluctuations, political changes, and tariff barriers."[25]

These arguments generated little enthusiasm among American businessmen. In 1943, McGowan said to Eric Johnson, the president of the U.S. Chamber of Commerce, who was then touring Britain, "I see no hope for collaboration between British and American business unless the United States repeals its Sherman anti-trust act."[26] It immediately became clear that the Briton's usually sharp diplomatic skills had deserted him, for the surprised Johnson replied, "No American can intelligently and sincerely promise you any cooperation in any system of worldwide cartels."[27] Johnson's answer in part reflected political realities—Congress simply was not going to repeal the Sherman Act—but it was also in accord with the opinions of most American businessmen. DuPont had extensive ties with ICI, and its top officers liked and respected McGowan, but their private correspondence indicates that they did not agree with him on this subject. One told Mc-Gowan, "If we remove the element of competition as it applies to large companies and combines, I am wondering if there is left to the public sufficient protection against high prices which might result either from high costs or high profits on the one hand, and, on the other, I am wondering if there is left to those large companies and combines that spur to great efficiency and effectiveness in their efforts which is furnished so well by the fury of the competitive storm and the profit motive."[28] These sentiments may seem bizarre in light of DuPont's extensive involvement in international cartels, but they are presumably sincere, because they appear in private correspondence. Throughout the 1930s, American businessmen had based their opposition to New Deal reforms on appeals to competition and the free market, which they claimed made government regulation unnecessary. Most of them had internalized these arguments. Although DuPont's executives could rationalize their own involvement in cartels, they could not bring themselves to defend these organizations in principle.

The differences between American and British business on this subject reflected experience as well as ideology. In Britain, government and business had cooperated fairly smoothly in the 1930s, often through cartels, whereas in the United States, the two had been in conflict over the New Deal. The impressive expansion of the American economy during the war gave U.S. businessmen confidence that peace would bring further opportunities. Cartels, most often the product of hard times, did not seem that useful to them. In contrast, the war cost Britain dearly in foreign markets and investments, and its businessmen were less sanguine about the future than their American counterparts. Cartels might help British industry hold its own in a difficult environment.

The Antitrust Revival

At the start of 1943, the antitrust drive seemed dead. The military had forced the Justice Department to suspend most cases, and the president had removed Thurman Arnold, the head of the Antitrust Division, sending him to the federal appeals bench. The subject appeared destined for an extended period of neglect, as had been the case during and after World War I. Antitrust prosecution, however, enjoyed a remarkable revival over the next few years—a revival centered, in part, on international cartels.

External factors contributed greatly to the change. When Washington had suspended prosecutions during early 1942, the Axis powers were advancing on every front. Mobilization had absolute priority. Two years later, the situation was different. In 1944, the Allies won a series of extraordinary victories—successfully landing armies in Normandy; liberating France, Rome, White Russia, and the Balkans (obliterating several German armies in the process); crippling the German Luftwaffe in air campaigns; and destroying Japanese naval power in a string of encounters in the Pacific. Victory seemed only a matter of time, and so military considerations weighed less heavily on decision makers.

The 1944 presidential election changed matters as well. President Franklin D. Roosevelt, running for a fourth term, sought to mobilize the New Deal coalition that had given him victory thrice before; suspicion of big business was one of the issues that held this coalition together. Attacks on international cartels allowed the president to emphasize his enduring commitment to New Deal reform. In his 1944 State of the Union address, Roosevelt enumerated an eight-point economic "bill of rights" that included "the right of every businessman, large and small, to trade in atmosphere of freedom from unfair competition and domination by monopolies at home or abroad."[29] In a September 1944 letter, addressed to Secretary of State Cordell Hull but intended for public consumption, the president declared, "Unfortunately, a number of foreign countries, particularly in continental Europe, do not possess . . . a tradition against cartels. On the contrary, cartels have received encouragement from some of these governments. Especially is this true with respect to Germany. Moreover, cartels were utilized by the Nazis as government instrumentalities to achieve political ends. The history of the use of the IG Farben trust by the Nazis reads like a detective story. . . . Cartel practices which restrict the free flow of goods in foreign commerce have to be curbed."[30] While campaigning, the president assured audiences that "small business will continue to be protected from selfish, cold-blooded monopolies and cartels. Beware of that profound enemy of the free enterprise system who pays lip-service to free competition—but also labels every antitrust prosecution as 'persecution.'"[31]

The Antitrust Division and its leader, Wendell Berge, ably seized on the available opportunities. Berge took over the bureau in the fall of 1943, after the brief tenure of Tom Clark, who moved on to head the more prestigious

Criminal Division of the Justice Department. Berge, a veteran of antitrust prosecution who had worked on the division's staff for over a decade, contrasted sharply with the dramatic, irreverent Thurman Arnold. Low-key and thoroughly conventional in his manner, he neither made the impression nor aroused the ire that Arnold had. Still, he was perhaps a better litigator, possessing the tenacity and mastery of detail needed to fight and win complex antitrust cases, which often involved thousands of documents and dozens of witnesses. Moreover, by 1943, Arnold had made himself unpopular in Washington, and so Berge's mild manner probably benefited his cause. Like Arnold, Berge was from west of the Mississippi—in this case Nebraska, where Berge's father had been a leader of the populist wing of the Democratic Party, even running (unsuccessfully) for governor. Wendell inherited his father's dislike of big business, which both believed had reduced Nebraska to an economic colony of the Northeast. This view shaped Wendell Berge's understanding of international as well as domestic conditions. Over and over again he denounced international cartels as devices of economic imperialism.

A suit against DuPont and Imperial Chemical Industries of Britain marked the resurgence of the Antitrust Division. DuPont and ICI had a broad alliance dating back decades. As early as the 1890s, the American firm, then almost solely a producer of explosives, had agreements with Nobel Explosives, one of ICI's forerunners, dividing markets and exchanging patents. As the firms expanded during and immediately after World War I, branching into new lines of business, they systematically broadened their alliance, a process that culminated in the 1929 Patents and Processes Agreement. This ten-year accord, which the signatories renewed in 1939, effectively eliminated competition between the two firms. Under it DuPont received exclusive rights to almost all of ICI's patents in the United States, and ICI to almost all DuPont's patents in the British Empire.[32] At regular intervals the two firms would calculate the value of the exchanges and, if they did not balance out, arrange compensation. Because the accord rested on patent rights, DuPont's attorneys believed it would survive an antitrust challenge. In third markets where both firms did business, the two operated through jointly owned subsidiaries, the most important of which were Canadian Industries Limited, Duperial of Argentina, and Duperial of Brazil. The Patents and Processes Agreement, however, did more than simply restrict competition. In the 1920s, ICI and DuPont were relative newcomers to many fields of the chemical industry, fearful of resurgent German competition personified in IG Farben. Because Farben's unmatched research establishment constituted its foremost competitive weapon, DuPont and ICI hoped by pooling their patents to put themselves in a better position to deal with the Germans.

By the early 1940s, the Antitrust Division had turned its attention to these arrangements, which it found distinctly sinister. DuPont had always been something of a bête noire among the foes of monopoly, who were suspicious of the firm's size, its extensive domestic and international contacts (which included a predominant stake in General Motors), and the strongly anti–New Deal politics of the DuPont family. Two members of the Antitrust Division described the company as "the nearest facsimile of economic feudalism in this country." [33] A 1942 Justice Department memo asserted that DuPont "has been steadily engaged in building up a series of alliances on a worldwide basis, the logical conclusion of which would be to destroy commercial competition, not only among the great chemical companies, but likewise among the industries directly dependent upon these companies for supplies." DuPont's agreements with ICI "constitute market-sharing arrangements masquerading as arrangements for cooperation in scientific research." Moreover, the accord was merely one part of a larger chain of alliances. "When Imperial Chemical Industries makes an agreement with IG Farben, Anglo-Persian [Oil] or Solvay [Chemical of Belgium]," the memo noted, "it must introduce into this agreement restrictions which adequately recognize and protect its commitments to DuPont."[34] As another memo put it, "Through its relationship with ICI, DuPont has been bound indirectly to other cartels in which ICI is a member"—and Imperial Chemical was party to about eight hundred agreements.[35]

The Justice Department filed suit against ICI and DuPont on January 6, 1944, seeking to terminate their alliance. Wendell Berge stated publicly, "The cartel system which has plagued us with shortages of critical material, lack of know-how and industrial skills during war, and unemployment and idle plants during peace, must not be disregarded in this country." ICI and DuPont, he claimed, "combined to control the operations of the chemical industry throughout the world for their special purposes. They treated the world as a kind of colonial empire to be divided up between them and cooperated to eliminate the competition of small manufacturers." He concluded, "The antitrust laws are going to be enforced wherever these arrangements restrict or affect American trade and commerce. I hope that the bringing of this case will serve as a warning to American and foreign monopolies."[36]

DuPont and ICI denied the allegations. Walter S. Carpenter, DuPont's president, engaged in the sort of semantic quibbling common among firms accused of cartel ties, declaring, "The DuPont Company denies that it is now or ever has been party to any cartel arrangement using the term cartel in its very generally accepted sense. The DuPont Company has for years had an agreement with Imperial Chemical Industries providing for a mutual opportunity to acquire patent licenses and technical and scientific information relating to the chemical industry." He "asserted unequivocally that this agreement has been of the greatest public benefit in giving to the American public products and processes which have materially raised the standard of living. Even more importantly in connection with the present war effort, the knowledge resulting from this agreement and the products made available as a result of it have been of inestimable value." Carpenter concluded trenchantly, "The existence of the agreements which are the subject of the present attack have never been concealed. Copies have been in the possession of Government agencies for approximately ten years. . . . With the government having had full possession of these agreements over a considerable period of time, the action of the Department of Justice at this particular time in our war effort is difficult to understand."[37]

ICI made a far angrier response. Although American businessmen were accustomed to attacks from government officials, their British counterparts were not. Lord Harry McGowan, ICI's chairman, issued a statement "denying utterly and totally any suggestion that any action of ours during the war and indeed before the war was of any other character than designed to assist both the British and Allied governments by any means within our power."[38] To colleagues within ICI he sent an emotional letter pointing out that, while serving in the British military against Germany, one of his sons had been seriously wounded, a son-in-law captured, and another son-in-law killed.[39]

The Antitrust Division nevertheless won the publicity battle. Just two days after filing the suit, Berge wrote to friends, "We hit the jackpot with this DuPont–ICI case. Front page clippings are rolling in from everywhere."[40] A few were critical. The *Philadelphia Inquirer* noted that DuPont and ICI were "deeply involved in war production, busily turning out millions upon millions of dollars worth of arms and ammunition for an Allied victory. On what strange principle are the labors of the heads of these companies now to be diverted from the job of helping to win the war to a defense against charges of promoting industrial monopolies?"[41] More typical, however, was a piece in the *Lincoln* (Nebraska) *Star*. It declared that the cartel "has no place in Nebraska's 'way of life.' It should have no place in the 'way of life' of the American people, the British, the French, the Germans, or any other race."[42]

The suit enjoyed a less enthusiastic reception on the other side of the Atlantic. ICI was Britain's largest war contractor, and the prosecution naturally concerned the government there. London did not share the Justice Department's aversion to cartels, and it feared that the case might damage relations with the United States. A memo from the British Foreign Office to the embassy in Washington noted, "We realize that the statement of the Assistant Attorney General [Berge] in advance of legal proceedings is normal American practice with a political object. None the less, we think it would be salutary if you could draw to the attention of Mr. [Secretary of State Cordell] Hull or the Attorney-General [Francis Biddle] to the effects upon ourselves of Mr. Berge's public allegations which we believe to be unfounded as far as ICI are concerned, that they have traded with the enemy or hindered the war effort. . . . A measure of the mud thrown at cartels will certainly stick to us, for even the friendly *Chicago Sun* has now contrasted the British commercial system ridiculously alleged to be founded upon cartels, unfavorably with the American. We feel that as a partner of the United States in a common effort we should be spared statements by the Administration that provoke this mud-slinging."[43]

ICI and DuPont had different strategies for dealing with the suit. The American firm was inclined to fight. Although the company could make a strong case for delaying prosecution for the duration of the war because of its extensive defense work, a report by Lord Halifax, the British ambassador, noted, "DuPont are [sic] anxious that no steps should be taken by anyone to postpone hearings of suit at this moment. . . . They want to answer the charges before court and at the bar of public opinion rather than sheltering behind delaying actions." Halifax also noted, "They are not mentioning the word cartel in any of their publicity and are most anxious that ICI's publicity should be on similar lines."[44]

In contrast, ICI sought delay. Restrictions on travel made it difficult to send officers to the United States. As a wartime security measure, the U.S. government read all cable traffic into and out of the country, raising the possibility that the Justice Department might have access to communications between ICI and its lawyers. Manpower, however, constituted the chief problem. Lord McGowan noted in April 1944, "DuPonts [*sic*] . . . has had fifty people working on this answer [to the antitrust charges] and nothing else for the last few months. It was impossible for ICI to adopt the same procedures. Very many of their staff had been loaned to Government Departments and the whole burden of the work would have been thrown upon key men, who were already fully engaged in war work."[45] ICI wanted to postpone not only the trial but also the formal answer to the charges, which the defendant would normally file soon after the indictment. The British government supported ICI, asking Washington to postpone both the trial and the formal answer until the war was over.[46]

The American service departments soon intervened, invoking their authority to postpone antitrust cases. They acted both out of deference to the British and to protect DuPont, a vital supplier of munitions. In April 1944, Secretary of War Henry Stimson wrote to Attorney General Francis Biddle, "As of November 30, 1943, DuPont and its subsidiary Remington had prime contracts with the Army totaling $1,431,966,504. In addition, it was operating for the government nine ordnance plants, which were constructed at a cost of $580,000,000. . . . It seems clear that interference with the war effort would be the inescapable result of trial of this case at this time." Stimson requested the Justice Department to delay not only the trial but also the formal answers by the defendants to the charges against them. "Counsel for the defendants," he wrote, "are positive in stating that the preparation of an answer will consume an additional three or four months, in consultation with key personnel of the defendant organizations."[47] The navy supported Stimson's request. James Forrestal, the acting navy secretary, stated the case for ICI, noting that it "is the largest supplier to the [British] government or to government contractors of military explosives, small arms ammunitions and components, high octane aviation fuel," and other vital materials; "that all its plants are operating to full capacity on direct war work or essential civilian requirements; and that apart from its own plants it has constructed and is now operating for the [British] government a series of agency factories, construction of which has involved an expenditure of over £60,000,000." Even more than DuPont, ICI was stretched thin and could not afford the time that a trial, or even making a formal answer, would consume.[48]

The case quickly became the subject of government infighting. According to its 1942 agreement with the military, the Justice Department had no choice but to postpone the trial. It had specifically ceded this authority to the service chiefs, who had exercised it on several previous occasions. The answer was another matter, however. This subject had not come up before. Although the antitrust laws allowed the Justice Department to file cases in either criminal or civil court, it usually went through the criminal courts because conviction there involved more severe penalties. The suit against ICI and DuPont, however, was a civil one—perhaps in deference to a foreign defendant or because the patent issues involved were convoluted. Yet the formal answer to charges in a civil case is far more important than in a criminal one. In the latter, the answer consists of a simple denial, whereas in a civil action it must squarely address the charges, giving reasons why they lack merit. If the presiding judge considers the answer in a civil case unsatisfactory, the bench may issue a summary judgment for the plaintiff. The 1942 agreement between the military and the Justice Department allowed the former to suspend "investigations, suits, and prosecutions," but heretofore the secretaries of war and the navy had intervened only to postpone actual trials, not answers.[49] But as one American official noted, "Previous cases stayed had all been criminal."[50] The Justice Department had no doubt about the matter. Attorney General Biddle wrote to Stimson, "I do not believe that our arrangement . . . is correctly applicable to pleadings on motions."[51]

The responsibility for mediation fell on President Roosevelt, who was already overworked. The war was entering a critical phase with the Normandy invasion at hand. He also had to plan his upcoming reelection campaign, and his health was poor. Both sides lobbied the president hard. Biddle told Roosevelt, "The preparation of pleadings and motions consumes the time of private counsel. It does not consume the time of executives and employees who might be engaged in war production." He could not "see how it is possible to determine whether a trial of this case will seriously interfere with the war effort until the nature of the defense is known. It may be, for instance, that after the defendants have filed their answers we may be able to dispose of the case on summary judgement."[52] Biddle also assured the president privately that he had intelligence that DuPont and ICI had almost finished their answers.[53]

Partisans of the companies denied Biddle's arguments. Lord Halifax stated, "It is obvious that the answer will have to be considered with the greatest care, since the judgement might alone depend on these pleadings. I am informed that as many as 100,000 documents may have to be examined in the preparation of the answer, and that some of the matters complained of go back as far as 1897; that the territory concerned comprises a large part of the world; and that the problems involved include the most complex questions of patent law, thus going far beyond the Sherman Act. To unravel the true facts of the case will thus be a gargantuan task, involving months of labor. Imperial Chemical Industries obviously cannot afford to let these matters go by default, and yet so many of their staff have been lent to government departments, that the whole burden will be thrown upon key men who are already engaged on vital war work."[54]

In May, the president tried to refer the matter to James Byrnes, his "mobilization czar." Byrnes hesitated, however, reminding Roosevelt, "At the cabinet meeting last Thursday you advised Biddle and Stimson that you had decided the case in favor of Biddle. . . . I suggest that, having decided it, the best thing to do is to let your decision stand."[55] The president did not follow this advice—he apparently refused to consider as binding what seems to have been a snap decision. Nevertheless, he knew that only he could reverse himself. Roosevelt did extract an opinion from Byrnes, who when pressed supported the companies and the military. Byrnes wrote, "The lawyers must get from the executives the facts upon which to base an answer. . . . Even allowing for exaggeration, it seems to me, in the case of each company, lawyers would require the constant assistance of executives in order to explain documents and transactions referred to in such documents." Moreover, Byrnes pointed out that DuPont was deeply involved in the atomic bomb project, code-named S-1.[56] Another, unsigned memo transmitted to Roosevelt reported that the head of the project, General Leslie Groves, "states work of DuPont's executives is key to the success of the S-1 and any diversion of their time would be disastrous."[57]

Roosevelt finally resolved the matter in mid-June. He wrote to Lord Halifax, "It seems to me that the Attorney General's view is appropriate and I have accordingly so advised him." He did order Biddle to extend the deadline for filing the answers to July 31, 1944, and to permit the defendants to amend their answers later if they so desired, which protected the companies against a summary judgment.[58] The motives for Roosevelt's decision are unclear. He may have agreed with Biddle that by delaying the filing of an answer, the government would set a bad precedent. He may have concluded that, with the success of the Normandy landing on June 6, the needs of mobilization no longer overrode the antitrust laws. The positive public reaction to the announcement of the suit in January could have convinced Roosevelt, a thoroughly political creature, that the case was good politics.

The president may have seen the suit as a way to strike back at the DuPonts, who had been particularly fierce critics of him and the New Deal. Or he may simply have concluded that, after so many defeats, the Antitrust Division deserved a victory. In any event, though it caused inconvenience, the preparation of answers does not seem to have seriously hampered DuPont's or ICI's contributions to the war effort.

President Roosevelt's decision had consequences far beyond the filing of a few documents in court. His show of support heartened the Antitrust Division and made it clear that prosecutions would indeed resume after the war. A few days after Roosevelt's decision in the ICI/DuPont case, Attorney General Biddle asked for permission to proceed with trials in two other cases involving international cartels. The first concerned an agreement among ICI, DuPont, Rohm & Haas of Philadelphia, and IG Farben governing the production and sale of certain plastics, and the second sought to overturn accords between Bendix and European firms involving the rights to various aviation instruments. Biddle insisted that in both suits the prosecution would need only a couple of weeks to present its case. The attorney general argued that, in the plastics case, the war had not ended but had merely suspended agreements, and these "would require that Rohm & Haas and DuPont withdraw and stay out of the important Latin American market upon the termination of the war." It was necessary, therefore, to invalidate them as soon as possible. In the Bendix case restrictions had actually continued in force during the war, although because the U.S. government purchased the entire output of the aircraft industry they had little impact. Nevertheless Biddle wanted to act before the end of hostilities to free "this industry now of artificial, uneconomic and unlawful limitations in order to insure efficient preparation for the postwar development of the aircraft industry in this country." In both instances, the president gave the Justice Department authority to proceed.[59] The cases themselves were not that important—in fact, the courts eventually decided against the Justice Department in the plastics suit[60]—but they offered more proof that the vigorous prosecution of cartels would proceed.

The Antitrust Division also went after Webb-Pomerene corporations. These organizations, authorized in 1918 by Congress, allowed American firms to cooperate in export markets. During the 1920s and 1930s, U.S. companies had often negotiated with international cartels through Webb-Pomerene corporations, a practice that the Federal Trade Commission, the regulator of these organizations, had tolerated. In March 1944, however, the Justice Department filed suit against the American Alkali Export Association

(Alkasso), the California Alkali Export Association (Calkex), and Imperial Chemical. The two American organizations were Webb-Pomerene companies that, between them, managed almost all exports of synthetic alkali from the United States. They had agreements with ICI that allocated each certain foreign markets and divided others according to a fixed ratio, providing for joint sales agencies in shared markets. As was the case with the alliance between DuPont and ICI, this accord formed part of a larger cartel structure. ICI had agreements with most of the world's other producers of alkali, of which the Belgian firm Solvay was the most important, dividing export markets. Invariably these accords took into account the interests of Alkasso and Calkex.

The defendants contended that these arrangements did not violate the law because they did not affect the American market. According to the FTC's "silver letter," which defined policy toward Webb-Pomerene corporations, these organizations could legally enter into cartels apportioning foreign markets as long as the agreements did not affect conditions at home.[61]

The Justice Department responded in two ways. Relying on information gathered by the Federal Trade Commission, it claimed that the alkali agreements *did* affect the American market. The accords, it claimed, implicitly banned imports. Shipments of foreign alkali to the United States were virtually nil despite good prices and a tariff that was not prohibitive. Moreover, Alkasso and Calkex allegedly stabilized prices in the United States by disposing of surplus alkali abroad. Alkali (bicarbonate soda, soda ash, and caustic soda) is a basic industrial commodity used to produce soap, glass, textiles, and much more, and the price of such commodities usually fluctuates with the business cycle. A special factor ought to have made alkali prices particularly volatile. Many American firms manufactured alkali through the electrolytic process. Alkali, however, was merely a by-product of this process—the chief output was chlorine. To a large degree, the output of alkali depended on the demand for chlorine, a situation that made it difficult for producers to adjust output to demand. Despite these factors, alkali prices had changed little since 1931. The Justice Department attributed the situation to Alkasso and Calkex. Both sold abroad for prices lower than those in the United States, often much lower, and would at times maintain stocks far larger than ongoing business required. The Antitrust Division argued that Alkasso and Calkex siphoned off "excess" supplies of alkali to keep domestic prices stable.[62]

More important, the Antitrust Division asserted that Webb-Pomerene associations could not legally take part in foreign cartels, even if they did not touch the American market. Wendell Berge argued, "The Webb Act was intended to strengthen American competition against foreign cartels. It was enacted by Congress in the belief that it would provide a means of assistance to American business in combating the power of foreign cartels dominating world markets."[63] The FTC's "silver letter" was simply wrong. To support its position, the Antitrust Division extensively investigated the legislative history of the Webb-Pomerene Act, finding much to support its claims.[64] Berge reported that Senator Pomerene had stated in floor debate on the measure that "there is nothing in this bill authorizing the division of territory abroad."[65] The Antitrust Division's case threatened not just Alkasso and Calkex but any Webb-Pomerene company that participated in an international cartel.

This argument seemed to challenge the Federal Trade Commission. The FTC had authority over Webb-Pomerene companies, and it had actually provided the Antitrust Division with much of the information on which the alkali suit rested. Yet the FTC had no role in the prosecution, a fact that according to some sources irritated the commission.[66] The Antitrust Division also failed to check with the FTC before challenging the "silver letter." Although the Antitrust Division may simply have been overeager, it could have been trying to push the FTC out of antitrust enforcement. Because both agencies had authority in the field, rivalry was natural. The permissive attitude displayed by the commission during the 1920s and 1930s toward Webb-Pomerene associations may also have convinced the Antitrust Division that the FTC was "soft" on international cartels. The commission had few ways to respond to the challenge, but in the summer of 1944 it did, on its own authority, launch a series of studies of international cartels that eventually yielded several substantial monographs that in some cases would shape antitrust policy.[67]

The alkali case itself, like most other antitrust prosecutions during the war, remained in limbo until the conflict ended. Yet just by filing it, the Antitrust Division raised doubts about Webb-Pomerene associations. Companies preparing for the postwar era were unlikely to adopt plans involving such organizations until the courts resolved these legal questions.

The Cartel Committee and Postwar Economic Planning

The attack on cartels also advanced under the banner of free trade. Political and economic considerations led the U.S. government to support measures to promote international trade after the war by cutting restrictions like tariffs. Cartels, which limited and channeled trade, became an object of this program. Washington sought a worldwide agreement regulating trade practices, including the operations of cartels.

Although the United States had followed a policy of protection since at least the Civil War, by 1940 there existed an influential group centered around the State Department committed to reducing tariffs and other obstacles to international trade sharply. Various sentiments motivated these people. Most economists believed that rising protection had contributed mightily to the Great Depression, which had destabilized world politics and greatly facilitated the rise of the German Nazis and Japanese militarists to power. The experience led the State Department to conclude that peace required prosperity and that prosperity required healthy international trade. American officials were also reacting against Nazi Germany's strict regulation of foreign trade, which had aimed to secure maximum political and economic advantage. Washington wanted to ban such discriminatory practices in the future. Alongside these calculations, however, existed an almost mystical belief that trade mitigated conflict and promoted peace. This faith had led President Woodrow Wilson to make free trade one of the famous "Fourteen Points" on which he hoped to base the peace settlement after World War I. Driven by the same creed, in the 1930s, Secretary of State Cordell Hull had negotiated a series of bilateral accords reducing tariffs and other trade restrictions between the United States and several of its trading partners. When the war started in Europe in 1939, the State Department drew up a projected peace settlement that included reductions in trade barriers. After the attack on Pearl Harbor, Washington began to plan for a substantial liberalization of trade throughout the world.[68]

The British viewed the American program warily. Although London had abandoned its traditional policy of free trade in the interwar years, it had done so reluctantly. The United Kingdom was still the world's largest trading nation, importing food and raw materials and exporting manufactured goods; before 1939, British subjects had also dominated international shipping and related services like insurance. The island nation might benefit handsomely from the reduction of barriers to international exchange. Yet good reasons for caution existed. It was clear that when the war ended and American aid ceased Britain would face a huge payments deficit that would require strict control over foreign exchange for several years. London had also enshrined full employment as its chief postwar economic aim, and many in Britain feared that the country could not achieve this goal without regulating international trade and capital flows.[69] Finally, in the 1930s, the British Empire and Commonwealth had developed a system of "imperial preference" under which members awarded one another preferential (lower) tariffs. Few Britons thought of their empire as a self-sufficient economic block, but most did believe that preferences made it more cohesive and prosperous. Yet American policy makers made little secret of their desire to dismantle this system, which they believed distorted trade—not to mention put U.S. firms at a disadvantage in empire markets. Despite these concerns, London cautiously embraced the liberalization of trade, in part because it elected to follow its hopes rather than its fears and in part because its economic and military dependence on the United States made the outright rejection of such a high American priority impractical.

Britain and the United States outlined their objectives in a clause of the February 1942 Lend-Lease Agreement, which London signed in part in exchange for an American promise not to seek repayment after the war for its military aid.[70] The two countries agreed to explore steps "directed to the expansion, by appropriate international and domestic measures, of production, employment, and the exchange and consumption of goods," including the elimination of all forms of discrimination in international commerce and the reduction of tariffs and other trade barriers.[71]

The Antitrust Division of the Justice Department argued that the trade program should include measures against international cartels. One memo asserted, "Free trade, however, involves more than governmental policies as to tariffs, quotas, and exchange controls. It implies freedom to buy from competitive sellers, and to sell to competitive buyers. . . . If we are to abolish governmental trade restraints, it would be absurd to leave in private hands a power or prerogative denied or foregone by nations as incompatible with world order."[72] This analysis was not confined to the American Justice Department. As a British economist noted, "It is possible for producers to make international [cartel] agreements . . . whereby free-trade policy is overreached by clauses reserving the home market to home producers."[73]

The State Department willingly placed cartels on the agenda of commercial talks. Though generally not as dogmatic as their counterparts in the Justice Department, its personnel conceded that cartels were part of the machinery of restriction that had retarded and distorted trade in the 1930s. Other concerns also drove State. As early as 1941, officials there worried, "There is a grave danger that work with respect to post-war economic policies will either be done independently by several agencies of the Government or else that it will be coordinated under other leadership than that of the Department of State."[74] Because the military and the White House had largely excluded State from decisions on the conduct of the war, the department was all the more determined to control postwar planning. In the spring and early summer of 1943, it organized under its aegis twelve interdepartmental committees to coordinate economic policy, including the Special Committee on Private Monopolies and Cartels. This body included not only officials from State but also representatives of the Justice and Agriculture Departments, the Tariff Commission, and the Office of Strategic Services (OSS), the government's intelligence arm.[75] From the beginning the committee sought an "agreement with other nations to forbid and prevent objectionable cartel activities."[76] The State Department's effort received reinforcement from the president's September 1944 public letter to Secretary of State Cordell Hull in which he asked Hull to "keep your eye on this whole subject of international cartels."[77]

Dean Acheson chaired the Cartel Committee. A Harvard-trained lawyer and the epitome of the "Eastern Establishment," Acheson was a conservative Democrat who in 1933 had quit a position in the Treasury Department to protest President Roosevelt's currency policies. In 1940, he had served as the lead counsel for the defense in the *Ethyl* case.[78] Nevertheless, Acheson firmly supported the president's stand against Nazi Germany and had returned to Washington during the war. By 1943, he was a rising figure at the State Department, in charge of economic affairs. Acheson held moderate views on international cartels. In a statement outlining postwar economic challenges he argued, "Most of these barriers and discriminations [restricting trade] are the result of government action," though he conceded that "a sound international economic policy must take cognizance not only of governmentally imposed restrictions but also the restrictive practices of international business agreements."[79] Acheson may have assumed the chair of the Cartel Committee to limit radical anticartel proposals. If such was the intention, however, it failed. Acheson's other duties left him little time for the Cartel Committee, and he rarely attended meetings. His memoirs, *Present at the Creation*, do not mention the subject at all.[80]

Effective leadership of the Cartel Committee fell to Edward S. Mason, an Iowa-bred economist on the faculty of Harvard who, during the war, had worked for the OSS. After 1945, he would become a pioneer in the economic subdiscipline of international organizations. Mason was one of the few leading figures in the drive against cartels not associated with the Antitrust Division, and his opinions on the subject reflected a balance rarely evident there. In a 1944 article in *Foreign Affairs*, Mason complained, "Very little of the recent literature is devoted to careful description or cool appraisal of their [cartels'] activities. Those opposed have relied on such words as conspiracy, monopoly, Fascism and treason." He also observed, "It was the depression of the thirties which produced that array of protective tariffs, exchange controls, quantitative limitations [quotas], currency depreciation, export subsidies and restrictions through cartels which by the end of the decade had put international economic relations in a strait jacket." In other words, cartels were more a symptom than a cause of the world's economic problems. Nevertheless, Mason's opinion was clear. "There can be little doubt," he wrote, "that international cartels on the whole restrict the total volume of world trade and divert its channels." "The political and economic interests of the United States," he concluded, "run so strongly in the direction of a liberal [economic] foreign policy that the appropriate attitude toward international cartels may be said to be predetermined."[81]

Corwin Edwards, an economist representing the Justice Department, also enjoyed considerable influence on the Cartel Committee. Although he was somewhat more dogmatic than Mason in his opposition to cartels, the two seem to have worked well together, and through talent and commitment they dominated the committee.

Surprisingly, the Cartel Committee included no representative from the Federal Trade Commission. The committee's organizers insisted, "Despite the obvious logic of a Federal Trade Commission representative, we were frankly unable to find any individual there who seemed to have any particular contribution to make."[82] The claim was improbable. The FTC maintained a large staff that was by 1943 supplying the Antitrust Division with information on international cartels. More likely, the State Department failed to include anyone from the commission because it saw no need to take into account the views of an agency with so little political influence. The FTC's exclusion from the committee, coupled with the leading role of the Justice Department's Corwin Edwards in the Cartel Committee's deliberations, did nothing to strengthen the FTC vis-à-vis the Antitrust Division, its chief rival in the antimonopoly field. Complaints from the FTC finally led to the appointment of one of its people to the Cartel Committee in February 1945, but by that time the group had been at work for almost two years.[83]

Farm policy constituted a far graver problem for the anticartel drive than squabbling between departments. During the 1930s, Washington had erected a complex system of price supports for agricultural commodities, controlling their production and marketing. These measures raised domestic prices over those of the outside world, requiring extensive protection. Despite restrictions on output, American farmers continued to produce more than the domestic market could absorb, forcing the government to dispose of the excess by subsidizing foreign sales at low prices—in commercial parlance, "dumping" it. Though not labeled as such, the system was a government-managed cartel. Nor was the American policy unique—many other countries had comparable schemes for agriculture. Because many of these programs contained provisions to dump surpluses, they created the risk of government-financed price wars over export markets. Exporting nations had avoided this by negotiating commodity accords that apportioned foreign markets—in effect, international cartels. The war had temporarily converted the surpluses of most commodities into shortages, but agricultural specialists generally expected the surpluses to return with peace.

It was hard to reconcile such programs with blanket denunciations of cartels. Their advocates justified farm programs on the grounds that they kept the supply and demand for agricultural commodities in balance and allowed farmers to earn a decent living, exactly the same terms used to defend private cartels. A few involved in the anticartel drive did address the issue squarely. Thurman Arnold stated, "I recognize that farmers cannot stand (or will not) the deflation of suddenly establishing an absolute competitive market. . . . The sudden liquidation of an entire group in the interest of free trade is never a political possibility."[84] The circumstances justified government-managed cartels, which, being accountable to the public, were unlikely to abuse their power. Such arguments, however, convinced few in the business community. If government cartels were acceptable under certain conditions, then as far as businessmen were concerned, so were private ones. If the latter were pernicious, then the former, clothed with the power of law and so able to compel adherence, were even more likely to cause harm. This interesting theoretical question received little attention because in practice it was moot. Farmers strongly supported agricultural programs, and they enjoyed considerable political influence. Washington was not going to abandon farm programs in the name of intellectual consistency on the cartel question. Instead, the State Department organized the Special Committee on Commodity Agreements and Methods of Trade. This body contained no one from the Justice Department, although Corwin Edwards did act as liaison between it and the Cartel Committee. Whereas the Cartel Committee sought to ban private accords restricting competition, the Commodity Agreements Committee aimed to define procedures for government cartels.

American and British officials held preliminary talks on trade in the fall of 1943. Military successes in North Africa and Italy had raised the hope of victory and encouraged the Allies to consider their postwar plans more carefully. As the leading capitalist powers among the Allies, the United States and the United Kingdom expected to dominate talks on the shape of world trade after the war. As one diplomatic dispatch claimed, "Representatives of small countries in particular feel that the commercial policies of their countries must be largely determined by the policies adopted by the larger states and in particular the United States and Great Britain."[85] John Maynard Keynes led a British delegation that traveled to Washington and met with a host of American officials, including members of the Cartel and Commodity Agreements Committees. Participants spent most of their time on financial questions, but they examined many other issues as well, including cartels.

The discussion of cartels surprised the British. As one State Department memo noted, "The British group came over here without any instructions on the subject of monopolies and cartels."[86] This did not discourage the Americans, who lectured their guests on the evils of cartels. A report on the talks stated, "The British participants, after a remarkable educational job by Mr. C. D. Edwards of the Department of Justice and Mr. E. S. Mason of the OSS . . . expressed themselves as personally much impressed by the merits of the American position."[87] The Americans may have overestimated their success. One month later Keynes produced a memo stating, "I believe that the future lies with . . . international cartels for necessary manufacturers."[88] In any case, lacking instructions, the British could agree to nothing. The Americans nevertheless took the opportunity to recommend a program involving the "registration of all private international agreements" and the "prohibition by international agreement of objectionable international cartel activities," which included price fixing, restrictions on output, and the allocation of markets among firms.[89]

The talks made greater progress on commodity accords. Here the Americans and British had different interests. A major exporter of commodities, the United States desired to sell dearly, whereas the United Kingdom, a leading importer, preferred to buy cheap. Keynes was enthusiastic about schemes for buffer stocks, under which a central authority would buy and store commodities when prices were low and sell when the market improved. This would not only even out swings in the market but, Keynes hoped, stabilize farm income and contribute to general economic equilibrium. The American with whom Keynes dealt in these particular discussions, William Clayton, was not so sure. Clayton was yet another conservative Democrat who had made his way to Washington during the war. In private life he had built the world's largest cotton brokerage firm; his expertise had secured him a position in the government's commodity bureau. In November 1944, he would move to the State Department, from which he would direct the government's commercial negotiations until retiring in 1948. In the 1943 talks with Keynes, Clayton argued, "The advocates of a buffer stock program underrate the constructive aspects of private trade on the commodity exchanges in regulating markets forces and . . . assume that a board of few men would be wiser in its decisions with respect to prices than the impersonal operations of the free market."[90] Clayton himself was an advocate of free markets and skeptical of government intervention, but other Americans present attacked Keynes's scheme because it lacked any controls on production, which they considered the only device capable of bringing long-term stability to commodity markets.[91] The minutes of the meeting indicate that, although not entirely convinced, "Lord Keynes thought that some restrictive schemes might be required in cases where the propensity to produce outruns the propensity to consume."[92] In the end, the two countries agreed to disagree. The final communication from the talks noted, "The U.K. group is hopeful that in practice it will be possible in the case of most commodities to allow long-term price trends to follow supply and demand and to constitute the primary means of effecting adjustments in productive capacity to balance demand. The U.S. group consider that it may well be necessary to have greater recourse to quantitative regulation schemes."[93]

Dissent over the exact shape of commodity accords did not prevent the two sides from agreeing on procedures to govern them. Both favored an "international commodity organization [that] would be charged with responsibility for reviewing, supervising and coordinating international commodity arrangements of all kinds and, if necessary, for initiating them." Individual accords would seek "the mitigation of violent short-term price fluctuations . . . which would help to counteract business cycles." In the long run, commodity agreements would aim for "a state of affairs under which price adjustments would follow changes in basic conditions of supply and demand and in which there would be increasing opportunities for supplying world requirements from countries able to furnish such requirements most effectively." No commodity accord would run for more than five years, although renewal would be possible at the end of that time.[94]

Diplomats made little further progress in the next two years, largely because the Allies had other priorities. Both the United States and Britain devoted much effort to working out the charter of the United Nations; in the economic sphere, they concentrated on the reorganization of the international financial system. When American military aid ceased after the war, the British would face a severe payments deficit, and they desired to put into place as soon as possible financial structures to help them deal with the problem. Certainly Keynes, perhaps the most important figure in the discussions, devoted most of his time to finance, his specialty. His efforts yielded fruit in the 1944 Bretton Woods Accords, which established a new framework for international finance.

Nevertheless, planning on cartels continued in the United States. In May 1944, the Cartel Committee laid out its ideal program. Noting that "the typical effects of cartels are to reduce output, raise and stabilize selling prices, increase profit margins, reduce employment, and protect high costs members," the committee recommended "the adoption of a coordinated program by which each nation undertakes to prohibit the most restrictive cartel practices." The International Office for Business Practices would administer the effort and suggest where "international conventions and national laws about patents, trademarks, and company organizations should be amended or supplemented to make such restrictive cartel practices more difficult." The Cartel Committee conceded that restrictive programs for "the furtherance of international security, the conservation of natural resources, the protection of public health and morals, or the relief of insupportable distress during the application of constructive measures to shift resources from over-developed industries to more productive uses" might be worthwhile, but they "should be agreed upon between governments rather than between private interests."[95] At the same time, the Cartel Committee set minimum goals. Corwin Edwards contended that any agreement should include at least "general language against private international agreements which are restrictive in character, [and] . . . the plan should include specific provision for some device . . . by which the things prohibited can be more fully defined from time to time." "We should insist," Edwards continued, "upon retaining the principle that international agreements for restrictive action shall be governmental in character. . . . We should insist, moreover, that the burden of proof shall rest upon the advocates of each restrictive arrangement."[96]

Planning for commodity accords proceeded as well. In October 1944, the Commodity Agreements Committee formally submitted its recommendations to the president. It argued that historically commodity prices had been unstable and suggested that free markets did not work particularly well in this area, permitting extended gluts. The committee also noted the "need for reconciling existing unilateral national policies in support of internationally-traded commodities." It believed that "a properly conceived and executed, selective program for international commodity agreements can be harmonized with a broad program of international economic expansion," though it conceded, "It will be necessary to provide adequate safeguards against possible abuses of international commodity agreements."[97]

The Cartel Committee well served the interests of both the State and Justice Departments. It gave the Antitrust Division and other foes of cartels a voice in postwar planning that they probably would not have enjoyed otherwise while lodging undisputed responsibility for the subject with the State Department. Put simply, State adopted Justice's program in exchange for recognition of its authority. This compromise entailed no great sacrifices. People at the State Department had little enthusiasm for cartels; the Justice Department's lawyers showed little desire to become diplomats. Still, without the Cartel Committee it is unlikely that the federal government would have spoken with such a firm, united voice against international cartels.

The Short, Unhappy Life
of the International Trade Organization

Allied victory brought no great acceleration of commercial talks. Political arrangements in Europe occupied much of the attention of national leaders, particularly with the development of the Cold War. Yet even in the economic sphere other matters came first. The disastrous state of the world economy in the years immediately after 1945 forced government officials to devote most of their time simply to staving off disaster. Long-term goals like commercial liberalization had to wait. Progress on trade did occur, but it was halting, and many objectives remained unrealized. Anticartel measures were among the casualties. They foundered because the nations of the world could not agree on general principles for organizing trade. Measures restricting cartels were not themselves particularly controversial, but they could not exist outside a broader context of agreement, which did not exist.

The chances for a general agreement on cartels seemed promising in 1945. By the end of the war, the British had conceded the need for reform. The State Department's Cartel Committee noted "a significant shift in British thinking about cartels. It is now generally recognized in the U.K. . . . that restrictive private arrangements often result in the contraction of trade and hence frustrate governmental policies directed toward trade expansion."[98] The change of opinion reflected, in part, the anticartel rhetoric emanating from the United States. The British had not ignored the 1944 indictment of ICI and DuPont—an anonymous pamphlet recounting the Justice Department's charges had circulated in the House of Commons, and the House of Lords had debated the case.[99] Publications attacking cartels had also appeared. Many of these originated in the United States—Joseph Borkin and Charles Welsh's *Germany's Master Plan* made a particularly strong impact—but British publications like *Patents for Hitler*, which examined ties among British, American, and German firms, had influence as well.[100] Cartels even lost ground in government circles. In 1944, a council of ministers devoted to postwar planning concluded that "restrictive practices of the type and scope prevalent before the war would be a major impediment to the full employment policy and expansionist economy which the government have adopted as their postwar aim."[101] Such opinions were hardly universal, but they indicated declining enthusiasm for cartels.

London, however, wanted to pursue a more flexible policy toward international cartels than did Washington. The authors of a Foreign Office memo drafted shortly before the end of the war noted, "It is, in our view, a proposition not entirely borne out by the facts that the best economic—or social—results can always be relied on to follow from the freest competition. . . . Our approach to cartels is quite empirical and does not derive from any moral judgement on the question whether international trade should be conducted on the basis of free competition or planned arrangements."[102] Such attitudes did not excite the American Cartel Committee. It observed, "The British leaned toward an examination of every restrictive practice. They wished to consider each on its own merits, and they believed that by a case-by-case analysis in each country a body of precedent would be developed."[103] Another memo noted, "Considerable doubt exists in the minds of the U.S. experts whether the consultative machinery of the U.K. Proposals could operate expeditiously."[104] Nevertheless, the prospects for some sort of agreement appeared good.

Restrictions on cartels constituted part of a broader program involving the creation of the International Trade Organization (ITO). This autonomous, supranational body was designed to oversee trade policy in the postwar era. It was to guarantee that the restrictive trade practices that had charac-

terized the 1930s, the complex networks of regulations created by governments to protect their balance of payments and, often, exert political pressure
on their neighbors, did not reemerge. In the fall of 1945, the United States
and Britain released the "Proposals for Consideration by an International
Conference on Trade and Employment," which called for a ban on various
discriminatory and protective practices, including cartels, and the creation
of the ITO to administer these prohibitions. Though technically an American document, the proposals were in fact a joint statement. British support
was, in part, a quid pro quo for a massive reconstruction loan granted on
favorable terms by Washington in 1945. Despite unease over some specific
points of the proposals, however, London nevertheless generally favored
them.[105]

William Clayton oversaw negotiations for the Americans. As a former
commodities trader he instinctively favored free markets, yet his vision tran-
scended business. Clayton was a convinced internationalist who believed
that healthy trade was vital to world prosperity and that prosperity was key
to peace. Cartels, he believed, violated the ideals of free trade and tended
to restrict and channel commerce. Although not as dogmatic on the subject
as some members of the Antitrust Division—Clayton never considered cartels the chief problem confronting the world economy—he worked hard to
include restrictions on cartels in the ITO charter.

The proposals reflected the minimum demands of the State Department's
Cartel Committee. They stated, "The [International Trade] organization
should receive complaints from any member . . . that the objectives of the
Organization are being frustrated by a private international combination."
The ITO would have the authority to investigate complaints and "make
recommendations to the appropriate members for action." The proposals
also left Washington free to act on its own against cartels, providing, "Any
act or failure to act on the part of the organization should not preclude any
member from enforcing within its own jurisdiction any national statute or
decree directed toward the elimination or prevention of restrictive business
practices."[106]

The document also provided for commodity agreements. Washington
had decided not to continue the bilateral arrangements through which it
had managed much of its commodities trade during the war, stating that it
"favors the use of private channels in international trade as most consistent
with the principles of liberal trade policy."[107] Although necessary in wartime,
state trading during peace represented an unacceptable departure from the

open economic system that the United States championed. Nevertheless, American officials realized that exceptions were necessary. Agricultural programs would not disappear with peace, and governments would not abstain from intervening in markets for commodities on which their economies were particularly dependent. A carefully regulated system of commodity accords seemed the best way to reconcile these realities with an otherwise liberal commercial regime. According to the Anglo-American proposals, the ITO would have the authority to determine whether a "burdensome world surplus" existed in any market. If such was the case, "The members which are important producers or consumers of the commodities should agree to consult together with a view to promoting consumption increases, to promoting the reduction of production through the diversion of resources from uneconomical production, and to seeking, if necessary, the conclusion of an intergovernmental commodity accord."[108]

Washington believed that British support for the proposals vastly increased the chances for an agreement limiting cartels. Though these organizations had many partisans in Europe, elsewhere they were unpopular. In 1945, the government of Canada issued to an enthusiastic public reception a long report alleging that international cartels had, before 1939, retarded the country's industrial development by keeping prices high and discouraging the growth of domestic producers.[109] At an international conference of businessmen in 1944, Indian representatives insisted that cartels had stymied economic progress in the subcontinent.[110] Many critics of cartels associated them with imperialism, in part because in cartel accords British and French firms usually reserved for themselves the markets of their colonial empires. Corwin Edwards claimed that "international cartels have usually acted as substantial deterrents to the industrial development of parts of the world which their members regard as colonial markets."[111] Considering the emphasis on national self-determination and industrial development after World War II, the identification of cartels with economic and political imperialism did not bode well for them.

The Soviet Union did not involve itself in the cartel issue or any aspect of the ITO. A State Department memo noted, the Russians "consistently attributed their absence [from talks] to a shortage of trained personnel."[112] Few American officials accepted this explanation. As the U.S. ambassador in Moscow wrote, "It is difficult to understand how a nation of 180,000,000 inhabitants and pretensions to world leadership cannot achieve the same degree of participation in international organs as a small country such as

Belgium, with its population of 8,000,000. . . . It would appear that the distribution of this personnel was one of conscious administrative decision."[113] Because the Soviet government controlled all that country's foreign trade, it had little stake in liberalization, and it may have feared that the ITO would impinge on its sovereignty. Moscow's opinion of cartels is not clear. The Soviet press had denounced them as instruments of capitalist aggression, but at the same time Russia had participated in some cartels during the 1930s.[114] In any case, the Soviet Union did not consider the issue important enough to warrant participation in the ITO talks.

Despite the favorable alignment among the great powers—American and British support coupled with Soviet indifference—the ITO faced serious opposition. Still, a preliminary meeting of eleven leading trading nations, held in London in late 1946, did yield promising results.[115] The Americans went to the conference eager to secure "acceptance of the American draft [the proposals] as the basis of the Committee's deliberations."[116] Because no one else had an overall plan the ploy succeeded, and as a State Department report noted, "From then on all the work of the Committee was directed toward our document. This gave us a great advantage in the negotiations. We had stated the problems, suggested the solutions, established the general pattern of the charter, and provided large sections of the text that have not been and will not be altered in any way."[117]

Participants accepted the cartel and commodity accord provisions of the proposals. Before the London meeting, Washington had received from several European countries "objections . . . to provisions in the Draft Charter [of the ITO] regarding cartels and inter-governmental commodity arrangements. . . . In particular they object to the presumption that the specific practices of cartels are bad and are inclined to feel that the burden of proof should be on the [international trade] organization to prove them so. Regarding commodity agreements they feel that the machinery is so cumbersome as to prevent or delay unduly the taking of needed action."[118] Nevertheless, thanks largely to American persistence, Canadian support, and the fact that the U.S. proposal formed the basis of discussions, the American delegates secured "a revised chapter [on cartels] that is stronger than our original proposals and far stronger than we thought was possible."[119]

Unfortunately, the ITO made little progress over the next year. Commercial negotiators turned to tariff reduction, and as a State Department memo noted, "In view of the thousands of tariff items involved, and the need for proceeding with tariff reduction on a selective, product-by-product basis, provisions effectuating actual tariff reductions cannot be incorporated into the [ITO] Charter itself."[120] Instead, participants conducted tariff talks in a separate forum, the General Agreement on Trade and Tariffs (GATT). These negotiations eventually succeeded, substantially reducing levies, but they took a long time. Talks on the ITO resumed in Geneva only in late 1947; their successful conclusion required a second round of meetings in Havana, Cuba, the next spring.

Final negotiations on the ITO did not proceed as smoothly as the preliminary talks in London. Several factors accounted for the difficulty. By late 1947, it was clear that the European and East Asian economies were recovering only slowly from the war, if at all, and that governments there would have to maintain tight control over foreign exchange and trade for the indefinite future. Most of these countries still favored the ITO in principle, but they did not think that they could implement its provisions for quite a while. The attitudes of Third World countries presented an even more serious obstacle. These nations wanted to industrialize, and contemporary theory on the subject favored "import substitution," restricting imports while subsidizing domestic manufacturing. Representatives of Third World countries pointed out that during critical periods of economic development the industrial countries had pursued comparable policies—Britain in the late eighteenth century and the United States and Germany in the late nineteenth century. Many developing countries feared that unless they could do the same their industries would remain stunted. Reconciling such a program with a liberal trade regime would be very difficult.

The problem had manifested itself at the preliminary meeting in London in 1946. According to a State Department memo, "The Indians came in with a chip on their shoulder. They regarded the Proposals as a document prepared by the U.S. and U.K. to serve the interests of the highly industrialized countries by keeping the backward countries in a position of economic dependence."[121] In London, the other participants had managed to mollify the Indians, but in Geneva and Havana, representatives of Third World countries constituted a much larger proportion of delegates and accordingly enjoyed greater power. In Havana, the leader of the Mexican delegation insisted, "Reduction of trade barriers must not be such as to hamper development in underdeveloped countries. These countries demanded the right to use the instruments of protection which other countries had used in the past to develop their industries. . . . Freezing the present pattern of world economy could not be tolerated."[122]

Import quotas soon became the center of dispute. With tariffs now set by GATT, protectionists saw quotas as the best way to regulate trade. Washington had hoped to ban quotas altogether but instead had to make concessions. The final draft of the ITO charter allowed countries to impose quotas either to encourage development or to deal with a severe balance-of-payments deficit. The United States had little choice but to agree to these exceptions if it wanted to secure approval of the ITO charter because Third World countries simply refused to forgo protection. The charter still included general language banning quotas. Nevertheless, many Americans feared that the prohibition against quotas contained so many exceptions that it would in fact institutionalize them in many circumstances.

Foreign investment constituted another problem. The United States and Britain wanted the ITO to guarantee their investments abroad. Developing countries, believing that the operations of foreign interests often impinged on their sovereignty, demanded the right to regulate foreign businesses. Negotiators compromised, accepting general language protecting foreign investments but allowing governments to transfer ownership of such property if they provided "just compensation," a term that was not defined. As with the provisions on quotas, many in both the United States and Britain believed that the exceptions would in fact institutionalize grave abuses.

Conflict between the industrialized nations and the Third World even touched the issues of cartels and commodity accords. Several Latin American delegations in Havana demanded that the ITO charter direct commodity accords to strive for "remunerative prices," which meant "prices which maintain a fair relationship with the prices which the producers of primary commodities are obliged to pay for manufactured . . . goods."[123] They believed that the prices of commodities tended to fall relative to manufactured goods, hurting the producers of raw materials to the benefit of industry. This tendency particularly affected Third World countries, which exported raw materials and imported manufactured goods. The suggestion had precedent— U.S. farm policy sought "parity" between agricultural prices and the costs of manufactured goods. Yet a requirement to strive for remunerative prices would make drafting commodity accords even more complicated, and many considered the entire concept flawed. The chief British delegate insisted, "The phrase 'fair relationship' could not be interpreted by inter-government commodity agreements. It was something which only general economic and social development might bring about *assuming* that there was any unfairness in past and present relationships."[124] The conference eventually rejected the proposed language.

The negotiators did, however, make a change in the cartel section. Some countries feared that the ITO's provisions directed against cartels might "be used to attack either the principle of public ownership or members' basic legislation."[125] Many countries had ambitious plans for postwar industrial development that entailed government rationing of scarce capital and resources among competing firms and, in some cases, creating government-owned companies or nationalizing private ones. Such programs restricted competition and so might run afoul of the ITO's anticartel measures. The final draft of the charter exempted government-owned firms from anticartel provisions. At first glance the exception seemed sizable, as even the governments of capitalist nations often owned large firms.[126] Yet the construction of an effective international cartel by government-owned companies alone was generally impossible. In almost every industry some private companies remained powerful, and an agreement that ignored them would not last. Barring a massive shift toward public ownership, this exception was not likely to be critical.

With respect to cartels and commodity agreements, the ITO charter actually followed the 1945 Anglo-American proposals fairly closely. In contrast with the provisions on quotas and foreign investment, Third World nations had little at stake in cartels, in which their companies rarely had a place. Many believed that these organizations had actually retarded their economic development. An official summary of the final agreement noted that the ITO had the authority to investigate "price-fixing, territorial exclusion, discrimination, production quotas, technological restriction, misuse of patents, trademarks and copyrights," and that "members are obligated to take action against restrictive business practices in international trade wherever they are contrary to the principles of the charter." The summary did note, "The powers of the ITO will be limited mainly to instructing the offending member to correct the abuse and to publication of the facts." Nevertheless, this language, in theory, banned most of the practices of international cartels. The ITO charter also laid down fairly strict procedures for commodity accords. The summary noted, "Members are obligated to enter into new control type agreements only through Charter procedures," which permitted action "only when there is a burdensome surplus or widespread unemployment, which could not be corrected by normal market forces alone."[127]

In the United States, the ITO charter generated little enthusiasm. Business groups, which had provided critical—albeit at times grudging—support for the Bretton Woods Accords and the loan to the British in 1945, refused to endorse it.[128] They particularly objected to the clauses on import quotas and foreign investment, but the cartel and commodity provisions also caused annoyance. Business groups noted the contradiction between provisions condemning private cartels and those regulating and thereby implicitly endorsing government commodity accords. The U.S. International Chamber of Commerce stated that it "rejects as unsound the notion that one standard of conduct can be applied in the case of private agreements and a different one in the case of similar agreements between governments."[129] The National Association of Manufacturers argued that the ITO charter "leaves the position of cartels in the world economy pretty much unchanged. True, it allows complaints to be made and outlines a procedure for dealing with them; but nothing in this Charter resembles even distantly a moderate version of anti-trust commitments."[130] As for commodity agreements, NAM stated, "They are especially to be condemned as an invasion of free enterprise, since the production, processing, and distribution of raw materials and foodstuffs are properly the responsibility of private management and operation. . . . They aim at fixing these monopoly prices at the height at which production pays also for the submarginal producers. They raise average costs of production. They result in monopolistic exploitation of the consumers for the sole benefit of the producers"[131]

The cartels and commodity provisions of the ITO did have defenders. A report issued by two congressmen, James G. Fulton and Jacob K. Javits, noted, "The provisions relating to restrictive business practices fall short of the ideal, but they are comprehensive, and given support by the governments should effectively serve . . . [to prevent] restrictive practices which limit the expansion of production or trade." The two lawmakers also observed, "It is an exaggeration to say that the charter provisions open the door wide to commodity agreements. The limitations applying particularly to commodity control agreements are significant. . . . No existing or prewar commodity agreements could meet all the standards laid down in the charter."[132] Besides, no better agreement was likely.

The ITO never came close to securing congressional approval. The business community was generally hostile. Many executives were reluctant to dispense with protection, which American manufacturers had enjoyed in many cases for eighty years. Others feared that the provisions on quotas and foreign investment would permit foreign governments to shut American firms out of lucrative markets by restricting imports and direct investment. More broadly, the idealistic enthusiasm for international cooperation that had carried the approval of the United Nations and the Bretton Woods Accords had subsided. The failure (thus far) of European reconstruction and the growth of Soviet power had soured many Americans on broad initiatives like the ITO that relied on supranational bodies. Finally, the Truman administration had other priorities. For most of his tenure, the president's support in Congress was precarious, and during 1948 and 1949, he devoted his limited political capital to winning approval of the Marshall Plan for European reconstruction. The White House considered it more important than the ITO and more likely to win passage. The Marshall Plan promised to contain Soviet power, whose growth alarmed both the public and policymakers, whereas the ITO offered no such geopolitical dividends. Congress never even voted on the ITO, and in 1950 the administration officially gave up on securing its approval.[133]

The failure of the ITO reflected the lack of consensus among nations on economic policy. They disagreed on how to treat private property and on how much control governments should exercise over trade and the economy in general. Concessions necessary for Washington to attract the support of other countries alienated the American business community, whose support was necessary for approval. The GATT talks on tariff reduction, which after the demise of the ITO became the vehicle for trade liberalization, succeeded because they operated on a quid pro quo basis, with countries making reciprocal concessions on specific rates. The ITO, a statement of principles, offered no such flexibility.

International cartels numbered among the less contentious issues surrounding the ITO—a consensus apparently existed for restricting them. Considering the enthusiasm lavished on cartels just a decade earlier, the shift was remarkable. The stream of denunciations emanating from the United States had apparently had an effect.

Yet the fate of the ITO also demonstrated the limits of the cartel issue among Americans. Despite grumbling, the provisions on cartels and commodity accords were not a center of debate. Indeed, they were probably acceptable to most members of Congress. Yet no one seriously suggested that the ITO's restrictions on cartels, however appealing, justified accepting an otherwise flawed agreement.

The Triumph of Antitrust

In contrast with commercial talks, the judicial offensive against international cartels enjoyed spectacular success. Throughout the war, the Justice Department had been preparing cases against these organizations, and by early 1945, it had at least nineteen ready for argument.[134] Peace sent the Antitrust Division back to court.

The Justice Department had good reason to expect a sympathetic hearing from the courts. In his twelve years as president, Franklin D. Roosevelt had remade the judiciary. Once the federal courts had been the bane of reformers, stoutly defending property rights against most forms of government interference. During the 1930s, the Supreme Court had struck down so much New Deal legislation that in 1937 Roosevelt had, in frustration, proposed his notorious "Court-packing" plan, which would have allowed him to create a slew of new justices. Although the measure failed in Congress, its prospect had frightened the judiciary into a more accommodating stance. More important, as time passed, Roosevelt was able to appoint more and more judges sympathetic to economic reform. By 1945, the Supreme Court included such notable New Dealers as Hugo Black, Felix Frankfurter, William O. Douglas, and Robert Jackson. Equally dramatic changes occurred in the lower courts. Although never monolithic in opinion, Roosevelt's appointees usually embraced a doctrine known as "legal realism," which at the risk of oversimplifying held that the law was not a science or a set of divine truths but a practical method for managing disputes whose interpretation ought to adapt to social change. They generally gave the government wide latitude in implementing economic reforms, an attitude that encouraged firm application of the antitrust laws. By 1945, the Antitrust Division believed that the Supreme Court was ready to overturn the legal precedents that permitted cartel agreements, particularly the 1926 *General Electric* decision regarding patent agreements, a key support for international cartels.[135]

The *National Lead* case provided the vital precedent. Among other things, the National Lead Company produced titanium oxide, a white pigment used chiefly in paint. By 1940, output in the United States totaled 100,000 tons, worth approximately $40 million. Legally the industry rested on three sets of patents taken out around World War I, each developed separately by groups in the United States, Norway, and France. National Lead, already a large maker of paint, had purchased rights to the American titanium oxide process and, in the early 1920s, had reached an agreement with the Norwegian group, exchanging all patents and apportioning the world's markets. National Lead received North America; the Norwegians got the rest of the world. The agreement eliminated both competition and the possibility of vexing patent litigation. Meanwhile, DuPont had obtained the American rights to the French process. In 1933, it signed an accord with

National Lead exchanging all patents and submitting to the existing international division of territory. Within the United States, DuPont and National Lead competed vigorously for customers, cutting prices and increasing output on a regular basis, although their joint control of patents prevented the emergence of any serious outside challenger.[136]

In the summer of 1943, the Antitrust Division filed suit to break up this arrangement. Wendell Berge wrote, "It is difficult to believe that the public interest has been adequately served by having the most valuable of white pigments subjected to complete control in this country and throughout the world by a cartel. . . . One may be quite sure that when the cartel shackles are broken, titanium will take its rightful place as not only the most important and useful of all pigments but also for a wide variety of other industrial uses."[137] The military forced the suspension of prosecution until the end of the war in Europe, but the case went to trial in the summer of 1945.

In October 1945, the federal district judge decided, "When the story is seen as a whole, there is no blinking the fact that there is no free commerce in titanium. Every pound of it is trammeled by privately imposed regulation. . . . It was more difficult for the independent outsider to enter this business than for the camel to make its proverbial passage through the eye of the needle." He continued, "Whether the form of association they created be called a cartel, an international cartel, a patent pool, or a 'technical and commercial cooperation' is of little significance. It is a combination and conspiracy in restraint of trade; and the restraint is unreasonable. As such it is outlawed by Section 1 of the Sherman Act." The court ruled against the cartel's domestic and foreign aspects alike, noting, "No citation of authority is any longer necessary to support the proposition that a combination of competitors, which by agreement divides the world into exclusive trading areas, and suppresses all competition among the members of the combination, offends the Sherman Act."[138] Though phrased in an off-handed manner, this statement represented a daring claim of power by the court, bringing into the province of U.S. antitrust law most international cartels. Other judges quickly recognized the value of this doctrine—decision after decision concerning international cartels quoted this section of *National Lead*.

The authority of National Lead's and DuPont's patents did not impress the court much. The original rights had expired by the 1940s, and the firms relied on patents to various incremental improvements in the product and the way it was made to keep competition at bay. The court noted that "the newcomer [to the titanium dioxide field] is confronted by a veritable jungle of patent claims through which only the very powerful and stouthearted would venture, having a regard for the large initial investment which this business requires. These patents, through the agreements in which they are enmeshed and the manner in which they have been used, have, in fact, been forged into instruments of domination of an entire industry. The net effect is that a business, originally founded upon patents which have long since expired, is today less accessible to free enterprise than when it was first launched." The court ordered National Lead and DuPont to license their titanium patents at a reasonable royalty to all applicants.[139]

The decision rested on law, not economics. The court conceded, "During the regime of the combination, the art has rapidly advanced, production has increased enormously and prices have sharply declined." Nevertheless, "the major premise of the Sherman Act is that the suppression of competition in international trade is in and of itself a public injury; or at any rate, that such suppression is a greater price than we want to pay for the benefits it sometimes secured."[140]

Decisions from the Supreme Court further weakened the status of patent cartels. In 1947, the High Court upheld the *National Lead* decision.[141] The next year it issued two opinions, *United States Gypsum* and *Line Material*, which further restricted patent cartels. *United States Gypsum* dealt with the producers of gypsum, a natural substance used to make plasterboard. As the Supreme Court noted, "By development and purchase, it [the U.S. Gypsum Company] has acquired the most significant patents covering the manufacture of gypsum board, and beginning in 1926, United States Gypsum offered licenses under its patents to other concerns in the industry, all licenses containing a provision that United States Gypsum should fix the minimum price at which the licensee sold."[142] *Line Material* involved a comparable situation. Several firms held patents on electric fuses; in some cases, one firm's patent represented a refinement of a technology controlled by another company. Accordingly the firms, of which Line Material was perhaps the most important, exchanged patents. The agreement, however, not only licensed rights but also stipulated minimum prices for fuses.[143]

The Antitrust Division, under Wendell Berge's leadership, filed suit to break up both the Gypsum and Line Material arrangements. The Supreme Court decided that Gypsum's patent agreements formed part of a larger effort to control the market for all gypsum products, some of which were not patented. It concluded, "Conspiracies to control prices and distribution, such as we have here, we believe to be beyond any patent privilege." More broadly it asserted, "Patents grant no privilege to their owners of organizing the use of those patents to monopolize an industry through price control, through royalties for the patents drawn from patent-free industry products and through regulation of distribution. Here patents have been put to such uses as to collide with the Sherman Act's protection of the public from evil consequences."[144] In *Line Material*, the Supreme Court decided, "Where two or more patentees with competitive, non-infringing patents combine them and fix prices on all devices produced under any patent, competition is impeded. . . . Even when, as here, the devices are not commercially competitive because the subservient patent cannot be practiced without consent of the dominant, the statement holds true." It concluded, "As the Sherman Act prohibits agreements to fix prices, any arrangement between patentees runs afoul of that prohibition and is outside the patent monopoly."[145]

Although the High Court did not say so, its conclusions effectively overturned the 1926 *General Electric* precedent, which had granted companies broad latitude to regulate competition through patent accords. These decisions imposed many of the restrictions on patent rights that the foes of economic concentration had been seeking for years from Congress, without success. Any patent agreement that restricted marketing or set prices was liable to challenge. Of course, if a firm owned rights to a key technology it could simply refuse to license competitors and enjoy a monopoly. Such patents were rare, however, and a company that possessed one might well run afoul of Judge Hand's *Alcoa* decision, which argued that monopoly by its very existence violated the Sherman Act.[146] The cases in question dealt with domestic arrangements, but as one student of antitrust law noted, "The rules applying to international patent licensing are no more and no less stringent than those applying within the United States."[147]

DuPont and ICI realized that their situation was hopeless. In November 1946, Lord McGowan conceded, "The Sherman Antitrust Act is capable of so many interpretations that it may well be that DuPonts and ourselves have contravened some sections of it," though he insisted that any violation was inadvertent.[148] The firms tried to negotiate a settlement with the Justice Department in 1946 but failed to come to terms, in part because of McGowan's determination to make as few concessions as possible.[149] Nevertheless, the two companies backed away from their traditional alliance. In 1946, DuPont revised an agreement concerning nylon with British Nylon Spinners (BNS), a cooperative effort between ICI and Courtaulds, Britain's leading producer of synthetic fibers. The initial contract, a cartel accord camouflaged as a patent agreement, had granted BNS exclusive rights to nylon in the British market while restricting exports, and it had provided for ongoing technical cooperation between BNS and DuPont. The new contract was simply a licensing agreement, granting BNS rights to DuPont's technology in exchange for a royalty. It provided for neither the division of territories nor ongoing technical cooperation.[150] The revision of the BNS agreement represented merely the first step of an industrial divorce. In 1948, DuPont and ICI terminated the patent and processes agreement, the basis of their alliance, and DuPont began "to make a survey of sales possibilities in the British Empire."[151] In 1950, ICI purchased Arnold, Hoffman, & Company, a chemical firm headquartered in New England, with the intention of using it as a foundation on which to build an American presence.[152]

When the federal district court finally handed down a decision in the ICI/DuPont case in 1951, after a long and complex trial featuring over 3,500 exhibits, the result surprised no one. The judge concluded, "We deem irrelevant any inquiry into whether the arrangements between the parties actually injured the public interest, or whether the public benefited thereby." The court enjoined any resumption of the patents and process agreement and ordered that the two firms dissolve most of their jointly owned foreign subsidiaries, dividing the assets. This order applied to Canadian Industries Limited and the Duperial companies of Argentina and Brazil.[153] ICI and DuPont had hoped that the decision would allow them to cooperate in other countries, but the court adhered to the principle that restrictions on competition abroad violated American law, noting, "Restraints were placed [by DuPont and ICI] upon the commercial activities of these joint companies, and restrictions were placed upon the exports to the United States." In ordering these dissolutions, the court apparently did not consult with the governments of Canada, Argentina, and Brazil. It did, however, exempt ICI's and DuPont's joint operations in Chile as well as a Brazilian enterprise devoted entirely to making ammunition. The court concluded that these organizations owed their existence solely to policies of the Brazilian and Chilean governments favoring locally made products at the expense of imports and that their operations had no appreciable impact on American commerce.[154] The Sherman Act had a broad reach, but limits did exist.

In the long run, the change probably benefited both ICI and DuPont. In the 1920s and 1930s, with both firms threatened by formidable German competition and general economic instability, alliance made sense, strengthening the two companies and the chemical industries of the United States and Britain in general. After 1945, conditions were different. The two companies were far more formidable than in the 1920s, and the war had temporarily removed German competition. New technologies, particularly in petrochemicals and synthetic fibers, opened up promising avenues for growth. DuPont and ICI no longer needed each other, and a continuation of their alliance would merely have reduced their flexibility. Yet without antitrust prosecution, cooperation probably would have continued. The alliance between the firms had existed in one form or another for two generations, and institutions rarely abandon such entrenched practices without outside pressure.

General Electric, which fought hard to retain its cartel arrangements, did not fare as well. In 1948, a federal district court overturned GE's tungsten carbide cartel, which was based on a patent agreement with the German firm Krupp.[155] A more serious blow fell early the next year when another court dissolved GE's long-standing lightbulb cartel. This complicated case, which had been in the courts for years and also involved GE's American licensees and the Dutch company Philips, produced a decision that ran over 150 pages.

First the court had to decide whether the government's argument differed from that in 1926, when the Supreme Court had ruled GE's lightbulb cartel legal, setting the key precedent in favor of patent cartels. Although the *Ethyl*, *National Lead*, *Gypsum*, and *Line Material* cases had severely limited this precedent, they had not formally overturned it. The federal district court deftly avoided the whole question, arguing, "The very passage of time has evolved new activities upon the part of the defendants and is essentially a factor bearing upon the continuing validity of patents and their efficacy as a basis for contractual relationships."[156] In 1926, the lightbulb cartel had rested on the patent to the tungsten filament, which was very strong. No serious legal challenge to it had emerged, and the tungsten filament was the basic component of the lightbulb. This patent had since expired. By 1949, GE was relying on its rights to incremental improvements such as frosted bulbs. This, the court asserted, created a different situation. The argument had validity, but in all likelihood the changing legal atmosphere was more important to the outcome than the changing patent position of the cartel. Had it held the tungsten filament patent in 1949, General Electric still probably would have lost.

Once the court had disposed of the 1926 precedent, the verdict was inevitable. The court cited fifteen different ways in which GE and its cartel allies had suppressed competition, concluding, "The aggregation of the fore-going activities and manifestations inevitably leads to the conclusion that General Electric monopolized the incandescent electric lamp industry in violation of the antitrust act." The decision conceded, "The record of General Electric's industrial achievement has been impressive. Its predecessors pioneered the lamp industry and it organized through the years an establishment that stands as a model of industrial efficiency. It early established the policy of making the best lamps as inexpensively as possible." "Admiration for the business acumen of General Electric, however," the court continued, "cannot avoid adherence to the philosophy of political economics enunciated in the antitrust laws of the United States." Nor did the court spare GE's foreign operations. It concluded, "The evidence overwhelmingly supports the Government's contentions[,] for it is a fact that I[nternational] G[eneral] E[lectric, GE's foreign arm,] was the manipulator which brought into being the Phoebus cartel and General Electric activities in the United States were geared to the Phoebus agreement." The judge discerned in GE's policies both at home and abroad "the plain intent to monopolize the incandescent electric lamp industry in the United States and protect their dominant position from foreign competition."[157]

The decree in the case, finalized in 1953, required GE to license its technology at reasonable prices to all applicants and to abstain from interfering through its position as a stockholder in the operations of otherwise independent producers of lightbulbs like Philips. The decision led GE to reconsider its entire position abroad. Many of the foreign companies in which it held stakes were not doing very well, and the court's order foreclosed any sort of cooperative arrangement with them. GE could better use the capital invested abroad at home. After 1953, General Electric disposed of most of its minority stakes in foreign companies, retaining only its wholly owned foreign subsidiaries (mainly in Latin America) and its shares in AEG and Tokyo Electric, for which it could not find buyers. GE became a passive investor in these two firms. The company returned to Europe, the world's second-largest market for its products, only after 1960. General Electric, the international leader in its industry during the 1920s and 1930s, was in retreat after 1945 thanks in large part to antitrust prosecution.[158]

The Antitrust Division also won its campaign against Webb-Pomerene companies. These organizations allowed U.S. firms to work together in export markets and often cooperated with international cartels. The Justice Department had challenged this practice in a suit against Alkasso and

Calkex, Webb-Pomerene companies that dominated foreign sales of synthetic alkali made in the United States and that had cartel ties with ICI. Although the sudden death of the presiding judge delayed a final decision until 1949, the Antitrust Division secured an unqualified victory in this case. The court rejected the authority of the FTC's "silver letter," in which the agency had sanctioned the participation of Webb-Pomerene companies in foreign cartels, noting, "Administrative interpretation must fall where clearly unsanctioned by law or in conflict with judicial decision." It went on: "Viewing the Webb Act in the light of contemporaneous interpretation of antitrust laws, considering the import of the Act when read as a whole, and giving careful attention to the entire legislative history of its passage, the conclusion is irresistible that the Webb-Pomerene Act affords no right to export associations to engage on a world-wide scale in practices so antithetical to the American philosophy of competition." The court also agreed with the government that the alkali industry used Alkasso and Calkex to manipulate the domestic market.[159] The decision effectively banned American firms from participating in international cartels through Webb-Pomerene companies, although the FTC itself did not formally abandon the "silver letter" until 1955.[160]

Another decision further restricted the utility of Webb-Pomerene companies. In the 1950 *Minnesota Mining and Manufacturing* case, a federal district court ruled that a Webb-Pomerene company could not own or operate plants abroad. The leading American producers of abrasives, which included Minnesota Mining and Manufacturing, had organized a Webb-Pomerene firm in 1929 to handle their exports. Subsequently, the growth of sales abroad, coupled with protection against imports in the most lucrative markets, encouraged this organization to construct plants in other countries—a step that, the Justice Department contended, exceeded the legitimate powers of Webb-Pomerene companies. The court agreed, concluding that "when a dominant group of American manufacturers in a particular industry combine to establish manufacturing plants in a foreign area to which the evidence shows that it is legally, politically and economically possible for some American enterprises to export products in reasonable volume, . . . [it] proves a violation of . . . the Sherman Act." "It is no excuse," the court asserted, "for the violations of the Sherman Act that supplying foreign customers from foreign factories is more profitable." The prohibition on foreign investment, however, applied only to Webb-Pomerene companies, not American firms operating on their own.[161]

Another decision involving foreign investment, *Timken Roller Bearing*, did apply to all American firms. Since before World War I, Timken Roller Bearing, the nation's leading producer of tapered, frictionless bearings, had agreements with a British firm that provided for the exchange of patents and technology, as well as for the division of world markets. In 1927, the American firm had purchased a 50 percent stake in its British ally, which assumed the name British Timken. Management of the British firm took the other 50 percent. Subsequent public offerings reduced the American firm's stake to 30.25 percent, although it remained the largest stockholder. Meanwhile, the British firm had, with financial aid from its American parent, organized a French subsidiary, French Timken, in which the other two Timken firms held a controlling stake. The three Timken companies coordinated their activities through agreements exchanging patents and technology and dividing markets. The Justice Department, as part of its campaign against patent cartels, filed suit to break up these arrangements. Timken defended itself on the grounds that the British and French firms were its subsidiaries. It claimed that the agreements in question were simply management arrangements and that the Sherman Act did not obligate different divisions of the same organization to compete against each other.[162]

Ruling in 1949, the district court found this reasoning unconvincing. It noted that anti-competitive arrangements predated the American firm's investment in the British and French companies. The purchase of stock in these organizations "did not mark the beginning of new business contacts. [It] merely extended the restrictive arrangements which had existed for almost twenty years." Perhaps more important, the American firm did not control a majority of the stock in the British and French firms. The court noted, "British Timken and French Timken retained their corporate independence and jealously guarded their interests in dealings with the defendant," adding that the "defendant had no control over the business conduct of either." Because the companies retained their operating independence, they "were potential competitors in the tapered bearing market." The court ordered the Timken companies to terminate their alliance and the American firm to dispose of its stakes in the British and French concerns.[163]

The Supreme Court upheld the principles laid down by the lower court. It concluded "that [to claim] the trade restraints were merely incidental to an otherwise legitimate 'joint venture' is, to say the least, doubtful." The court continued, "The fact that there is common ownership or control of the contracting corporations does not liberate them from the impact of the antitrust laws." It did relent on one point. It did not require American Timken to dispose of its holdings in the British and French firms but merely to sever the illegal agreements. The High Court also implied that the decision did not apply to agreements between American firms and their wholly owned subsidiaries.[164]

The *Timken* decision provoked great controversy. Justice Robert Jackson, hardly an apologist for monopoly, complained in a dissent, "I doubt that it should be regarded as an unreasonable restraint of trade for an American industrial concern to organize foreign subsidiaries, each limited to serving a particular market area. If so, it seems to preclude the only practical means of reaching foreign markets by many American industries. . . . I think this decision will restrain more trade than it will make free."[165] Subsequent decisions did retreat somewhat from *Timken*. Nevertheless, the case struck a serious blow against the joint subsidiaries that members of international cartels had often used to coordinate their activities.[166]

Taken together these decisions represented perhaps the greatest victory for antitrust prosecution since World War I. They made the participation of American firms in international cartels through patent accords, joint ventures, or Webb-Pomerene corporations illegal under most circumstances, even if the cartels in question were not directed specifically at American markets. Exceptions to this rule did exist, like DuPont's and ICI's Chilean venture, but they had to meet very strict standards. The implications reached far beyond the United States. Because American firms were among the leading concerns in most industries, the ban on their participation in international cartels made the construction of such organizations an uncertain proposition at best. These court decisions also established the right of the federal government to sue foreign firms involved in cartels that affected American markets, even if the companies in question had simply agreed to stay out of the United States.[167] Theoretically such firms were beyond American jurisdiction if they did no business in the United States, but the American courts usually concluded that any activity within the country, no matter how small, brought firms under their purview. ICI had only one office in New York, dealing mainly with patent matters, but the U.S. courts considered this presence sufficient to subject the entire company to American law. Besides, most large foreign firms wanted access to the lucrative U.S. market. Forced to choose between the profits they could earn in America and participating in cartels, they usually opted for the former.

International cartels did not suddenly vanish from the world economy. In some cases, such as the De Beers diamond cartel, they managed to reconfigure themselves outside the reach of American law. In other cases, like shipping, American legislation explicitly exempted the international cartel from the antitrust laws. Cartels often persisted at the national level where protection or the cost of transportation insulated domestic producers from foreign competition. Nevertheless, few of the great international cartels of the 1930s, particularly in high-tech fields like electrical machinery and chemicals, recovered from the blows administered by the U.S. courts.

5   Among Unbelievers:
Antitrust in Germany and Japan

Allied victory in World War II inaugurated perhaps the most ambitious social science experiment in world history: the reconstruction of Germany and Japan. After war, the losers usually cede territory and pay reparations to the winners, which sometimes occupy the defeated powers to enforce these obligations. But after 1945, the Allies occupied Germany and Japan not only to extract land and wealth but also to reorganize their societies, eliminating the authoritarian and militaristic tendencies that had made both countries a threat to world peace. For Americans these reforms involved first and foremost promoting political democracy, but economic reorganization also received high priority. Proponents of economic deconcentration were particularly eager to play a role. No matter how effective, the American attack on international cartels did not touch other industrial countries' many domestic cartels and monopolies. The occupation, however, allowed Americans to reach into Japan and Germany, which had highly concentrated, thoroughly cartelized economies. The results, reformers hoped, would set precedents for the rest of the world.

Theories of Occupation

Although eager to reshape Germany and Japan, Americans did not agree how to go about it. Many saw these societies as inherently flawed, requiring revolutionary reorganization. Others contended that Germany and Japan contained many healthy elements that could, with encouragement, form the basis for peaceful, democratic societies. Radical change would destroy the good with the bad. Antitrust reformers generally fell in the first group, arguing in particular for a complete restructuring of the German and Japanese economies.

Many in the United States attributed World War II to the machinations of German business. Explanations usually began with Germany's rapid industrial development in the late nineteenth century. Drawing on arguments first advanced by Thorstein Veblen, an economist and a leading intellectual of the Progressive Era, they claimed that the traditional elite, the German aristocracy and military, had commandeered the economic transformation, harnessing it to authoritarian political ends. Unlike the situation in the United States and Britain, industrial growth in Germany had not proceeded alongside political liberalization but had actually strengthened dictatorship. A long memo prepared by the Cartel Committee stated, "The tardy and rapid development of large-scale industry [in Germany], together with a tradition of absolutist government, fostered the growth of monopoly unparalleled in the western industrial nations. A highly efficient monopolistic industry, in turn, has been driven to seek control over markets outside the borders of the Reich. German industrialists have therefore persistently worked to enlist the support of the public, and have used their great influence upon the Government, in the interest of foreign expansion."[1]

Although defeat in 1918 had temporarily halted Germany's drive for conquest, it had not changed the complexion of the country's industry. As a Senate report on international cartels noted, "A federated Germany emerged from war with her imperialist-minded industrial hierarchy intact." If anything, defeat had further consolidated German business. The Senate report continued, "In the period following the war, German industries were reorganized into closely knit, highly integrated combines whose productive and technological capacity constituted a menace to large producers in other countries."[2] These organizations had clear objectives. The Cartel Committee's memo asserted, "Almost from the end of World War I Germany's arms manufacturers, for the most part great combines which constituted the very heart of heavy industry, set about preparing Germany for another effort at conquest."[3]

German industry played a critical role in Adolf Hitler's rise to power. The Senate report noted, "Krupp, Thyssen, and other powerful figures on the

German industrial scene provided the Nazis with indispensable financial and political support."[4] The publication of steel magnate's Fritz Thyssen's memoirs, *I Paid Hitler,* reinforced this view.[5] The Cartel Committee argued that "the expansionist and anti-democratic yearnings of German industrialists . . . seem to have been fully satisfied—even if it turns out to be only for a brief moment—in Hitler's Third Reich."[6]

German business, operating through international cartels, participated in Nazi aggression. The Senate report claimed, "Almost immediately, as a consequence of this unholy alliance between Hitler and the cartelists, Germany's plans for economic warfare, aimed at ultimate world domination, were expanded. . . . American businessmen were induced to enter into cartel agreements by the promise of freedom from German competition. In exchange for a guaranteed domestic market, American participants accepted restrictions on their own production and sales." The results were disastrous. "Shortages and scarcities in strategic sectors of industry," the Senate report claimed, "visible even before our entry into the war, became ominous following Pearl Harbor. The evidence shows that many of these must be attributed to the operations of international cartels."[7]

Military victory would not eliminate the threat posed by German big business, which had survived defeat before. "To crush German imperialism permanently," the Senate report noted, "the structure and control of German industry must be so altered that it cannot serve again the purposes of war. . . . Punishment of 10,000 of the leading imperialist-minded German industrialists would be more effective than punishment of 1,000,000 Nazi underlings who carried out the orders of the conspirators."[8]

Taming German business required the destruction of international cartels. Whereas before the war cartels had served as avenues for economic aggression, after the peace they would allow German industry to recover by providing access to markets and capital. Recovery would then open up the prospect of new aggression. The Senate report noted, "Any efforts to retain the international cartel system will . . . help to keep in power the German militarist-industrialist clique who have already planned and launched two world wars."[9]

Lasting peace, however, required more than the elimination of international cartels, which represented only one aspect of German industry. The real problem was the concentrated power of German business, which also operated through domestic cartels and large firms like IG Farben that dominated entire sectors of the economy. A lasting peace required the termina-

tion of the former and the dissolution of the latter—a policy of "decartelization and deconcentration."

This analysis was and is controversial. Although Germany's business community certainly harbored a substantial number of Nazis, many historians
have argued that industry as a whole contributed no more to Hitler's rise to
power than other segments of Germany society and may have contributed
less than some.[10] Businessmen like Fritz Thyssen and Halmar Schact did
provide the Nazis with valuable help, but other business figures, just as
prominent, supported the nationalist or liberal parties. Jewish industrialists
and financiers naturally opposed the Nazis. Up until 1934, when Hitler
purged the party, the Nazis included many who embraced various types of
socialism.[11] Relations between large German firms and the Nazi regime were
often tense, with each at times pursuing quite different objectives.[12] Few
Americans in the 1940s were familiar with the extraordinary complexity of
German politics between the world wars. German business was in many
cases implicated in the crimes of the Nazi regime, but New Dealers' attri-
bution of fascism to the machinations of big business was a gross oversim-
plification that reflected the influence of Marxist thinking and reformers'
fear of American big business, not a sound understanding of German history
and society.

Nevertheless, U.S. policy toward occupied Germany initially reflected
these ideas. Orders governing the occupation, issued by the joint chiefs of
staff to General Dwight D. Eisenhower in April 1945, stated, "You will prohibit all cartels or other private business arrangements and cartel-like organizations," continuing, "It is the policy of your government to effect a dis-
persion of the ownership and control of German industry."[13] The July 1945
Potsdam Conference, a meeting of the American, British, and Soviet heads
of state near Berlin, endorsed this policy. The three nations agreed that "at
the earliest practicable date, the German economy shall be decentralized
for the purpose of eliminating the present excessive concentration of economic power as exemplified in particular by cartels, syndicates, trusts, and
other monopolistic arrangements."[14]

Policy toward Japanese business occasioned more debate within the
government. Some of the State Department's Far East specialists saw this
community as a logical counterweight to militarism. Businessmen had
been closely associated with the parliamentary regime that had governed
Japan in the 1920s, and several prominent industrialists had fallen victim
of ultranationalist violence in the 1930s.[15] As late as the winter of 1945,

some U.S. experts argued that "if we are looking for a party which might lead the Japanese people to a more reasonable government during the transition period, the business leaders might well emerge at an early stage as a focal point for collaboration with an Allied military administration."[16]

The State Department's Cartel Committee vigorously resisted this reasoning. It claimed, "Voluntary participation by the large industrialists in Japan's program of aggression is a historical fact. . . . Participation in the national program was advantageous to the industrialists. Aggression solved the problem of export markets and likewise assured the large business organizations control over strategic raw materials." The argument continued, "Through political maneuvering and skillful tactics carried out at high levels of government, the large industrialists by 1944 achieved virtually complete control over the economic phases of the Japanese domestic economy and monopoly control over the raw materials of the Far East conquered under the program of aggression."[17]

Concern centered on the Zaibatsu, family-dominated combines active in every segment of the Japanese economy but particularly strong in finance, heavy industry, and foreign trade. By 1945, the ten largest Zaibatsu controlled approximately half of Japan's heavy industry and financial resources.[18] In no other large industrial country did so few companies wield so much power. The war had substantially strengthened the Zaibatsu because the Japanese government had relied on them to build up wartime industry and to manage the economic affairs of conquered territories. Even if they had not instigated aggression, the Zaibatsu had profited from it.

Interestingly enough, international cartels did not figure prominently into analysis of the Japanese economy. Japanese companies often organized domestic cartels, but they dealt with international ones warily. Relative latecomers in most industries, Japanese firms often had to challenge established cartels for foreign markets—they were the nemesis of the lightbulb and synthetic alkali cartels. However, when offered sufficient inducements, Japanese companies would join cartels. They were particularly open to arrangements based on patents and the exchange of scientific know-how, which they wanted to obtain from the more technically advanced economies of Europe and North America. Still, the Cartel Committee emphasized not the role of Japanese firms in international cartels but rather how these organizations had furthered the concentration of business in Japan, arguing, "These corporate devices enhanced the power of the already powerful combines, and placed them in the practical position of monopolistic importers, custodians and dispensers of industrial technology in Japan."[19]

Washington finally came down in favor of economic reform for Japan. Americans were in a vindictive mood—they were not quick to forgive the attack on Pearl Harbor—and breaking up Japan's largest firms accorded with this sentiment. Moreover, the publication in the United States of many books and articles denouncing the Zaibatsu had turned public opinion against these organizations.[20] President Harry S. Truman, who succeeded Franklin Roosevelt upon the latter's death in April 1945, charged General Douglas MacArthur, the head of the occupation in Japan, "to favor a program for the dissolution of the large industrial and banking combinations which have exercised control of a large part of Japan's trade and industry." Subsequent orders directed MacArthur to "terminate and prohibit all Japanese participation in private international cartels."[21] As in Germany, policy fell under the heading "decartelization and deconcentration," but with even heavier emphasis on the latter. In Japan economic reform began with the Zaibatsu.

Decartelization and deconcentration did not have to operate in tandem. The United States had relatively few cartels but many large companies. Defenders of cartels often argued that by putting a floor under prices they actually made it easier for small firms to survive on their own. Nevertheless, the Americans officials who led the attack on cartels were, for the most part, deeply suspicious of all types of economic concentration. Organizations that put economic power in a few hands, be they cartels or integrated combines, were inimical to political democracy as well as to technical efficiency. The evolution of some of the largest German firms such as IG Farben and the steel maker Vereinigte Stahlwerke from cartels further linked the two issues.

Legally and practically, the occupations of Germany and Japan differed in important respects. In the former, the four chief Allied powers—the United States, Britain, the Soviet Union, and France—divided responsibility. Each controlled a designated occupation zone. They were supposed to coordinate their policies, but in practice they often ignored one another, ruling their zones as they saw fit. In contrast the United States ran Japan more or less on its own with only nominal consultation with the Allies.

Despite considerable discussion of the subject during the war, American occupation authorities had little in the way of specific plans for economic reform when they took over the defeated Axis powers. Several factors accounted for the situation. Most officials in Washington had grossly underestimated the economic problems they would face. One memo, drawn up in early 1944, suggested that immediately after the war, "It was probable that a large portion of German resources would be available," freed up by the termination of that country's war effort. "There would be surpluses of labor and some products such as steel, coal, and artificial fertilizers."[22] Such had been the case after World War I. In fact, when Germany formally surrendered in May 1945, the country was in desperate shape. Most of its cities were in ruins. The transportation system had ceased to function, and almost every factory lacked raw materials, especially fuel. Food rations were barely enough to sustain life, and without outside assistance they were likely to decline further. Moreover, the Allied invasion had destroyed government at the higher levels, eliminating the organizations that normally would have coordinated reconstruction. Economic conditions in Japan were perhaps even worse. The country had literally no petroleum, and food rations were not enough to keep the population alive for long, although because Tokyo had surrendered before invasion the government did still function. Instead of the battered but going concerns they expected to find, the Allies assumed responsibility for economic wastelands requiring heavy infusions of aid. The United States would have to subsidize both West Germany and Japan into the 1950s. In Japan's case, the timing of end of the war, September 1945, caught Allied planners by surprise. Ignorant of the existence of the atomic bomb, they had assumed that Tokyo would not capitulate until after invasion of the home islands, which they did not expect until 1946.

Bureaucratic factors added to the confusion. The military ran the occupations of Japan and Germany, whereas most postwar planning had occurred in the State Department and (to a lesser degree) the Treasury. Washington enjoyed imperfect control over the occupation regimes. In Japan, General Douglas MacArthur was virtually autonomous. In Germany, General Lucius Clay, who became the head of the occupation soon after Germany's surrender, lacked MacArthur's status as a war hero and so was slightly more malleable. Nevertheless, he was a forceful man who did not fear to act on his own authority, and he had numerous contacts in Washington on whose support he could count. A West Point–educated staff officer who had compiled an impressive record during the war, Clay carefully monitored all aspects of the occupation, keeping final authority in his own hands.

Yet intellectual shortcomings rather than economic or bureaucratic ones constituted the chief impediment. During the war, whenever people spoke of establishing a durable peace, they emphasized the need to avoid the mistakes of the Treaty of Versailles, which had ended World War I. Yet no consensus existed on the nature of these errors. Some argued that Versailles failed because it had not crushed German power once and for all. They usually considered Nazism the logical culmination of the German political, economic, and social systems and assumed that the only way to prevent another war was to keep Germany weak and to reorganize its society radically. Others considered Versailles too harsh, crippling Germany's relatively pacific Weimar Republic before it was firmly established and thereby opening the way for the Nazis. They generally attributed Nazism to the chaos spawned by the Great War and the Depression and assumed that prosperity and social order were the keys to a lasting peace. Advocates of a "hard" peace wanted to break up Germany, dismantle much of its industry, and subject it to thoroughgoing reforms that included decartelization and deconcentration. Proponents of a "soft" peace imagined that, after a suitable period of reconstruction under the watchful eyes of the Allies, a united, democratic Germany would resume its place in Europe.

The dichotomy between a "hard" and a "soft" peace obscures both gradations of opinion and areas of consensus. Officials could, and sometimes did, favor both the rapid rehabilitation of German industry and the division of the country into several states. All concurred on punishing war criminals, disarming Germany, and instituting democratic government there. Still, disagreement on the objectives of occupation could affect even such apparently uncontroversial matters. Did disarming Germany entail simply dismantling the military and banning weapons or did it also require restrictions on the production of metals and chemicals (aluminum, synthetic nitrates) that could be used to make arms? Did the term "war criminal" encompass only leading Nazis and those guilty of specific atrocities, or did it include the entire elite—professionals, businessmen, government officials, and so on? These questions went back to the central issue: Should the Allies concentrate on punishing and reorganizing Germany or on rehabilitating it? Many Americans simply ignored these questions, assuming that Germany could recover quickly even as the Allies upended its society. Yet it was not clear that Germany could survive without the heavy industries that had been the core of its economy or function without its traditional leadership.[23]

These divisions affected opinion on deconcentration and decartelization. Many of the advocates of this program contended that it would benefit the German economy, at least in the long run, by eliminating bloated industrial giants and opening up new opportunities for entrepreneurs and innovators.

At the same time, by destroying the power of big business it would make German society more democratic. Yet many doubted that it was possible to reorganize completely the German economy, gutting the institutions that had long governed industry, without substantially disrupting production and slowing recovery.

Attitudes toward the Soviet Union would further complicate the issue of German occupation. Even before the war ended, many U.S. officials were suspicious of Russian intentions in Europe, and after victory, relations deteriorated fast. How to deal with Soviet Russia soon became the chief issue of foreign policy. Americans eager to conciliate the Russians often urged a tough line toward Germany on the assumption that the chief objective of Soviet foreign policy was to prevent that country from ever again emerging as a great power. Those suspicious of Soviet intentions tended to advocate a generous settlement with Germany because a prosperous, stable Germany would form a bulwark against communist expansion.

Washington wavered on its plans for Germany throughout the war. At first, State Department supporters of a generous peace seemed to hold sway, but the revelation of Nazi atrocities and the general wartime desire to punish the enemy strengthened the hand of those pushing "hard" terms. In 1944, Treasury Secretary Henry Morgenthau persuaded President Roosevelt to endorse a plan to dismantle Germany's manufacturing industry and to refocus its economy on agriculture. By 1945, however, the administration had discarded Morgenthau's plan, largely because it realized that without industry Germany could not support anything like its current population, even at subsistence levels. A somewhat less punitive policy, in effect when Germany surrendered in 1945, envisaged a reduction of the role of heavy industry (steel, chemicals, machinery) in favor of the production of consumer goods (textiles, processed foods). Yet effecting such a shift would be difficult in the best of circumstances, which most certainly did not exist in Germany in 1945. Moreover, support persisted for policies that emphasized rapid economic recovery over reform. Many army officers managing the occupation feared that without substantial improvement in the German economy their task would be impossible. Economic specialists worried that an impoverished Germany would pull down Europe as a whole, inhibiting general recovery. General Clay's orders acknowledged the situation, noting, "This directive sets forth policies relating to Germany in the initial post-defeat period. As such it is not intended to be an ultimate statement of policies of this government concerning the treatment of Germany in the post-war world."[24] Nonetheless, the failure to decide in a sense constituted a decision. Germany was in terrible shape, and without a concerted effort by occupation authorities recovery simply would not occur.

At first glance, debate during the war over the occupation of Japan involved different issues. The key question was whether to retain the imperial system. A faction in the U.S. government, centered around Joseph Grew, ambassador to Japan before the war and then undersecretary of state, urged that the United States keep the emperor as a constitutional monarch, whereas others in Washington wanted to try him as a war criminal and turn Japan into a republic. Yet the underlying issue was the same as in Germany: Were the Japanese militarists who had waged World War II essentially historical anomalies created by the political and economic chaos that flowed from the Great War and the Depression, or were they a natural product of Japanese society? The former conclusion dictated a generous occupation policy; the latter, a rigorous one.[25]

Deconcentration and Decartelization in Germany

At the end of the war, reformers had high hopes for decartelization and deconcentration in Germany. They had support in the occupation bureaucracy as well as in Washington. Yet the requirement of coordination among the Allies made it difficult to implement a comprehensive program. During the first two years of occupation, reformers initiated much but concluded little.

Advocates of deconcentration and decartelization initially enjoyed a strong position in the American occupation regime in Germany. A team of cartel specialists had followed behind the U.S. Army as it marched into the collapsing Reich, securing corporate records and questioning captured industrialists. James Stewart Martin, a lawyer and former chief of the economic warfare unit of the Justice Department's Antitrust Division, headed the group. He left during the summer, not long after Germany's formal surrender, but once home he began to urge publicly that the occupation employ members of the Antitrust Division to reorganize the German economy. In December 1945, General Clay recalled Martin and put him in charge of the newly constituted Decartelization and Deconcentration Branch of the military government. Martin had a relatively large staff of 162, many of them drawn from the Antitrust Division of the Justice Department, and he answered to the head of the occupation's Economics Bureau, who reported directly to Clay.

Although this arrangement seemed logical—deconcentration and decartelization were economic matters—it produced friction. In the United States the Antitrust Division was part of the Justice Department, and its employees were generally lawyers who did not concern themselves much with economic policy. Their counterparts in Germany often got along poorly with the other members of the Economics Bureau, who were usually businessmen for whom the revival of the German economy took precedence over reform.[26] Even before Martin's return, American officials eager to break up cartels and large firms had clashed with those responsible for economic policy. It was this conflict that had persuaded Clay to create the Decartelization Branch and recall Martin. Unfortunately, bureaucratic reorganization had not erased the basic disagreement over policy.[27]

Despite such tension, or perhaps because of it, members of the Decartelization Branch exhibited great esprit de corps. Most of them believed that their labors were absolutely vital to creating a peaceful, democratic Germany. One insisted, "Decartelization policy if carried out, might be one step toward delaying the coming war," presumably by forcing German society into a more pacific mold and maintaining good relations with the Soviets.[28] As late as 1951, after the branch had experienced many changes in fortune, one of its members stated, "I became accustomed in finding myself . . . being called a fanatic. I think the characterization is very apt and correct. . . . In the States, antitrust is almost a religion. It is similar to a religious doctrine and expresses the belief of people to freely compete to the best of their abilities."[29]

Others did not consider fanaticism so endearing. The British, lacking the Americans' aversion to cartels, complained of the application of U.S. standards to Germany and grumbled that because antitrust laws "had not been able to produce contemplated results in America, the 'trust-busters' were all the more anxious to experiment in new fields."[30] This gripe had much truth in it. The American antitrust tradition had no counterpart in Germany or Europe, and U.S. authorities in Germany drew precedents almost solely from American law, largely because no others existed.[31] Perhaps more important, members of the Decartelization and Deconcentration Branch often sought to impose in Germany more rigorous standards than applied in the United States itself, apparently in the hope of setting precedents that would have impact at home as well as in Europe.

The enthusiasm of the Decartelization Branch could not easily overcome the limits inherent in the American position in Germany. Theoretically, policy had to reflect the wishes of all four occupying powers. Even had the United States acted alone on decartelization and deconcentration, it could accomplish only so much. Its occupation zone covered southern Germany—the states of Bavaria, Hesse, and Baden-Württemburg—which were not the country's most heavily industrialized. The largest and most capital-intensive firms generally operated out of Berlin or the Ruhr Valley, beyond the direct reach of the Americans. Without an agreement with the other three powers, the Decartelization Branch "could do little but make studies, and their whole large force did little else before [a limited agreement was reached in 1947]," the historian of the branch noted.[32] These investigations were extensive and aggressive. One memo from late 1945 proudly reported, "Twenty-one leading bankers are under arrest pending interrogation which will reveal the role played by German finance in the preparation and waging of aggressive war."[33] The Decartelization Branch ultimately conducted enough studies to fill a bookshelf. At best, however, such activity merely constituted a prelude to action.

The Allies had great difficulty agreeing on decartelization and deconcentration. Interestingly, the former was not particularly controversial. Cartels were alien to most Americans, including businessmen, and enjoyed almost no support among U.S. officials in Germany. Even the British and French, who had more experience with these organizations, considered their future a secondary matter and were willing to accommodate American preferences. Deconcentration, the dissolution of large companies, constituted the chief point of contention. Most people considered "the breakup of large industrial combinations . . . largely punitive and political," as the historian of the American deconcentration effort noted.[34] Certainly officials of the British, French, and Soviet governments took this view, as did most Germans. They all assumed that in economics, bigger was better. The Americans, however, had a more ambiguous attitude. Some regarded deconcentration a way to punish Germany or at least to limit its war-making capability. Members of the Decartelization Branch tended to consider radical deconcentration vital both to eliminating Germany's aggressive, militaristic tendencies and to maintaining good relations with the Soviets. Yet most of the Branch's members also sincerely believed that deconcentration would help the Germans, at least in the long run, by shutting down bloated, inefficient economic behemoths and opening their economy to competition. As a 1949 report insisted, "Rather than interfere with German production or the recovery of Germany, . . . deconcentration has increased production and strengthened the German economy."[35] The willingness of the Decartelization Branch to target the German subsidiaries of American and British companies like International Telephone & Telegraph and Unilever suggests that they did not envisage deconcentration chiefly as a way to punish the Germans.[36]

The different attitudes of the Allies toward the occupation further complicated the matter. The question of how generously to treat the defeated enemy, an issue that had split the U.S. government, also divided the Allies as a whole. The British were the most conciliatory toward Germany. They believed that the tough terms of the Treaty of Versailles had set the stage for World War II, and they thought that Europe as a whole could not recover economically unless Germany did so as well. In contrast, France, which had faced three devastating German invasions in the previous seventy-five years, took a hard line. Its leaders were particularly eager to partition Germany into two or more states. The Soviets, who had suffered perhaps even more terribly at German hands, adopted a tough stance as well, particularly on the issues of rebuilding German industry and extracting reparations. Yet at first they, unlike the French, seemed open to the eventual reemergence of a united Germany.

These attitudes made concerted action of any sort difficult. The Allies did reach tentative agreements on reparations and the "level of industry"—that is, the manufacturing capacity they would permit Germany to retain. The issues were linked because the Allies intended to take reparations in the form of capital equipment rendered surplus under the level of industry plan, which envisaged a sharp reduction in German manufacturing and the complete elimination of industries with important military applications like ball bearings and aluminum. Yet even these accords were vague on key points such as the exact value of reparations and the duration of restrictions on German industry. In other areas, cooperation did not exist. The French vetoed plans to create nationwide agencies in such basic areas as transportation, blocking the development of mechanisms through which the Allies could set common policies for all of Germany. In the end, each occupier made policy for its own zone in such key fields as labor law, the purging of Nazis, and the organization of local and provincial governments.

In these circumstances, talks on a general deconcentration statute for all of Germany yielded little. The initial American proposal, which would have banned "cartels and cartel-like arrangements" and would have created a commission to study large companies, satisfied no one because it contained few specifics on deconcentration.[37] In December 1945, the Soviets took the initiative, suggesting that the Allies dissolve any German company either employing more than 3,000 people, controlling more than a quarter of its market, or enjoying an annual turnover of 25 million or more (prewar) Reichmarks, although they did reserve to the Allies the right to exempt specific firms from sanctions. They also attached to their proposal a list of over a hundred companies that would automatically face dissolution. The Americans soon proposed their own version of this measure, raising the standard for deconcentration to 10,000 employees, 30 percent of the market, or capital of 50 million (prewar) Reichmarks and shortening the list of firms for automatic deconcentration to sixty-one. Only the unanimous consent of the Allies could exempt a firm from action. The U.S. suggestion also largely banned domestic cartels.[38]

The French and Soviets endorsed this proposal, but the British balked, encouraged, it seems, by some members of the U.S. Economics Division who feared that such a massive reorganization would cripple the German economy and forestall recovery.[39] Instead, London recommended a measure that set similar standards for economic deconcentration but subjected only nineteen firms to automatic dissolution. More important, it gave the commander of each zone the responsibility for enforcing deconcentration rather than creating a central body, as did the American plan. Although on its face innocuous, this provision would effectively allow one power to block action against a firm simply by refusing to cooperate. Finally, the British proposal contained no restrictions on domestic cartels, although it did ban German participation in international ones.[40] The United States rejected the British alternative, complaining of its tolerant attitude toward domestic cartels and arguing that the de facto requirement for unanimity among the occupiers to break up large firms constituted a recipe for deadlock, a fear borne out by the difficult history of four-power cooperation in Germany.[41] The Allies spent much of the next eighteen months maneuvering around the subject, generating a lot of paperwork but no decision.

In a few instances where the case for deconcentration seemed irrefutable, the Allies did act quickly. In July 1945, the U.S. military seized all the property of the giant IG Farben chemical combine in the American zone; by the end of the year, the other Allies had followed suit in their territories. All four agreed to work together to dispose of the company's assets.[42] In the interim, the Allies banned trading of Farben stock, severed the company's international cartel arrangements, and sold off the IG's securities holdings in other firms in cases where it owned less than 25 percent of the total equity.[43]

The Americans treated the IG firmly. The Decartelization Branch considered it a particularly egregious example of economic overconcentration. James Martin described the firm as "the greatest limitation on free enterprise in Europe and the single greatest economic threat to the peace of the world."[44] The Americans dismissed over 2,000 Farben executives working at facilities in their zone (which included the firm's headquarters in Frankfort), and U.S. Army officers assumed management positions at IG installations. By 1946, however, General Clay had realized that such control could not last indefinitely and had turned over Farben's facilities to German executives, who acted as trustees. Nevertheless, he required them to operate each plant separately, effectively dividing Farben's properties in the American zone into about thirty companies.[45]

The policies of the other Allies toward Farben did not always please the Americans. The French had only one (very) large installation in their zone that they managed as a unit, an uncontroversial policy. The British also continued to manage Farben's extensive properties in their zone as one company, even though they included several large installations that the Americans believed ought to stand separately. The continued unity of the plants around the town of Leverhusen was a particular point of conflict. One American official complained, "The failure on the part of the British to divide the Farben property in their zone into independent economic units has caused great inconvenience and disruption in our zone because the huge Leverkusen complex in the British zone which has always been a supplier of many of the intermediates used by the Farben units in our zone has been able to dominate the former Farben units in our zone. . . . There is no satisfactory explanation of the British failure in this field except for their general dislike of deconcentration and the incredible incompetence of their Farben Control Officer."[46] The Soviets eventually took permanent title to much of Farben's property in their zone for themselves, ignoring promises to negotiate its fate with the other Allies.[47]

The Allies also acted against the German coal and steel industry, although in this case the British took the lead. All four occupying powers were particularly concerned about the future of this industry because they considered steel central to the economics of both war and peace. Moreover, production concentrated in a handful of companies, the largest of which, Vereinigte

Stahlwerke (United Steelworks), had before the war accounted for about 40 percent of Germany's steel, more than the entire output of France. The large steel companies also controlled the coal mines of the Ruhr Valley, which were the chief source of coke for steel makers throughout continental Europe. This control allowed the Germans, in theory at least, to ration a vital raw material to their competitors. The British, whose occupation zone included the Ruhr (the center of Germany's steel industry as well as its coal-mining business), seized the region's steel and coal facilities. They placed these properties under the supervision of military officers, although in most cases the existing management remained in place. As with IG Farben, subsequent negotiations among the Allies would determine the final status of these assets.

Although pleased by this development, the Americans saw risks. In London, a Labour Party government was in the process of nationalizing the British coal and steel industries, an approach it might well encourage for Germany. Few Americans, even in the Decartelization Branch, endorsed this solution, which not only challenged the institution of private property but actually concentrated industrial control more tightly than private monopoly. As a U.S. government report noted, "Rather than bringing about competition and avoidance of the use of such properties for future war purposes, government ownership[,] for instance through socialization, may concentrate the properties in the hands of the government."[48] The issue of nationalization became a constant irritant to Anglo-American cooperation in the coal and steel industries.[49]

The fate of Reich-owned companies occasioned less division. The Allies, who now were the German government, seized these firms. The most important of them were the Reichwerke Herman Goering, an organization created to facilitation mobilization that was, among other things, Germany's second largest steel producer, and the Universum-Film Aktiengesellschaft (UFA), a de facto arm of Joseph Goebbels's Propaganda Ministry that had controlled the production and distribution of films. The Allies grouped the former with other steel companies, whereas they broke up the latter, severing the business of making movies from that of managing theaters. Although implementing these decisions was complex and time-consuming, the policies were not particularly controversial.

The Americans led the way in striking against concentration in German finance. Until 1945, a handful of "universal" banks, most notably the Deutsch Bank, had dominated the German financial system. They not only took deposits and made commercial loans but also underwrote securities and even held large blocks of stock in many of the country's leading companies, and they had branches throughout Germany. The situation horrified most Americans. The power of large financial institutions had been a contentious issue in the United States since the early days of the republic, when Alexander Hamilton and Thomas Jefferson had clashed over the creation of the First Bank of the United States. By 1945, U.S. law had separated commercial and investment banking and had placed strict limits on branch banking, effectively fragmenting the financial system. In line with this experience, as General Clay described it, "six of the largest banks in Germany were dissolved and their branches authorized to operate only as separate institutions limited in operation to the state in which located."[50] In this, British authorities agreed with their U.S. counterparts, applying similar restrictions in their own zone. Though less dogmatic than the Americans, they disapproved of the German practice of combining commercial and investment banking, which were usually separate in Britain. Although the situation remained unsettled, these measures constituted an important step toward financial reorganization.

A major breakthrough on decartelization and deconcentration occurred in early 1947. The British and Americans agreed on a statute for their zones, bypassing the French and Soviets in the process. Throughout 1946, as the Allies found themselves at odds on most major issues, economic conditions in Germany had deteriorated. Each power increasingly ran its occupation zone as a separate entity, imposing restrictions on trade with the outside. Yet the zones were artificial creations, unable to stand on their own economically without substantial aid and extensive restructuring. The United States was particularly concerned because its zone depended heavily on food imported from eastern Germany, which was under Soviet control, and relations with the Russians were getting worse. In the first half of 1946, a Soviet crackdown had strengthened the control of the Communist Party over their zone, while General Clay had terminated reparations shipments from the American zone to the Soviet Union.[51] In late 1946, despairing of a broader solution, London and Washington merged their two occupation zones in the hope that together they might contain the critical mass necessary for recovery and provide a foundation for the eventual reunification of Germany.

The merger led to joint action on deconcentration. The British were reluctant, but after General Clay made it clear that he was ready to issue a unilateral decree on the subject, they compromised.[52] In February 1947, the two powers issued identical laws on decartelization and deconcentration. These statutes eliminated cartels, banning practices used to regulate competition, including restrictive patent agreements. The Anglo-American laws also provided for deconcentration, declaring that any firm with more than 10,000 employees presented a "prima facie" case for dissolution. The decrees excepted the iron and steel industry as well as IG Farben, which were already under the control of the occupiers.[53] American officials estimated that, under the new laws, about sixty firms faced deconcentration.[54]

The provisions on cartels operated fairly smoothly. Although the Allies had ceased to enforce German cartel agreements (which before 1945 had possessed the force of contracts), neither had they formally terminated these accords. With the enactment of the British and American decrees, the situation changed. As the historian of the American decartelization effort noted, "Every person who was a party to a cartel agreement which had not expired by February 12, 1947 [when the Anglo-American orders went into effect] was required to serve a notice of termination on the other parties and to file a report of termination with the German Decartelization Agency in the Land [state] in which it maintained its headquarters. By the end of 1948 over 1,100 cartel agreements were formally terminated."[55] Some firms did continue to cooperate informally, much to the chagrin of General Clay.[56] Nevertheless, the Anglo-American decree wrecked the legal foundation on which cartels rested.

Deconcentration proved more difficult. Whereas the joint statutes unconditionally banned cartels, occupation authorities were supposed to investigate large firms to "determine . . . that these enterprises do in fact constitute excessive concentrations of economic power."[57] Size automatically invited investigation, but not action. Philip Hawkins, who became the interim head of the Decartelization Branch in 1947, noted, "The only way to proceed in the enforcement of [the] anti-monopoly program is the case by case method. No reasonable man desired to break up efficient mass production, nor yet to justify concentration beyond the point of efficiency."[58] Moreover, once the Allies did decide to act, breaking up a large firm required careful planning.

Despite the obstacles, the Decartelization Branch needed to move quickly. As Hawkins wrote, "The Decartelization Branch has now reached the point where it must show some dissolved combine in the next six months or else face defeat. We cannot close two years of operations on the continued promise that at some uncertain date in the future we will break up a German cartel."[59] The German state governments did have considerable authority under the American and British decrees, but few expected rapid action from them. They lacked both staff and enthusiasm for the job, which they believed would weaken the German economy. Whereas the American Decartelization Branch had plenty of enthusiasm, it too lacked numbers. One hundred sixty people could conduct a lot of studies, but they would have trouble reorganizing Germany's sixty largest companies. In recognition of this fact, Hawkins decided to concentrate on four firms: Henschel & Sohn, Germany's largest producer of locomotives; Robert Bosch, the world's leading maker of fuel injection systems; Siemens & Halske, Europe's chief producer of electrical machinery; and Metalgesellschaft, Germany's foremost processor of nonferrous metals.[60] At first, the Decartelization Branch had included a coal and steel company in its plans, but it dropped the firm because the occupiers were devising special legislation for that sector. Subsequently, the Decartelization Branch added the ball bearing industry to the list, in part at the urging of the Justice Department's Antitrust Division, which was conducting an investigation in the area.[61] Deconcentration would stand or fall on these five cases, setting precedents for the rest of German industry.

Challenges to Deconcentration

Changing international conditions led the United States to alter its occupation policies in Germany in the late 1940s. Right after the war, the occupation had emphasized the reform of German society, implicitly assuming that such efforts would not obstruct recovery and that, even if they did, the delay would create no problems for the United States. By late 1948, deteriorating economic conditions in Germany and Europe in general, coupled with worsening relations with the Soviets, encouraged the U.S. government to rethink its assumptions. The result was new policies that emphasized recovery and backed away from some, though hardly all, reforms. Among the casualties was deconcentration.

Even as the occupiers promulgated deconcentration statutes in 1947, changing international conditions strengthened foes of the program. Until that time, reformers had enjoyed considerable freedom in Germany, largely because few Americans cared about deconcentration there. The result was a policy more radical than ever implemented in the United States that targeted companies simply because they were larger than some arbitrarily determined size. The deterioration of relations with the Soviet Union, however, led Washington increasingly to look at Germany not as a defeated enemy but as a potential ally. Perhaps more important, after 1947, American policy in Europe centered on the Marshall Plan. The continent's economic recovery had stalled, and Washington feared that hard times could open the way for Communists to take power in western Europe, particularly in France and Italy. The U.S. government hoped that by providing aid through the Marshall plan it could restore prosperity to the continent, stabilizing the democratic regimes of western Europe and giving them the confidence and resources necessary to resist Communist pressure, both domestic and foreign. Yet as Secretary of State George C. Marshall said in late 1947, "Without a revival of German production there can be no revival of Europe's economy."[62] In August 1947, British and American authorities significantly relaxed restrictions on German economic output, the "level of industry" program, allowing both higher production and the continued operation of some industries, like aluminum, that they had planned to dismantle entirely.[63] New orders to General Clay stated, "Although the economic rehabilitation of Germany . . . is the task and responsibility of the German people, you should provide them general policy guidance."[64]

The new attitude affected all aspects of policy toward Germany. The western Allies ceased to concern themselves with reuniting the country or compromising with the Soviets on the occupation and instead devoted their efforts toward rebuilding the country's western zones. The program had several aspects, the most notable of which was the 1948 currency reform, which replaced the practically worthless Reichmark with the new Deutschmark. This measure, along with the termination of price controls and rationing, sparked economic recovery. At the same time, the Soviets, who had opposed currency reform and refused to allow the Deutschmark to circulate in their zone, ended all meaningful discussions with the western Allies on occupation policy.

The emphasis on economic recovery had grave implications for deconcentration. Although most members of the occupation's Decartelization Branch firmly believed that their program would strengthen the German economy, at least in the long run, many on the outside thought otherwise. In 1946, Philip Reed, an officer of General Electric dispatched to Germany by the Commerce Department, reported back to Washington that deconcentration was hindering German recovery; former president Herbert Hoover said the same after a tour the next year.[65] True, little deconcentration had actually occurred, but critics claimed that just the prospect made it difficult for large German firms to borrow, invest, or generally plan for the future.

Serious doubts also existed within the occupation's Economics Division, which the staff of the Decartelization Branch believed (probably with reason) had encouraged London's delay of a general statute. Foremost among the skeptics was the division's chief, General William H. Draper, an alumnus of the investment banking house of Dillon, Reed, which in the 1920s had done a lot of business in Germany. Draper was perhaps Clay's closest adviser, but his ties to German businessmen through Dillon, Reed had raised concerns in some quarters. Senator Harvey Kilgore, an opponent of cartels and a critic of big business in general, claimed as early as 1945 that American executives like Draper "are still sympathetic to their old cartel partners and they look forward to resuming commercial relationships with a rehabilitated German industry."[66] Members of the Decartelization Branch did not hide their contempt for Draper and his lieutenants, who unfortunately were also their superiors. James Martin charged in late 1946 that "serious damage has already been done to the decartelization program by a year's delay during which parts of the Economics Division have held to the attitude that their only function was to revive industry and trade by whatever means they choose."[67] In the summer of 1947, Martin had resigned from his job in Germany, complaining, "Through their activities in Germany [to rehabilitate industry], 'monopolistic' American corporations have strained the critical relations between the United States and Russia."[68]

The British remained as skeptical as ever despite having issued the decartelization statute. London considered the Anglo-American decrees an "uneasy compromise. They were looked upon as representing a minimum requirement by the Americans and a maximum by the British."[69] A few in the British government went so far as to assert that the decartelization statutes applied only to concentrations of economic power in Germany that threatened the security of other nations, and they contended that only IG Farben and the coal and steel industries fell into this category.[70] The proposition was dubious. Because the Anglo-American decrees explicitly exempted the IG and coal and steel firms, it was improbable that they were its sole object.[71] Nevertheless, dissension created problems, particularly in mobilizing German agencies behind deconcentration. Although the German state governments were supposed to do most of the work implementing the decrees, as a British memo noted, "This scheme went off at half-cock since we never succeeded in reaching . . . a firm Bipartite . . . policy as regards implementation upon which we could brief the German agencies."[72] Because most Germans were unenthusiastic about deconcentration, the lack of clear directives guaranteed inaction.

The 1948 merger of the French zone into the Anglo-American "Bizonia" added yet another layer of confusion. Paris was unenthusiastic about the prospect of German recovery, joining the effort mainly because its dependence on U.S. aid forced acquiescence to American desires. Yet at the same time, the important role of cartels in the French economy made Paris reluctant to endorse an aggressive campaign against these organizations. The French followed an inconsistent line, sometimes pushing for tough policies and sometimes opposing them.

The future of deconcentration hinged on the five cases initiated by the Decartelization Branch in the summer of 1947: Siemens, Bosch, Henschel, Metalgesellschaft, and ball bearings. Success would provide critical precedents, whereas failure would lead observers to conclude that the experiment was a sham. Much depended on the attitude of General Clay. If he backed deconcentration, there was a good chance for success, whereas opposition would almost guarantee failure. Heretofore he had supported the program, energetically pushing the Allies for a general statute. Yet he also sought economic recovery, and the Economics Division was warning him that deconcentration would retard the process.

As the investigations in these five cases moved toward conclusion in the winter of 1947/1948, Clay acted. Siemens did manage to sidestep the threat of reorganization by dexterous stalling, made possible in part because its headquarters was in Berlin, which raised complex questions of jurisdiction.[73] Two other firms were not so lucky. The Decartelization Branch recommended, and Clay approved, orders directed at Bosch and Metalgesellschaft. Before 1939, Bosch had dominated production of electric ignition and fuel injection systems for internal-combustion engines throughout the world, and even after 1945 it still possessed many foreign subsidiaries. Clay ordered the firm to sell off several of its foreign holdings and to license its technology on a "reasonable" basis to all applicants. Metalgesellschaft's situation was somewhat different. The Decartelization Branch determined that, in and of itself, the company did not constitute an "excessive" concentration of economic power. However, the firm was part of a larger "concert of interests" in the light metal and chemical industries involving two other large companies, the Deutsch Gold- und Silber-Scheide-Anstalt (DEGUSSA), which produced chemicals and metals using electrolytic processes, and Henkel, which made soap. Each of these firms held large blocks of stock in the other. Clay ordered the three to terminate their alliance and dispose of these holdings.

Clay, however, blocked action against Henschel and the leading producer of ball bearings, Vereinigte Kugellager-Fabriken (VKF), which was the subsidiary of a Swedish firm. In both cases he ignored the advice of the Decartelization Branch, which wanted to break the companies up into several smaller firms. Clay grounded his decision on Henschel on economics, stating, "I do not believe the breaking up of Henschel, the principle locomotive works in Germany, was a wise undertaking in a period in which transportation was almost at a standstill." He added that because the firm sold most of its output to Germany's government-owned railways, the authorities could easily control it. With respect to VKF, Clay asserted, "Since it was understood . . . that the production of bearings in Germany would in the future be prohibited [by the Allies to prevent German rearmament], nothing would be gained by breaking up this enterprise."[74] VKF itself had recently taken a step that probably made Clay's decision easier. In late 1947, VKF, at that time the only producer of bearings in Germany, had sought to deflect criticism of its monopoly by selling 2,600 machines to the firm that had before 1945 been its chief competitor, Kugelfischer, but whose facilities the Allies had confiscated and shipped abroad as reparations. This decision effectively ceded between 25 and 30 percent of the German bearing market to Kugelfischer.[75] When the Allies subsequently decided to permit the continued production of bearings in Germany, the two firms continued to compete.

Clay's decisions in these two cases represented the start of a general retreat from deconcentration, although not necessarily from decartelization. In the general's mind, the program had reached the point of diminishing returns. He later wrote, "Personally, I think that the process has been carried to about the right point, and that to carry it any further would result in inability [by the Germans] to compete in world markets."[76] American politics may have influenced Clay's timing. Most people assumed that the Republicans would win the 1948 presidential election, and as a personal letter from an American lawyer to one member of the occupation regime noted, there was "a very reasonable expectation that policy and procedure in this matter [deconcentration] is headed for a thorough review under the next administration."[77] In May 1948, Clay announced that henceforth the occupation authorities would apply the "rule of reason" in deconcentration cases, advancing on a case-by-case basis rather than just attacking big firms wholesale. Although not really a major change in policy—investigations under the Anglo-American decrees had in fact proceeded on a case-by-case basis—the order gave the impression that Clay had raised the requirements for deconcentration and disheartened advocates of the program. Meanwhile, Clay announced that in the future the Decartelization Branch would concentrate on consumer goods industries, where monopolies presumably affected German citizens most directly. In Germany, however, companies manufacturing consumer products were generally much smaller than those making capital goods and so in all likelihood less of a threat to free markets. Perhaps most important, Clay sharply reduced the staff of the Decartelization Branch, which by the end of 1948 numbered only thirty-seven.[78] He also ordered future actions to "emphasize the trade practices and decartelization [side] of the program" rather than deconcentration.[79] The general had always been more enthusiastic about the former than the latter. As he wrote, "It is perhaps unfortunate that these really separate measures were associated."[80] In January 1949, Clay remarked, "Basically our deconcentration of property has been completed."[81]

Clay acted on his own authority. To critics he responded slyly, "If I have interpreted my instructions wrongly either in the United States zone or in my negotiations with my colleagues [with the other Allied powers], I assume that the government will advise me and instruct me further in the premises."[82] Clay realized that such instructions were unlikely. Though a State Department memo noted that "a good case can probably be made out . . . that General Clay, without authorization, has altered the Government's occupation policy," it also observed, "Our present policy of giving Germany back to the Germans appears inconsistent with . . . active re-entry on a large scale into the field of deconcentrating German industry."[83] The State and Defense Departments seemed satisfied with the general's actions and perhaps even relieved that he had taken the onus for changing policy from them.

Clay's decision did spark a revolt in the occupation's Decartelization Branch. The branch was divided. After Martin's departure in 1947, Philip Hawkins, a lawyer attached to the Economics Division, had assumed temporary leadership, giving way in early 1948 to a permanent chief, Richardson Bronson. Neither Hawkins nor Bronson was a veteran of the Antitrust Division of the Justice Department, and the decartelization staff regarded them as agents of their superiors in the occupation's Economics Division, a view reinforced by Hawkins's marriage to General Draper's daughter. Hawkins and Bronson supported Clay's new policy, but most of the staff did not. The result was that, as Bronson put it, "all Hell broke loose."[84] Nineteen members, led by Johnston Avery, a former assistant to Thurman Arnold at the Justice Department, signed a memo (subsequently leaked to the press) asserting that Clay's new policy "excludes from decartelization action the principal group of monopolistic enterprises which the law says must be eliminated." It continued, "The law does not draw any distinction between capital goods industries and consumer goods industries. . . . It is our view that monopolies in the capital goods industries are far more frequent and more repugnant than are concentrations in consumer goods industries." The result of Clay's decision to concentrate on consumer goods industries "would be to leave the fundamental concentrations of economic power intact."[85] One of the nineteen subsequently went further, telling a committee investigating the subject, "It is no secret that the operations of the decartelization program have been hampered by Major General Draper and his associates in military government. . . . They have done whatever they could, by innuendo and misstatement, to discredit a program they either did not understand, or did not like."[86]

Clay initially tried to reason with the Decartelization Branch's disgruntled personnel. He met with them to reaffirm his decision, informing the group that German firms had to be large enough to compete in world markets and earn "a reasonable rate of return on investment." The branch's staff remained unmollified. One member asked the general why the military government ought to guarantee the profits of German firms. Clay, irritated by the hostility he encountered, walked out of the meeting.[87]

Clay subsequently came down hard on the dissidents. A military man, he was not sympathetic to those who publicly challenged the orders of their superiors. "The decartelization group," he wrote in 1950, "was composed of extremists, sincere but determined to break up German industry into small units regardless of their economic efficiency."[88] Their plans went beyond any antitrust program ever implemented in the United States, and the general said, "I held very much to the principle that we had no right to make Germans accept reforms that we had not been willing to get authorities in the United States to accept."[89] He placed in the files of the nineteen protestors formal letters of reprimand prohibiting their promotion without his approval, and he dismissed the one who had publicly denounced Draper, asserting, "The right to accuse his superior of dishonesty can be exercised only if the employee has resigned."[90] Wendell Berge, by this time retired from government and in private practice, defended the man and eventually secured his reinstatement.

People in the United States noticed the commotion. Articles in the *New York Times* chronicled the blow-up and cast the dissidents in a sympathetic light.[91] James Martin, back at home in Maryland, denounced Clay's policy as "a complete sell-out to the German heavy industrialists."[92] In his address accepting the third-party presidential nomination of the Progressive Party, Henry Wallace complained, "We have been maneuvered into a policy whose specific purpose has been this, and only this: namely to revive the power of the industrialists and cartelists who heiled Hitler and financed his fascism, and who were the wellspring of his war chest."[93]

It seems unlikely, however, that these events particularly excited the public at large. In the spring of 1948, a Communist coup extinguished democracy in Czechoslovakia. Meanwhile, the Soviets terminated all conversations with their former Allies regarding Germany. In the summer of 1948, Russian forces initiated the Berlin blockade, which continued well into 1949. Alongside these matters, the future of German producers of locomotives and ball bearings did not seem particularly important.

President Truman did pay attention, however. During World War II he had led the first congressional investigations of international cartels, and he remained hostile to anything associated with them. Within a month of his unexpected reelection victory in November 1948, the *New York Times* reported, "President Truman declared . . . that while he was President there would be no revival of the world-wide German cartels, which, he added, had tried to help us lose the war."[94] In December, the secretary of the army appointed a committee, headed by Garland Ferguson, a member of the Federal Trade Commission, "to sift accusations that the United States government's program for dissolution of the combines and monopolies that so materially furthered the Nazi war effort has been scuttled through the activities of top officials entrusted with its execution."[95]

The committee's staff drew largely from the Federal Trade Commission and the Justice Department's Antitrust Division, which almost guaranteed an outcome favorable to the advocates of further deconcentration. The committee's final report concluded, "The deconcentration of Germany industry under Law 56 [the Anglo-American decree] has not been effectively carried out."[96] It recommended transferring the Decartelization Branch from the Economics Division, which was hostile to deconcentration, to the Legal

Division, which would presumably be more supportive. More important, it urged the reopening of all major deconcentration cases, including those that General Clay had declared closed.

The Ferguson Committee's report, issued in April 1949, came at a propitious moment. Clay was a formidable individual, and as long as he was in charge in Germany, policy there would follow his wishes. In late 1948, however, the western Allies oversaw elections that set into motion the formation of the West German government the next year. These changes required a reorganization of the occupation. The Allies turned over many functions—although not decartelization and deconcentration—to the new German government in Bonn; oversight of American operations in Germany shifted from the Defense to the State Department.[97] Clay, who was exhausted after four years as military governor, retired, and John McCloy became the American high commissioner for Germany. After two years of frustration, the deconcentration program apparently had another chance.

Antitrust in West Germany

Under the new regime in Germany, decartelization and deconcentration assumed consistent form. Radical deconcentration failed, but German industry did not return to its old patterns. West Germany, prodded by the United States, adopted policies that resembled the American antitrust laws.

In 1949, the new regime in Germany raised both hopes for and fears about deconcentration. The new American high commissioner was John McCloy, a noted corporate lawyer who had served with distinction as an undersecretary in the War Department during the war. In Germany, he served not the Pentagon but the State Department, which apparently hoped that his military contacts would ease the transfer of authority. McCloy moved the Decartelization and Deconcentration Branch from the Economics Division to the office of the General Counsel, where it reported to Robert Bowie, a lawyer who had taught antitrust at the Harvard Law School before joining the government. Bowie, whose talents commanded almost universal respect, soon became McCloy's closest adviser. At the same time, McCloy expanded the much-shrunken staff of the Decartelization Branch, drawing many of the new additions from the Justice Department's Antitrust Division.

These steps generated much speculation, as conversations with British officials indicated. The notes of one meeting observed, "The Foreign Office viewed with some concern the reports that a new staff of some thirty officers

was being sent to Germany to work on decartelizations and feared that this
was an indication that the United States was preparing a great offensive."[98]
London also worried: "By making decartelization primarily a legal question
[by putting it under the General Counsel], . . . [the Americans] intend to
launch a program without regard to its disturbing effects on German production."[99]

These concerns were grossly exaggerated. McCloy was no friend of radical economic reform—he was a Republican who had displayed little enthusiasm for the New Deal—and he firmly supported efforts to revive the
German economy. The Decartelization Branch's staff may have had ambitious plans, but McCloy and Bowie pursued a more limited agenda. The
New York Times reported that on going to Germany in 1949, McCloy had
"deprecated domestic criticism of delay in the decartelization of Germany.
. . . Mr. McCloy indicated his belief that in Germany the progress had been
reasonably satisfactory. He declared that it was not enough merely to tear
down a monopoly, but that something must be created in its place to prevent
a collapse of the national economy."[100] According to the official history of
the decartelization effort, McCloy wanted "to introduce an element of competition into a German economic structure freed from the restraints of monopoly [and] restrictive agreements," not to disassemble large German firms
en masse.[101] He agreed with Clay that American policy in Germany should
not impose more exacting standards than those applied in the United States
itself. Bowie concurred with this prescription. He supported antitrust as it
actually operated in the United States, where the law tolerated big business
as long as it was efficient and faced competition.

McCloy and Bowie also realized that any successful program required
German cooperation. As an October 1950 memo stated, "Germany, rather
than being regarded as the sole object of Western precautions, is now called
upon to cooperate with the West as a partner in a common program of
defense against a new danger. Western treatment of that partner must be
reasonably commensurate with these changed circumstances."[102]

In truth, the Ferguson Committee's recommendations for more thoroughgoing deconcentration lacked support. President Truman as a rule
strongly backed antitrust enforcement, and it was during his administration
that the government scored its great court victories against international
cartels,[103] but in matters touching national security, Truman relied chiefly
on the State and Defense Departments, whose leaders he greatly respected.
These people were concerned first and foremost with the emerging Cold
War and eager to secure a friendly West Germany; most of them thought

that in the case of deconcentration Clay had done the right thing. Although the retreat from deconcentration momentarily exercised Truman, who had a temper and sometimes made snap judgments, the president showed little interest in the conclusions of the Ferguson Committee. Its report represented not a new beginning for deconcentration but the last manifestation of a policy that the government had abandoned.

Even before McCloy actually went to Germany, Ferguson himself had backed away from his report. Clay and his lieutenants had vigorously rebutted its charges. Clay characterized the report as "poor" and took personal responsibility for the decisions it criticized.[104] By this time, the successful resolution of the Berlin blockade had raised Clay's prestige to immense heights, and his uncompromising reply had forced Ferguson to declare, "Nowhere in the report is there criticism of General Clay," adding, "I know of no one who could have so ably and wisely made these decisions [on deconcentration]."[105]

In 1951, as part of a larger package involving the end of reparations, the western Allies agreed to shift responsibility for decartelization to the Germans. The government in Bonn promised to enact a decartelization statute on its own, while the Allies would finish the reorganization of the banking, chemical, and coal and steel industries.[106] McCloy realized that securing adequate legislation from the Germans would require tact because support for cartels still existed. In 1949, a respected German economist had warned that cartels were "becoming more indispensable from day to day as obstacles to trade are pulled aside. . . . Market and production regulations are needed as the basis for an organically growing national and international European economic organization."[107] In 1953, Fritz Berg, president of the Federal Association of German Industries, denounced the opponents of cartels as impractical theorists and warned that, without some sort of brake, price competition could drive small- and medium-size producers into bankruptcy and encourage further industrial consolidation.[108] "There can be no doubt," one High Commission memo stated, "as to the necessity for the U.S. to continue to bend every effort to bring about the passage of the German draft antitrust legislation. Our influence, however, in order to be more effective, should be brought to bear only behind the scenes. . . . This doctrine of competition cannot be imposed . . . from without nor from above. It must be accepted as the result of voluntary action."[109]

Fortunately for Washington, decartelization enjoyed the genuine support of Ludwig Erhard, the economics minister and arguably the second most important figure in Chancellor Konrad Adenauer's government. Erhard, an economist, favored free markets and had made his reputation in the late 1940s by abolishing price controls and rationing in Germany—measures that, in concert with currency reform, had contributed substantially to the country's economic recovery. As one historian wrote, Erhard "saw himself as the champion of American[-style] capitalism in West Germany," and anti-trust was a component of American-style capitalism.[110] Erhard even dispatched experts to the United States to meet with Edward Mason, Thurman Arnold, and Corwin Edwards and elicit their thoughts on the subject.[111]

Although it took several years, by 1957, Erhard had secured from the German parliament legislation strictly limiting, although not entirely abolishing, cartels. It required positive government approval for any cartel to go into effect, something that rarely proved forthcoming. The new measure was not as strong as the 1947 Anglo-American decrees—it did not unconditionally ban cartels and entailed few limits on the size of industrial firms. Nonetheless, it was strict enough, as one historian put it, "to shunt West German industry away from cartels and towards a system of oligopolistic competition on the American pattern."[112]

After 1950, the staff of the Decartelization Branch, as well as many other members of the occupation, concerned themselves chiefly with the reorganization of the banking, chemical, and coal and steel industries. The Allies had made clear their intention to restructure these industries and had in many cases actually seized control of them. Yet as of 1950, the future of these businesses remained undecided, and if the Allies intended to leave Germany and encouraged economic recovery there, they had to act. No industrial nation could afford to leave such key sectors in limbo indefinitely.

Deconcentration eventually failed in banking. Right after the war, the United States, Britain, and France had split the six largest full-service German banks along state lines, turning their operations in each state into a separate bank. By 1950, this arrangement had proved unsatisfactory. German critics of the system argued, "The new bank units are far too small to satisfy the financial requirements of German business and that, owing to the split-up of the larger branch banks, banking costs have increased substantially, with the result that the new banks cannot achieve satisfactory profits . . . that the new banks, being confined to operating within the Laender [state] boundaries, are in no position to distribute risks properly and that funds no longer flow smoothly from areas with excess liquidity to areas where credit needs are of the greatest urgency."[113] The French and British accepted these arguments wholeheartedly, and even the Americans conceded, "There remain weighty arguments to re-centralization that merit support."[114]

In 1951, the Allies loosened restrictions on German finance. A new statute allowed banks to operate in up to six of the nine West German states, except Rhineland-Westphalia, which, as the home of the Ruhr Valley, carried such weight in the West German economy that the Allies decided not to let its banks expand outside the state. This measure also settled the vexing question of who owned the banks, a serious problem since 1945, by distributing stock in the new institutions to the shareholders of the old, "universal" banks from which they had been formed. The statute contained provisions to prevent large shareholders in the old institutions from securing a controlling stake in more than one of the new banks.[115]

The retreat did not end there. Most Germans considered large banks a vital support to business, particularly to firms having substantial capital requirements or competing in international markets. Although technically separate institutions, the components of the old universal banks cooperated very closely throughout the occupation and the first years of the existence of West Germany. After 1957, when further changes in German law allowed reemergence of universal banks on a national scale, the various component banks merged into something approximating their prewar form. A handful of very large institutions continued to dominate both commercial and investment banking in West Germany.

The disposition of IG Farben accorded more closely with American desires, although even here the United States had to compromise. Conflict among the Allies had prevented progress on the reorganization of Farben before 1950. The Soviets had, of course, gone their own way, but the western nations had disagreements among themselves as well. Whereas the British had operated most of Farben's properties in their zone as a unit, the Americans had required Farben's facilities under their control to act independently. Neither side hid its disapproval of the other's policies. American officials complained about the managers of the giant Leverhusen complex in the British zone, who they claimed wanted to re-create IG Farben. "We have examples," the Americans complained, "of their using pressure on the independent units [in the U.S. zone] to observe policies laid down by Leverhusen."[116] The British were unimpressed. "As a result of the divergent action taken by the U.S. and U.K. elements," they contended, "there is today a general picture in the British zone of success and progress, compared with a much less satisfactory picture in the U.S. zone. . . . The principal difference between the German management of the Leverhusen complex in the British zone and that of the Hoechst/Main plants in the U.S. zone is one of competence."[117] Occasionally the exchanges became uglier. At one point, a Brit-

ish memo complained of an American official who was "an emigrant German Jew who had anglicized his German name."[118] Yet the Allies had to do
something. They could not leave the remains of Germany's largest company
in "trusteeship" indefinitely. Moreover, if they did not act, Bonn eventually
would, in which case the Allies would lose control of the process entirely.

Two factors made the reorganization somewhat easier. First, over half of
IG Farben's assets had been in East Germany, the parts of Germany ceded
to Poland, or abroad, and the firm had lost control of them.[119] The remainder
was still very large but nevertheless more manageable than the gargantuan
IG of 1945. Second, by 1950, most students of the matter had concluded
that Farben's management had never been able to control properly the firm's
countless subsidiaries, which had often operated autonomously. For this reason, even the more enthusiastic proponents of business concentration had
little desire to re-create the IG.[120]

To avoid disagreements among their regular staffs, the three western Allies
dispatched a joint, three-power commission to Germany to draft a plan for
the final distribution of Farben's assets.[121] The group reported in November
1950. First, it recommended that Farben spin off seven firms that, even
though legally part of the IG, had largely operated independently.[122] This
was not particularly controversial, but such was not the case with its other
suggestion. It recommended that the greatest part of the IG's property go
into six new companies, one each in the French and American zones and
four in the British zone. The companies in the French and American sectors
would roughly correspond to Badische Anilin- & Soda-Fabrik AG (BASF)
and Hoechst, respectively, which had been two of the three leading firms
involved in the 1925 merger that had created Farben. The new firms would
even assume the old names. This represented a major change of policy in
the U.S. zone, where the IG's installations had operated independently since
1946. The plan also called for big changes in the British sector. It proposed
to divide the Leverhusen complex, which had been the core of Bayer, the
third leading firm in the Farben merger, into four parts: AGFA (film), Dormagen (rayon), Titangesellschaft (titanium dioxide), and Bayer (dyestuffs,
pharmaceuticals, and heavy chemicals).[123]

The West German government, which had had no representatives on the
reorganization commission, resisted this plan, as did the British. They objected chiefly to the recommendations for Leverhusen. "The Federal Government," Bonn argued, "cannot see any valid reasons in favor of abandon-
ing the existing technical, organizational, regional, and historic integration

of the present Farbefabriken Bayer, by their proposed split-up into four parts."[124] The British agreed, arguing that the plan largely reflected the American grudge against Leverhusen, which U.S. officials had somehow communicated to the Allied commission.[125] The division soon hardened, with the British and Germans urging the creation of a united company, Bayer, at Leverhusen, the Americans recommending the breakup of the complex, and the French vacillating.

Mutual concessions resolved two of the outstanding issues relatively quickly. The Americans agreed to include AGFA in Bayer; the Germans agreed to sever Titangesellschaft from it.[126] The latter was a joint venture between National Lead and Farben created to produce titanium dioxide for the German market. As such it not only had operated with a fair degree of independence but also had become entangled in American law. Part of the antitrust judgment against National Lead required that the company either sell its stake in Titangesellschaft or expand it to 100 percent, turning the joint venture into a wholly owned subsidiary.[127] The German concession on this point allowed the American firm to purchase the facility.

The Dormagen plant, however, remained a point of dissension for almost two years. The Americans stubbornly contended that with this facility Bayer would be so much larger than any other German chemical firm that it could dominate the West German industry and perhaps even reassemble IG Farben. The Germans (and the British) responded that the plant simply could not stand on its own. Dormagen relied on raw materials from other Leverhusen facilities and on Bayer to sell its product. Dormagen produced rayon, and the development in the 1940s of improved synthetic fibers like nylon meant that it needed extensive investment to remain competitive, investment that alone Dormagen could not command.[128] Almost everyone associated with the plant, from shop stewards to the management, opposed severing it from Bayer.[129] The Germans also produced statistics demonstrating that the leading American chemical firms differed substantially in size and that, by world standards, none of the three central German firms (BASF, Hoechst, and Bayer) would be toweringly large.[130] But the Americans did not back down until 1952, when confronted with irrefutable proof from experience that Dormagen could not stand alone.[131]

The plan for IG Farben finally went into effect in the spring of 1953. Shareholders in the old IG received stock in each of the three main successor firms. Because the IG's securities had been widely dispersed, no one stockholder would be able to control any of the new firms. All the successor firms

(not just the three largest) received royalty-free licenses to all Farben technology, an arrangement that made participation of these firms in patent-
based cartels very difficult.[132] The reorganized firms did well. Although the
"big three" subsequently absorbed some of the smaller companies spun off
from the IG, BASF, Bayer, and Hoechst remained independent, and each
became a leader in the world chemical industry.

Had United States policy succeeded? The answer depends on the American goal. After 1953, the German chemical industry remained in the hands
of large companies. If the United States wanted to change this, it failed.
Nevertheless, the industry was far more open after 1953 than before 1945.
Instead of one company that dominated most sectors of the business, Germany now had three very large firms and several medium-size ones that
competed with one another, albeit cautiously. As such, the German chemical industry resembled that of the United States, becoming an oligopoly—
that is, dominated by several large firms—rather than a monopoly.

The reorganization of the coal and steel industries presented even greater
challenges than banking and chemicals. Coal and steel were Germany's
largest industries and had been the economic basis of its military strength.
Moreover, Germany was western Europe's chief coal producer, and throughout the late 1940s, a chronic fuel shortage had impeded the continent's
economic recovery. The future of these businesses occupied the highest
officials in the Allied governments. More was at stake than deconcentration.

The western Allies had a simple plan for these industries: break up the
large coal and steel enterprises into smaller concerns and, perhaps more
important, sever ties between the two types of business. German mines,
which the steel companies controlled, supplied coking coal to steel makers
throughout Europe, and many experts believed that the German steel makers used their control of this vital raw material to limit competition. Although
probably exaggerated, this concern did have foundation. In the late 1940s,
Germany was charging domestic consumers of coal lower prices than foreign
ones, a practice common among European exporters, including Britain.[133]
Tentative plans called for the occupiers to vest coal and steel assets in new
companies, each of which would operate a single complex of mines or mills.
The British, who had closely overseen the industry since 1945, had already
laid plans to divide the steel industry into twenty-eight firms and to completely separate them from the business of mining coal.[134] American authorities wanted to be involved in this important process, and they were
concerned that the British, if left to their own devices, might leave the new

companies under government ownership, effectively nationalizing these industries. In 1948, they persuaded London to acquiesce to a joint program to seize and reorganize the assets of the leading coal and steel producers.[135] The French participated as well, although their chief goal seems to have been ensuring that their steel industry received equal access to Ruhr coal. At the same time, the occupiers realized that they had at least to consult with the new government in Bonn as well as with the managers of these properties, whose expertise was necessary if the coal and steel industries were going to recover. Both were skeptical of reorganization. In particular, many Germans insisted that the ties between coal mines and steel mills had allowed substantial efficiencies and opposed separating the two types of business.[136]

The structure of the coal industry raised serious questions about the effectiveness of reforms. Since the 1890s, all the Ruhr coal mines had marketed their product through a cartel agency. German steel firms had often bought coal mines just to gain a place in this organization. After 1945, the British had allowed the cartel to continue to operate as the Deutsche Kohlenbergbau-Leitung (DKLB). Coal was in desperately short supply, and the DKLB was a convenient agency through which to ration it. Moreover, mine operators had no experience managing sales. After the creation of Bizonia in 1946, the United States acquiesced to the DKLB's continued existence.[137] German mining executives, none of whom had experienced life without a cartel, were happy with the situation. By 1950, operators in the Ruhr were talking about the benefits of a "self-governing body of the mining industry" to handle "coordination between the various interests" in the business.[138] To present abuses, the Allies created the International Authority for the Ruhr (IAR) to oversee the coal and steel industries. Unfortunately, this organization had few resources and commanded little respect from the Germans. In 1951, a U.S. official complained, "With the passage of time our ability to exercise the proper supervision over DKLB's activities . . . has diminished. DKLB has paid less and less attention to instructions from this group [IAR] and to the Allied policies."[139]

Nevertheless, Allied plans for reorganizing the Ruhr mines proceeded. By 1952, they had broken up the seven largest mining combines, all of which had been under the control of steel firms and that together accounted for 49.5 percent of output, into twenty-one companies. After tough negotiations with German mine and mill operators, the Allies conceded that steel companies could own coal mines capable of supplying up to 75 percent of their own needs, but no more. Nine coal firms, accounting for 13.5 percent of total production, went to steel companies. The other twelve companies would operate independently.[140] The continued existence of the DKLB, however, rendered problematic the creation of a free market in coal.

The story of the steel industry resembled that of coal. Despite Allied seizure, after 1945, management of the mills had remained largely in the hands of German executives who had grown up professionally in a world dominated by cartels. No other group capable of running the factories existed. Reorganization did proceed fairly smoothly, with the steel industry divided into twenty-four firms whose securities the Allies distributed to stockholders in the old, more concentrated steel firms. As with coal, however, reorganization did not necessarily preclude the reemergence of a Germany steel cartel. Indeed, informal cooperation between the steel companies seems to have continued throughout the occupation period and into the early history of West Germany.

Even worse from the American point of view, by the end of the 1940s, the international steel cartel seemed about to reemerge. National cartels had survived the war in many western European countries (Britain, France, Belgium), and German steel makers still cooperated extensively among themselves, albeit less formally. In a series of meetings in late 1949 and early 1950, representatives of German, French, Belgian, Dutch, Luxembourger, Swedish, Swiss, and possibly British steel producers tried to forge arrangements for the sale of many goods.[141] The talks were inconclusive, but Washington was concerned.

The drive for European integration offered a way around these problems. From a political point of view, the reorganization of Germany's coal and steel industries had not resolved the basic question—whatever their structure, German producers had the power to dominate European steel production. The Allies did impose a ceiling on total German steel output through the IAR, but this was only a temporary solution. The moment of reckoning came in 1950, as German economic recovery pushed steel production up against the ceiling. The Allies would have to either lift restrictions and allow the German industry to reassert itself or clamp down and cripple German recovery, and quite possibly hopes for a democratic, pro-western Germany.

Jean Monnet and Robert Schumann devised a way out of this dilemma. Monnet was the *eminence grise* behind French economic planning and a convinced internationalist who would play a key role orchestrating European integration. Schumann was the French foreign minister. In 1950, they negotiated the European Coal and Steel Community (ECSC), which eliminated barriers to trade in coal, iron, and steel among Germany, France, Italy, and the Benelux countries (Belgium, the Netherlands, and Luxembourg). It also created a central agency, the High Authority, to coordinate modernization of the industry. The ECSC would integrate German steel makers into a European framework, reducing—ideally erasing—their national character. At the same time, it lifted restrictions on German output and treated the West German government as an equal partner with its neighbors, the first time Germans had enjoyed such parity since the war.

Monnet hoped that the ECSC would prevent the reemergence of steel cartels. Although restrained in his enthusiasm for the free market—Monnet was a pioneer in economic planning—the Frenchman believed that to develop efficiently, Europe's steel makers needed access to a large continental market such as that enjoyed by American firms. By dividing up territories and channeling sales, cartels had precluded the emergence of such a market in Europe. Cartels also encouraged participants to think largely in national terms, because countries were the basis of organization and cartels generally guaranteed producers' home markets. Monnet also knew that restrictions on cartels would reassure the United States, which favored European cooperation but feared that the ECSC might resurrect the international steel cartel. Monnet, who had spent much of the war in Washington and whose contacts in the United States were legion, was familiar with American antitrust law. Thanks to his insistence, the ECSC accord contained what his biographer described as "Europe's first strong anti-cartel law."[142] He had Raymond Vernon, an American economist who had helped plan Japan's deconcentration program and, in 1950, worked for the State Department, go over the ECSC agreement and draft language that sharply restricted cartels. Corwin Edwards later reported that the Coal and Steel Community's anticartel provisions "were written in Washington and adopted as written."[143] Monnet subsequently became the first chief of the High Authority, with responsibility for enforcing these rules.

The creation of the ECSC did not suddenly banish cartels from the coal and steel industries, but it greatly facilitated the effort against them. Simply by expanding the market, it made the formation of cartels more difficult. The greater the number of producers and consumers, the harder devising effective restrictions. More important, it changed the context of the issue, particularly for Germans. Before 1950, decartelization was part of an alien (if on balance benign) occupation. After 1950, it was part of an idealistic and generally popular program to build a united Europe and overcome the continent's sad history of war.

The long and sometimes ugly debate over deconcentration obscured the substantial successes of American decartelization policy in Germany. General Clay had a point when he argued, "There has never before been a like effort to reduce concentration of economic power."[144] Before 1945, the German economy was probably the world's most cartelized. Largely at the insistence of U.S. officials, the occupiers of western Germany terminated almost all cartels and persuaded the government in Bonn to enact laws that, in most cases, prevented their reemergence. Cartels had deep roots in Germany, and without strong action they no doubt would have continued to play an important role in the German economy. Although deconcentration was not nearly so thoroughgoing, the reorganization of IG Farben and the coal and steel industries did transform two of Germany's most important industries, effectively replacing monopoly with oligopoly. The United States had succeeded in imposing on West Germany an antitrust policy roughly comparable to that it followed at home. Some reformers had wanted to go further, perhaps even setting precedents for the United States. Yet Clay was right when he declared that Americans could not in good conscience force on the Germans a policy they were unwilling to adopt for themselves.

The Anti-Zaibatsu Program

Although economic reform in Japan initially took an even more radical course than in Germany, it ultimately accomplished less. Reformers had fewer brakes on their activities than in Germany both because the other Allies had far less influence on occupation policy in Japan and because the American public and business community were not as interested in policy toward Japan as toward Germany. Yet economic conditions in Japan were less hospitable to deconcentration and decartelization than in Germany. In the end, these factors were decisive.

At first glance, reformers seemed to have a free hand in Japan. The United States effectively ran the Japanese occupation by itself, consulting with the Allies but giving them little real authority. The reorganization of Japanese business did not involve the endless inter-Allied talks that characterized the same process in Germany. Yet the structure of occupation gave the Japanese themselves the capacity to stymie reform. Their government continued to operate throughout this period, and the American authorities invariably worked through it. This was in sharp contrast to Germany, where the central government had ceased to exist and the Allies exercised sole political authority. The Japanese government was supposed to follow directives laid down by the Americans, but there were many ways in which it could sabotage decisions it opposed, particularly because the United States did not have enough personnel on hand to closely monitor its activities.[145]

During its first two years, the occupation imposed a variety of sweeping reforms on Japan. It dissolved the military, punished war criminals, and purged from positions of authority those deemed too close to the old regime. It imposed a new constitution that redefined the emperor as a purely symbolic leader, reinforced the authority of elected officials, guaranteed civil liberties, expanded the franchise, and banned the country from going to war for any reason. The occupiers decentralized education and law enforcement, strengthening local governments at Tokyo's expense. The Americans redistributed land, transforming Japanese farmers from a class of tenants into one of independent freeholders. Finally, the occupiers encouraged the formation of labor unions, which grew very fast in the immediate postwar period. For the most part, reforms proceeded from the assumption that Japanese society was basically unhealthy and that only dramatic changes could eliminate its authoritarian and militaristic tendencies. Although most of these reforms were not in a strict sense punitive—the occupation officials who imposed them sought to make Japan a better place in which to live—they did entail severe economic, social, and political disruption.

Economic hardship cast a pall over reforms. Industrial production was terribly depressed. Foreign trade had practically ceased except for American charity. Inflation ranged as high as 10 percent a month, and food rations remained barely adequate to keep people alive. This situation reflected not only the physical destruction of the war, which was immense, but also the collapse of Japan's colonial empire and trade relations. A densely populated island nation with few natural resources, Japan had to import large quantities of food and raw materials to survive, paying for these goods by exporting manufactured products. With the end of the war, the other countries of Asia, Japan's chief trading partners, had largely severed commercial ties. The result was a situation so desperate that, for much of the next decade, American authorities despaired of ever again making Japan economically viable.

Deconcentration and decartelization played out against this background. The program had little support in Japan. As an official historian of the occupation pointed out, the Japanese considered legislation against monopolies "a luxury which only the rich nations could afford, and that competition was wasteful to a country with limited resources. Some were positive that a nation as poor as Japan in natural resources needed to pool its available stockpiles, capital and talents in order to survive in a competitive world. There were also the predictions that the Japanese economy would be made ineffectual and weak by breaking up the trusts, cartels, and private monopolies, and be reduced to an economy of small-sized industries only."[146] This attitude affected leftists as well as conservatives. The former thought not in terms of deconcentrating industry but of achieving nationalization and worker control. Japan's Communist Party denounced deconcentration as "a scheme of the traitorous, monopolistic capitalists."[147]

The Americans in charge of decartelization and deconcentration nevertheless plunged ahead. Responsibility for this program rested with the occupation's Antitrust and Cartels Division, which reported to the Economics and Science Section, which was in turn directly under General Douglas MacArthur, the military governor. Edward Welsh, who headed the division for most of its history, was an economist who had worked for the Temporary National Economic Commission in 1940 and had held important posts in the Office of Price Administration (OPA) during the war.[148] As in Germany, much of the deconcentration staff came from the Antitrust Division, although the OPA, the only major wartime agency dominated by New Dealers, also provided a substantial number. There was no doubt about their enthusiasm. Welsh insisted, "People can talk and write about democracy, but they cannot really live democracy without deconcentration of economic power." "Those opposed to democracy are opposed to the deconcentration plan."[149] He also contended that decartelization and deconcentration would help the Japanese economy. "Deconcentration or the breaking up of large spider-like combinations should decrease the non-productive labor currently hoarded in overstaffed head offices, as well as in non-operating or non-essential plants, and should increase the employment, through increased efficiency and better allocation of materials, in the actual enterprises producing essential goods."[150]

Realizing that change was inevitable, the Japanese government and business community sought to contain and control it. In October 1945, they proposed to break up the four largest Zaibatsu: Mitsui, Mitsubishi, Sumitomo, and Yasuda. These combines, each dominated by a single extended family, centered on holding companies that controlled dozens of operating firms, many themselves huge. The Japanese planned to create the Holding

Companies Liquidation Commission (HCLC) to take over these organizations, compensating their owners with ten-year, non-negotiable government
bonds and selling off their many subsidiaries as separate firms. Because compensation was in non-negotiable securities (holders could not sell them before maturity), the former owners could not convert it into money and buy
back their property.[151] Members of the leading Zaibatsu families would also
resign all their offices in the companies they had controlled. The HCLC
would report directly to the occupation authorities even while technically
remaining part of the Japanese government, an arrangement that would give
the Antitrust and Cartels Division an unusually large voice in its operations.
The occupiers approved this plan with the provision that, in doing so, they
did not preclude further reform.[152]

If the Japanese expected their plan to forestall more radical changes, they
were mistaken. Soon after the initial Zaibatsu proposal, the State and Justice
Departments dispatched an eight-man commission to Japan led by Corwin
Edwards—who through the Cartel Committee had ties to both agencies—
to study economic deconcentration and recommend further reforms. All
members were experts on antitrust, with four (including Edwards) hailing
from the Justice Department. After an extensive tour of the country, the
commission issued a report in the spring of 1946 that urged measures well
beyond those already taken. Action was slow, however. General MacArthur
and his staff resented outside meddling in the occupation, and they may
have considered Edwards's report an implicit rebuke of their willingness to
accept the Japanese deconcentration program. MacArthur declared that the
report was "too liberal" and "unworkable" and did nothing for a year.[153]
Nevertheless, in the spring of 1947, the general reversed himself and embraced Edwards's suggestions. The reasons are not entirely clear. He did not
closely monitor the details of the occupation, and it is possible that in this
matter the Antitrust and Cartels Division acted on its own, pulling him
along. MacArthur also wanted the Republican presidential nomination in
1948, and he may have believed that a more aggressive deconcentration
program would help his prospects, perhaps softening his ultraconservative
image. Whatever the cause, the Edwards report became the basis of decartelization and deconcentration.[154]

The Edwards commission urged not simply the dissolution of a few of
the largest firms but a thoroughgoing reform of Japan's business structure.
First, it recommended the dissolution of all Zaibatsu, which it defined as
any organization "which, by reason of its relative size in any line or the

cumulative power of its position in many lines [of business], restricts competition or impairs the opportunity for others to engage in business independently, in any important segment of business; and any individual, family, allied group, or juridical person owning or controlling such an enterprise or combination." In practice, this meant holding companies that were very large, that were active in several different lines of business, or that joined substantial financial interests with manufacturing or commercial ones, as well as the people involved in these enterprises.[155]

The occupiers deployed the HCLC against all suspect firms. By 1948, the HCLC had taken over not only the 4 leading Zaibatsu, its initial targets, but also several smaller ones as well, eventually seizing 83 holding companies with a staggering 1,151 subsidiaries. It targeted fifty-six members of the Zaibatsu families, seizing their assets and taking control of their personal finances. The HCLC also "purged" several hundred non-family Zaibatsu executives considered too loyal to the old organizations, not only dismissing them but banning them from working for any former Zaibatsu firm for ten years.[156]

The Zaibatsu program imposed immense administrative burdens on the HCLC. Zaibatsu had extremely complex structures that often involved several layers of subsidiaries. The distinction between operating and holding companies, so neat in theory, broke down in practice. Many firms that managed physical assets (factories, land, ships) also held stock in other firms, and because the HCLC did not want to shut down going concerns, it had to reorganize these companies by separating operations from stockholding. Nor did the HCLC rapidly dispose of the vast reserve of securities it accumulated. In part, the expansion of its authority in 1947 forced it to concentrate on seizing assets rather than selling them, but other factors also hindered progress. Even before the war, Japan had had few people with the capital to invest in securities; defeat had impoverished many of them. At the same time, war-related losses had rendered many—if not most—Japanese companies insolvent, making them unattractive investment prospects. Finally, high inflation made large-scale financial operations impractical.

The HCLC exercised strict oversight of the firms it controlled. They had to get its approval before paying dividends or bonuses, borrowing money, disposing of assets, or expanding or rehabilitating facilities. The HCLC even set allowances for the members of the Zaibatsu families.[157] Although on the whole the HCLC seems to have acted fairly, the need to get its approval for every major decision must have been a burden for its charges.

According to the Edwards report, the Zaibatsu constituted only part of the problem, however. Collusion of various types permeated the Japanese economy, and the report suggested a variety of remedies. First, it urged the dissolution of control organizations, technically private companies established during the war by the Japanese government to regulate various industries by setting prices, allocating scarce raw materials, and so on. To the extent that they performed vital functions, political authorities should take over their responsibilities. At American urging, the Japanese parliament (Diet) banned these bodies, although endemic shortages forced the government to continue their work rationing critical materials.[158] At the same time, the Japanese government, at the occupier's behest, promulgated legislation regulating trade associations, preventing them from fixing prices, allocating markets, or otherwise acting as cartels.[159] Most important, the Edwards commission recommended a strict antimonopoly law. In April 1947, the Diet implemented this suggestion, prohibiting Japanese firms from entering price-fixing or market-sharing agreements or international cartels or from owning stock in competing enterprises. The law also banned holding companies (firms that invested most of their capital in the stock of other firms) and interlocking directorates (the same individuals sitting on the boards of competing firms), and it limited mergers. To interpret and enforce these restrictions, the bill created the Fair Trade Commission (FTC), modeled on the American Federal Trade Commission.[160]

The Edwards commission contended that reform of the Japanese economy required one more step. By breaking up the Zaibatsu and banning various anticompetitive practices, the occupation had sharply restricted collusion among companies, but it had done nothing about the existence of very large firms. For instance, Mitsubishi Heavy Industries, a part of the Mitsubishi combine, had in 1945 employed approximately 400,000 people making ships, airplanes, trucks, and more. The Edwards report argued that the very existence of such economic behemoths impaired competition. To remedy this problem, the report recommended a deconcentration law to break up excessively large companies. This one-time measure would open up the economy, creating an atmosphere in which the antimonopoly law and the FTC could function effectively.

In December 1947, at the bidding of the occupation authorities, the Japanese government issued a measure authorizing the HCLC to dissolve "any private enterprise conducted for profit, or combination of such enterprises, which, by reason of its relative size in any line or the cumulative

power of its position in many lines restricts competition or impairs the opportunity of others to engage in business independently."[161] Armed with this
sweeping mandate and urged on by the members of the Antitrust and Cartels
Division, the HCLC announced in early 1948 that it had targeted 257 industrial firms and 68 service companies for possible reorganization.[162]

Reverse Course: The Fate of Deconcentration in Japan

As with Germany, the changing international situation led Washington
to reorient policy toward Japan in the late 1940s. The intensification of the
Cold War and, particularly, the increasing likelihood that the Communists
would win the Chinese civil war led the United States government to view
Japan not simply as a beaten foe but as a potential ally. Yet shortages of food,
economic stagnation, and high inflation were imposing terrible hardships
on the Japanese population, rendering the country politically volatile. Conditions were so bad that many Americans feared that Japan would remain a
ward of the United States indefinitely. Economic recovery constituted the
first step toward stabilizing the country and making it a reliable partner.
William Draper played a key role in the change. Promoted in August 1947
from his job in Germany to undersecretary of the army, where he had responsibility for the occupation regimes, Draper quickly concluded that
change was in order. In early 1948, he led a mission to Japan that announced
that henceforth the occupation would emphasize economic recovery over
reform.

Deconcentration, breaking up Japanese firms, was among the chief casualties of this new policy. The Japanese had never been enthusiastic about
it, believing that the program would damage their economic performance,
and they enacted measures only because the occupation authorities insisted.
Yet the program was controversial on the other side of the Pacific, too.
George Kennan, who as head of planning at the State Department played
a key role in shaping policy during the early years of the Cold War, was one
of deconcentration's leading critics. Kennan believed that Japan's industrial
potential made it the most important country in the Far East and that, if
prosperous and stable, it could contribute substantially to American security.
By early 1947, he had concluded that deconcentration was hindering economic recovery there.[163] His departmental colleagues agreed. One of State's
experts on Japan complained in 1948 that deconcentration "rest[s], as far as

I can see, on the strong views and convictions of a relatively small group of people who view the respective problems exclusively from the standpoint of economic theory. . . . Our preoccupation with matters of this sort reflects a serious lack of sense of proportion with regard to the problems of occupation in Japan."[164]

Some within the occupation itself had doubts. General F. W. Marquat, who as head of the Economics and Science Section of the occupation had ultimate responsibility for deconcentration, complained to Edward Welsh that "he had to be convinced that it was possible to separate a large number of the major Japanese companies into groups of new corporations; staff them with directors, managers, technicians and workmen who were willing to take over the responsibilities involved; obtain the . . . credit necessary to finance a new enterprise; manufacture an end product at a cost competitive with old established companies which remain as active but small[er] organizations, all *without* decreasing production output."[165] Most important, William Draper had doubts. He had opposed deconcentration in Germany and so was naturally inclined against the more radical program under way in Japan. Nor was the information he was getting encouraging. A friend in Tokyo warned him, "The sword-of-Damocles-like effect of the present program [on firms designated for possible deconcentration] is absolutely killing initiative and planning for the future."[166] By the fall of 1947, even before the enactment of the deconcentration statute, Draper had concluded that the program had gone far enough.

Those behind deconcentration defended it. Edward Welsh insisted that the question was "whether the United States decides to make a healthy, democratic Japan or whether the pressure of events and influential people is such as to cause a decision to forget such an objective and to take only such measures as will develop quickly a Japan which would be most readily transferable into an ally in case of war."[167] To those concerned with Japan's economic recovery, he replied, "Deconcentration should reduce substantially the cost of producing Japan's basic commodities" by pruning overstaffed bureaucracies and eliminating monopolistic practices.[168] Welsh hinted darkly at the role of American businessmen in opposition to deconcentration. "One would be naive," he wrote, "to overlook the personal advantages which sometimes come to 'foreign' investors from the reestablishment of previous reactionary groups with whom such investors have had such close relationships in the past."[169] It was vital to continue the "anti-monopoly progress which certain American businessmen fear both at home and abroad."[170]

More important, MacArthur stood firm. A man of immense vanity, he interpreted attacks on the deconcentration program as assaults on his own record, and he feared that they would injure his presidential hopes. He may also have found it embarrassing to abandon a program that he had taken up in earnest less than a year earlier. MacArthur argued, "If this concentration of economic power is not torn down and redistributed peacefully and in due order under the Occupation, there is not the slightest doubt that its cleansing will eventually occur through a blood bath of revolutionary violence."[171] When, in October 1947, Draper urged MacArthur to delay passage of the deconcentration law, the general ignored his recommendation and secured enactment by the Japanese Diet. The HCLC's subsequent decision to re-organize 325 firms indicated that the occupation's commitment to decon-centration had not wavered.

The issue soon became public. In an article published in the December 1, 1947, issue of *Newsweek*, James Kauffman, a New York lawyer returned from a tour of Japan, asserted that the deconcentration law reflected "an economic theory which has, I think, no counterpart anywhere else in the world. It is not communistic but it is far to the left of anything tolerated in this country." It "not only provided for the abolition of the Zaibatsu but also for a virtual destruction of Japanese business and the sale of its assets at nominal prices to select purchasers, including Japanese labor unions, of which about one-half are communist-dominated."[172] Soon Senator William Knowland of California, a Republican stalwart, took up the issue. The sen-ator denounced deconcentration policy in Japan, which he attributed to "doctrinaire New Dealers who found their activities limited in Washington and signed up for overseas occupation service." He particularly objected to the purging of Zaibatsu officials "without any provision for a prelude of accusation, trial, or conviction for war crimes or other offences."[173] Draper apparently encouraged these statements in the hope of forcing a change in occupation policy. He had been in contact with Kauffman for months, and he was cooperating with *Newsweek*'s editor, who had an abiding interest in Japan and opposed many of the occupation reforms. Draper also seems to have provided Knowland with information on which to base his speeches.[174]

To clear up the furor that he had helped engineer, Draper dispatched the five-man Deconcentration Review Board to Japan in the spring of 1948 to go over the HCLC's decisions. It consisted of three businessmen with experience in government (one of whom MacArthur knew fairly well), a member of the Securities and Exchange Commission, and a lawyer recommended by Attorney General Tom Clark. The last, Walter Hutchinson, had worked on antitrust investigations both as a U.S. district attorney in Iowa and with the Justice Department in Washington.[175] Though not formally in charge of the committee, Hutchinson seems to have had more influence over it than anyone else.

The commission demonstrated little enthusiasm for deconcentration. One of the business members stated, "Fundamentally I am not predisposed to breaking up 'concentrated' industry or 'big business' in Japan—especially at this time when the need to speed economic recovery in Japan is so acute."[176] Hutchinson, despite his experience with antitrust, shared this sentiment, complaining that deconcentration had "permitted those individuals who believed in the ideology of atomization or fragmentation to implement their ideologies by encouraging the enforcement of the law along those lines without any basic requisite of evidence of restriction of competition."[177] The Review Board reduced the list of firms to be reorganized from 325 to 19. The occupiers broke up eleven of them into two or three companies; they reorganized the other seven in a less radical fashion, terminating objectionable practices.[178] The Review Board also blocked deconcentration action against Japanese banks, which had been under way.[179]

These reversals infuriated the occupation's Antitrust and Cartels Division. One memo implied that American businessmen eager to move into Japan had forced the change. William Draper was the villain—he had used the Review Board "to change policy, while apparently not changing policy."[180] In truth, the division had only itself to blame. It is hard to believe that 325 Japanese firms each significantly restricted competition or that reorganizing a large number of them would not have disrupted the Japanese economy in a major way. Some of the targets were extremely questionable—small shipbuilders that operated only one yard, or companies that managed a single department store. Even some advocates of the program subsequently conceded that it had gone too far.[181] The HCLC would not have acted against every one of these companies and indeed had already released some from consideration before the Review Board arrived in Japan. Yet considering both the wretched state of the Japanese economy and the way designation under the deconcentration law placed the targets in a legal limbo that made it difficult to carry on business, critics of the program had solid ground for complaint.

The retreat from deconcentration constituted part of a program known as the "reverse course," designed to revive the Japanese economy. The Americans forced the Diet to impose strict monetary and fiscal austerity, subduing inflation and stabilizing the yen at the cost of sharply higher unemployment. The occupation, enthusiastically supported by Japanese conservatives, purged leftists from positions of responsibility and restricted the right of workers to strike. Reparations, which had never been extensive, ceased. Together these measures restored financial stability and labor discipline, putting Japan in a position to profit from the boom associated with the Korean War. By the early 1950s, the island nation once again enjoyed a measure of prosperity.

The "reverse course" did not, however, entail reconstitution of the Zaibatsu or emasculation of the antimonopoly law. The deconcentration statute encountered opposition in Washington because it was far more radical than anything ever attempted in the United States and because it threatened to paralyze much of Japanese industry. By the time of the reverse course in 1948, the Zaibatsu were already gone, and the antimonopoly law banned practices that not only were illegal in the United States but were believed by most Americans to be inimical to commercial efficiency. As in Germany, the issue was not whether to abandon decartelization and deconcentration but whether to adopt standards roughly comparable to those in the United States or to impose stricter ones.

The HCLC completed its work by 1951. In 1948, in the wake of the activities of the Review Board, it reduced restrictions on the many companies it controlled, allowing them to operate more freely, and it began to concentrate on selling their securities.[182] The HCLC completed this gigantic task by 1951, assisted by the return of prosperity and financial stability. Among the largest purchasers were employees of the firms being sold, although many subsequently disposed of their holdings.[183] Once it had marketed all its securities, the HCLC ceased to exist. Its demise completed a program that, despite the setback with respect to deconcentration, had been quite successful. The occupation had effected a major change in the Japanese economy, breaking up the Zaibatsu and some of the largest companies and prohibiting both domestic and international cartels.

Up to this point, developments in Germany and Japan resembled each other. In both countries the occupation had imposed reforms roughly comparable to American antitrust law but had abandoned more radical measures. The end of occupation in Japan, however, had different results than in Germany. Whereas McCloy and Bowie were confident of securing German backing for decartelization, in Japan, the Antitrust and Cartels Division feared that, left to themselves, the Japanese would dismantle reforms. One of its reports noted "a distinct and increasing effort on the part of major Japanese political and business figures to undo the accomplishments" of the program. "It is recognized fully," the report continued, "that implementation of this policy [decartelization and deconcentration] will be effected by the Japanese only if the most careful supervision over their performance is maintained."[184] Within the American government, however, enthusiasm for such oversight was fading. As a State Department expert on Japan stated in 1948, "Our main problem today is to get them [the Japanese] to accept the responsibility implicit in democratic institutions and to strike out on their own in a really democratic way. If their decartelization laws are still not perfect, Japanese society will now have to find within itself the impulse and inspiration to correct the remaining deficiencies."[185]

The durability of the occupation's accomplishments in this area depended on the Fair Trade Commission. It had the authority to prevent the reemergence of the Zaibatsu or of cartels, but as a new agency grafted onto a bureaucracy not particularly sympathetic to its goals, success was not guaranteed. Certainly the initial record was not encouraging. The FTC held only eight hearings during 1947 and 1948 and found itself overwhelmed by the massive number of requests that flooded into its offices for the approval of mergers, of agreements between Japanese and foreign firms, and of the purchase of the securities of one company by another. By late 1950, the situation had improved somewhat. The FTC had its paperwork under better control and hearings were more common. Nevertheless, the agency continued to work slowly, to conduct superficial investigations, and to impose light penalties on those violating its rules.[186]

The FTC failed to prevent a substantial reconcentration of Japanese industry after the occupation ended in 1952. It approved mergers of several of the firms broken up under the deconcentration law. More important, it allowed the Zaibatsu to reemerge in the form of Keritsu. The member companies of the old Zaibatsu exploited a loophole in the antimonopoly law that permitted firms that did not compete directly to own stock in one another. Firms from the old Zaibatsu corporate "families" exchanged large blocks of securities, creating a web of mutual interests that allowed a high degree of coordination.[187] Although lacking the central management through holding companies that had characterized their predecessors, the Keritsu still represented immense concentrations of economic power. Finally, the FTC showed a willingness to approve cartels to oversee the orderly retrenchment of overbuilt industries, programs often devised by other government bureaus. Such "rationalization" cartels became a regular feature of economic life in Japan.

The reorganization of Japanese business during the occupation did change things. The Antimonopoly Law established at least the principle of competition. Cartels remained the exception rather than the rule—left to their own devices, private companies in Japan often fought fiercely over markets. Few Japanese firms participated in international cartels, and the Keritsu were less monolithic than the Zaibatsu. Nevertheless, the accomplishments fell well short of the goals of the Edwards report. If deconcentration and decartelization in West Germany rated as a qualified success, then in Japan the program was a qualified failure.

Differences between Germany and Japan account for these outcomes. Japan had no equivalent to Ludwig Erhard and Jean Monnet, powerful politicians and officials who genuinely believed that antitrust, at least in its more moderate forms, was a good idea. This was in part because, economically, Germany and Japan existed in very different worlds. After the war, the nations of western Europe pursued a series of initiatives that reduced trade barriers among themselves, giving German firms access to a very large market. In this atmosphere, restrictions on trade through cartels seemed counterproductive. In contrast, after 1945 most Asian nations sharply limited trade with Japan, and because of the Cold War Japan had no ties at all with China, which before 1940 had been its chief commercial partner. Japan joined the General Agreement on Trade and Tariffs, the international forum for liberalizing trade, only in 1955, and even then some important members used "escape clauses" in the accord to deny Japanese goods the lowest tariffs.[188] The island nation had to regulate imports and coordinate exports to survive economically—it could not risk unrestrained competition.

6   The New Order in Practice: The Cases of Oil and Steel

In the early 1950s, as the western nations achieved a measure of prosperity and stability, cartel policy too achieved a certain equilibrium. On one hand, radical decartelization had failed in Germany and Japan, whereas on the other court decisions in the United States had struck serious blows against international cartels. Germany and the European Coal and Steel Community had adopted measures strictly limiting cartels. The result was a sort of implicit compromise in the international sphere roughly comparable to that which had existed in the United States since the Progressive Era. Although monopoly was suspect and cartels largely forbidden, big business was acceptable as long as competition persisted, even if it involved only a handful of firms. In practice, of course, some cartels did exist when the participants could cite special circumstances or command substantial political support. The histories of the oil industry and of the European Coal and Steel Community demonstrate both the limits and the possibilities of the new system.

Looking the Other Way: Petroleum

The petroleum industry was arguably the most important of the postwar era, supplying the industrial democracies with a vital commodity. The leading oil companies were among the largest firms on earth and had operations in almost every non-Communist country. Yet the conditions under which the industry operated differed greatly from place to place, and this inconsistency, coupled with the central role of petroleum in the world economy, led the United States and other governments to overlook practices that they would not have tolerated elsewhere.

Cartels had played an important role in the oil industry between the world wars. In the immediate aftermath of World War I, most experts had projected a petroleum shortage, and the leading firms had concentrated on finding new supplies. The situation had encouraged IG Farben to develop hydrogenation, which led to its accords with Standard Oil of New Jersey.[1] By the late 1920s, however, output was increasing throughout the world, most notably in Texas and Oklahoma, where drillers made huge new discoveries. The shortage became a glut, and in the United States the price of oil went from $1.88 a barrel in 1926 to $.65 in 1931.[2]

The oil companies did what firms in other industries confronting overcapacity were doing: they organized a cartel. In 1928 the heads of the three largest oil companies—Standard Oil of New Jersey, Royal Dutch/Shell, and Anglo-Iranian Oil (British Petroleum)—met in Scotland, where they negotiated an agreement. The document, known as the "As Is" accord, stated that the glut of petroleum required that "economies must be effected, waste must be eliminated, and expensive duplication of facilities curtailed." The central clause of the agreement, however, required "the acceptance by the units of their present volume of business and their proportion of any future increase in consumption," although in deference to American antitrust law it noted that this rule did not apply to "the domestic market in the U.S.A. and imports into the U.S."[3] As one critic later noted, "Oil is a major commodity in international trade, [and] could hardly be subject to such a far-reaching stabilization scheme without inevitably affecting the imports and exports of the United States."[4] Yet Washington's relatively permissive attitude toward international cartels in the 1920s and 1930s made this clause sufficient to protect the signatories from prosecution.

The "As Is" agreement was a statement of principles, the implementation of which proved more difficult than the signatories anticipated. They had hoped to stabilize prices by regulating output, but the growing flood of oil from Texas and Oklahoma proved impossible to control. In most countries with large petroleum reserves, the government retained the sub-soil rights and so could grant oil companies the ownership of petroleum under huge tracts of land, which allowed firms to control entire fields. In the United States, however, each property owner had rights to the mineral wealth under his or her land. Because large pools of oil usually extended under the property of many individuals, each of whom was free to pump as much as possible from the common pool, this system created chaos as everyone extracted petroleum as fast as possible before their neighbors did. In such circumstances, restricting output was nearly impossible for private companies, no matter how powerful. Standard of New Jersey did create a Webb-Pomerene company involving seventeen U.S. producers to coordinate sales abroad, but it never worked well. The members rarely agreed on a common policy, and even when they did, they accounted for only 45 percent of U.S. petroleum exports.[5] Yet the "right of capture," as the extraction system was called, did more than disrupt market-control schemes—it led to the premature exhaustion of oil fields. Drillers counted on underground pressure to bring petroleum to the surface; the greater the number of wells, the faster pressure dissipated. In the long, run a few wells, carefully spaced, would produce more oil than many drilled helter-skelter.

In the early 1930s, the major oil firms changed their tactics, turning to marketing agreements to regulate prices.[6] In each important market they devised accords including all the major sellers. A "Draft Memorandum of Principles," finalized in 1932, set forth general rules for agreements, fixing quotas in line with the "As Is" formula and creating a system of fines and rebates to enforce them. A central secretariat, headquartered in London, oversaw the negotiation and operation of these accords.[7] By this time, the "As Is" group had expanded to include such important firms as Gulf Oil, Texaco, and Standard Oil of New York (Socony or Mobile), in addition to the initial three.[8] When war broke out in 1939, marketing agreements covered most of the world outside the United States.

In some cases, companies developed provisions for even closer cooperation. Anglo-Iranian and Royal Dutch/Shell merged their marketing organizations in Britain as well as east of Suez.[9] When Standard Oil of California (Socal or Chevron) discovered oil in Bahrain in the Persian Gulf, members of the "As Is" group, fearful that the newly discovered crude would disrupt marketing arrangements in the Far East, besieged Socal with merger offers. In the end, Socal combined its Persian Gulf operations with Texaco's East Asian marketing organization, already part of the "As Is" framework. Socony and Standard of New Jersey also merged their East Asian operations. Although intended to limit competition, these mergers often had other objects as well. Both Shell and Texaco sold more oil east of Suez than they produced there, requiring them to bring in the balance from the outside. It made sense for them to cooperate with Anglo-Iranian and Socal, both of which pumped more oil in the region than they could easily sell.[10]

Cooperation among the large oil companies also extended to production in several important instances. The Iraq Petroleum Company, organized in 1928 after years of unspeakably complex negotiations between companies and governments, involved Standard of New Jersey, Royal Dutch/Shell, Anglo-Iranian, Socony, and Compagnie Françoise des Pétroles of France. The venture not only controlled production in Iraq but also bound its members to act in concert anywhere else in the old Ottoman Empire, an area defined to include the rich but heretofore undeveloped oil fields of Saudi Arabia. In Venezuela, Standard of New Jersey, Royal Dutch/Shell, and Gulf controlled almost all output. They had no overall agreement comparable to the Iraq Petroleum Company's, but they often cooperated, particularly where more than one had rights in the same oil field. United action, the history of Standard of New Jersey explained, made it "possible to apply the growing knowledge of the nature and mechanics of oil reservoirs and the new production engineering to reduce costs and ensuring more efficient production." These companies also jointly owned several pipelines.[11] Though arrangements like those in Iraq and Venezuela no doubt made it easier for the large companies to control the oil market, as long as the United States remained the chief source of crude, they had limited impact.

The success of the international oil cartel depended at least in part on the outcome of efforts in the United States to control output, work centered in the state of Texas. In 1931, when oil was fetching as little as $.02 a barrel at the wellhead in some fields, the Texas legislature authorized the state's Railroad Commission to regulate the output of oil fields in the state to conserve oil and stabilize prices, a practice dubbed "prorationing."[12] As was usually the case with cartels, execution proved more difficult than conception. The Railroad Commission had no control over output in other states, and producers in Texas tended to cheat, selling "hot" (over-quota) oil outside the state. Order came only after 1935, when Congress passed the Connally Act, banning the shipment across state lines of oil produced contrary to state regulations. At the same time, most of the producing states signed the Interstate Compact to Conserve Oil and Gas, which coordinated the activities of the Texas Railroad Commission with like bodies in other states. The arrangement was imperfect because California and Illinois refused to take part. Yet as the history of Standard of New Jersey noted, "In place of the wasteful, erratic, high-cost industry that had prevailed in the United States since the beginning of oil production in Pennsylvania, most oil states had achieved a more stable and efficient production which promised the ultimate recovery of a far larger percentage of the oil in each reservoir than had been possible in earlier times."[13] They had also stabilized oil prices in the vicinity of $1 a barrel.

Taken together, these measures restored order to world oil markets, relieving the gross oversupply of petroleum. Nevertheless, the power of the oil cartel remained far from absolute. Outsiders, usually but not always Americans with oil from the Southwest, regularly challenged the cartel throughout the world. For example, although Standard of New Jersey, Royal Dutch/ Shell, and Anglo-Iranian managed to stabilize their relative position in the British market (the world's largest after the United States), their combined share of sales fluctuated. The situation was not critical—Standard had 29 percent of the market in 1931 and still held 27 percent in 1938.[14] Yet Britain was among the best-organized markets. Elsewhere challengers caused more trouble.

Modern armies run on petroleum, and World War II not only absorbed all excess capacity but taxed producers to the utmost. The leading companies, all based in Allied countries, rose to the challenge, but officials in Washington nevertheless worried about long-term trends. The United States was drawing down old reserves faster than it was finding new ones. Unless the trend changed, the United States would in the foreseeable future become an importer of oil. Harold Ickes, the secretary of the interior, sought to provide against this. A veteran of Progressive Era reform who had led Interior since 1933, Ickes combined overweening self-righteousness with fierce ambition and great administrative talent. Unlike many New Dealers, he effectively made the transition from peace to war, taking responsibility for the Petroleum Administration, where he worked closely with oil executives— just the sort of people he had spent much of the 1930s denouncing.

Ickes fixed his attention on the vast oil fields of the Middle East, hoping to secure them for the United States. He first suggested that the federal government itself acquire part of the petroleum concession held by Socal and Texaco in Saudi Arabia, which had immense untapped reserves. In this Ickes was following the example of the British government, which owned a majority stake in Anglo-Iranian. Opposition from the oil companies, however, forced him to abandon the plan. They did not want competition from Washington and feared that the investment might be the first step toward nationalization. Another plan for the federal government to finance a key

Middle East pipeline for Socal and Texaco in exchange for a guaranteed supply of oil failed as well, for the same reason. The secretary concluded from these exasperating defeats that cooperation with oil companies was necessary for his plans.

Another wartime experience convinced Ickes that cooperation would be easier with the large firms than with the smaller ones. During the war he had found himself arrayed with the big oil companies in political campaigns in California and Illinois to get both states to adopt prorationing and join the Interstate Compact to Conserve Oil and Gas. The efforts failed, largely because of the opposition of small oil producers who opposed regulation of their business and fought under the banner of "free enterprise." In a public letter Ickes denounced the "vicious and mendacious campaign instigated [in California], and in the main carried on, by certain unscrupulous oil companies that were perfectly satisfied with a situation that permitted them to drain through their own ill-begotten wells oil that did not belong to them." He blamed the defeat of prorationing schemes on "men as selfish and un-scrupulous as have ever been found in the oil business, notwithstanding that they adorned themselves with the halo of 'small independent' producers."[15] The big international companies at least shared Ickes's goals, even if they often balked at his tactics.

Ickes also reached out to the British government. The United Kingdom considered the Middle East its sphere of influence and looked askance at U.S. plans to expand its presence there. London had blocked the develop-ment of a concession in Kuwait held by Gulf Oil (an American firm) until 1933, when Gulf agreed to take Anglo-Iranian as an equal partner in the venture, and throughout the war Whitehall competed with American dip-lomats for the favor of Ibn Saud, the king of Saudi Arabia. Britain's wartime dependence on U.S. aid made London somewhat responsive to American desires, but any grand scheme for Middle Eastern oil would have to take its concerns into account.[16]

In the summer of 1944, the United States and Britain negotiated a treaty to govern the future of the oil industry. The document declared, "The two governments agree that the development of petroleum resources for inter-national trade should be expanded in an orderly manner." To this end, "The two governments hereby agree to establish an International Petroleum Commission. . . . To prepare long-term estimates of world demand for pe-troleum. . . . To suggest the manner in which, over the long term, this estimated demand may best be satisfied by production equitably distributed among the various producing countries . . . [and] to recommend to both governments broad policies for adoption by operating companies."[17] The delighted Ickes, who had played a leading role in the talks, wrote to President Roosevelt, "If it [the agreement] succeeds it will have pointed a new and better road in international economic relationships, and will have established a most valuable pattern."[18]

The two sides disagreed on the exact nature of the accord. Lord Beaverbrook, who had led the British delegation, described it as a "monster cartel." The Americans denied his assertion, claiming, "The Petroleum Agreement under discussion has been formulated on a basis altogether different from anything associated with the expression 'cartel.' . . . This was an intergovernmental commodity agreement predicated upon certain broad principles of orderly development and sound engineering practices."[19] American officials may have deceived themselves, but they convinced few others—"orderly development" and "commodity agreement" were well-worn euphemisms for cartels.

In the United States, the Petroleum Agreement created a political furor. Despite the attempts at camouflage, it obviously created an organization to allocate markets—in short an international cartel—something regularly denounced by leading officials including Ickes himself. Most of the backers of the oil accord came from the national security and mobilization establishments and simply did not understand how touchy the issue was.[20] A thoroughly political creature, Ickes should have known better, but he allowed his enthusiasm for the agreement and his sense of his own integrity to distract him from how the public might perceive the treaty.

Objections came from both right and left. The prospect of a state-sponsored cartel involving the leading oil companies horrified most reformers, whereas the intervention of the government in one of the country's largest industries appalled conservatives. One liberal journalist reported, "Informed Washington sources see [in] the International Oil Agreement, just concluded here, the first wedge of an attack designed to break down the Justice Department's power to attack international cartels through the Sherman Act." Noting that "the State Department did not clear the international agreement with the Department of Justice," he continued, "if such a cartel agreement receives Senate approval, the way might well be opened to the chemical, rubber, steel, tanning material and other industrial colossi to dominate markets, kite prices, cut down production and otherwise exercise extreme monopoly control as they did before the war."[21] Although *The Nation* reserved judgment and expressed hope that the agreement would encourage greater production at lower prices, it pointed out that the accord "can also be read as providing a government front for the Anglo-American [petroleum] cartel whose representatives took part in the discussions leading to its adoption."[22]

The oil industry itself provided the most formidable opposition. Howard Pew, one of the nation's leading independent oil men, said of the Petroleum Agreement, "This is a deliberate attempt to place the American petroleum industry under the bureaucratic control of the Federal Government. . . . The effectuation of its objectives can be achieved only through embroiling our domestic petroleum industry in a vicious cartel system." Pew repeated the sentiment common among businessmen: "Cartels under the aegis of government are *far more reprehensible* and *detrimental* to the public welfare than cartels entered into by individual companies," because the government had greater power to enforce its will than private entities. The oil man ended by asking, "What is the difference between an economic system where the government dominates an industry, such as is comprehended in this agreement, and the Nazi system of National Socialism against which we are fighting in a war in Germany?"[23] Pew undoubted reflected the views of most independent producers, who feared that the agreement would subordinate them either to the federal government, to the big oil companies, or to both.

The large international firms—Standard of New Jersey, Socony, Gulf, Texaco, and Socal—were more confident of their ability to bargain with governments on a basis of equality and so were less suspicious of the oil accord. Yet neither were they wildly enthusiastic. The agreement subjected them to a measure of regulation but, by way of compensation, created a government-sanctioned cartel that would reinforce what they had constructed under the "As Is" system. Still, the large firms were concerned that the accord did not explicitly exempt companies following the dictates of the International Petroleum Commission from the antitrust laws and feared that, unless it did, the Justice Department could indict them for executing its orders. This concern was not academic. In the late 1930s, the Justice Department had sued the industry for measures designed to stabilize prices, measures that oil men believed Ickes himself had endorsed.[24] Washington, however, hesitated to include such a provision in the accord because doing so would effectively concede that it did indeed create a cartel. The omission, however, led the primary international firms to remain neutral on the agreement. Yet even had the large companies intervened, they had less political influence in the United States than the far more numerous independent producers.

In January 1945, realizing that Senate approval was impossible, the administration withdrew the Petroleum Agreement from consideration. Despite attempts by Ickes in 1945 and 1946 to revive it, the accord was dead. Many factors accounted for its failure, but the most important was the fiercely independent attitude of southwestern oil men. Although willing to follow the dictates of the Texas Railroad Commission, over which they had substantial influence, they refused to accept outside control, and they had considerable political resources.

Yet American hostility to international cartels did not, in the end, affect the oil industry much. Changes in the business in the aftermath of World War II forced the petroleum cartel to reorganize itself, but Washington acquiesced to and even condoned these measures. It apparently accepted Ickes's belief that oil was too important to leave to the free market.

The end of the war found the oil industry in a strong position. The demand for petroleum was robust and seemed certain to grow. Oil supplies were plentiful, but the glut of the prewar era had disappeared. Output was under control. Production in Venezuela, Iran, Iraq, and Indonesia remained in the care of the major oil companies, whereas the Texas Railroad Commission and its sisters in other states regulated American output. The war had disrupted the "As Is" framework, but the machinery of cooperation continued to operate in many individual markets.

The only serious threat to the industry's prosperity came from the Arabian peninsula. There a joint venture between Anglo-Iranian and Gulf was developing substantial new oil fields in Kuwait while Texaco and Socal were opening up even larger sources of supply in Saudi Arabia. These operations would soon dump huge amounts of petroleum on world markets. The firms producing in Kuwait and Saudi Arabia had belonged to the "As Is" cartel, but if they wanted to dispose of their new crude they would have to challenge the existing division of markets.

By acting in concert, the leading oil companies neutralized this threat, absorbing Kuwaiti and Saudi output without disrupting world markets. Standard of New Jersey and Socony bought their way into the Saudi Arabian concession, known as the Arab-American Oil Company (Aramco), purchasing 30 percent and 10 percent of it, respectively.[25] The two companies then disposed of much of the Saudi crude through their extensive marketing organizations, at the same time using their authority within Aramco to make sure that it charged the same prices for oil as other producers.[26] Another device, long-term supply contracts, guaranteed that Kuwaiti crude did not upset petroleum markets. In 1946, Standard of New Jersey agreed to purchase 110,000 barrels of oil a day for the next twenty years from Anglo-Iranian's Kuwaiti operations; Royal Dutch/Shell signed a twenty-two year accord with Gulf for 150,000 barrels per day from Kuwait.[27] These contracts diverted much of the emirate's output into existing marketing channels. Socal, Texaco, Gulf, and Anglo-Iranian acquiesced to these arrangements because the cost of building their own marketing facilities and challenging Standard, Royal Dutch/Shell, and Socony would have been prohibitive. The development of the new oil fields in Arabia, an area with almost nothing in the way of modern infrastructure, had already absorbed a lot of capital and continued to demand heavy investment. Cooperation offered the most secure road to profit.

These arrangements resurrected the international oil cartel, albeit in a new guise. Instead of using its hold on marketing to regulate prices, as had been the case before 1939, the cartel now relied on its control of production. In 1952, the Federal Trade Commission estimated that just seven companies—the famous "seven sisters": Anglo-Iranian, Royal Dutch/Shell, Standard of New Jersey, Socony, Gulf, Texaco, and Socal—controlled 88 percent of the oil reserves outside the United States and the Soviet Union. As the FTC noted, "Each of these companies has pyramids of subsidiary and affiliated companies in which ownership is shared with one or more of the other large companies. Such a maze of joint ownership obviously provides opportunity, and even necessity, for joint action." These arrangements brought "the seven international oil companies, controlling practically all the Middle East oil resources, together in a mutual community of interests."[28] Texas remained a major source of petroleum, but production there was under the control of the Railroad Commission, which had as strong an interest in stable prices as the international companies. Besides, the United States increasingly consumed its oil at home. Moreover, production costs in the Middle East were lower than in the American Southwest, giving the seven sisters a great advantage over U.S.-based rivals in international markets.

From a legal point of view, these arrangements had a great advantage over the "As Is" system. Whereas the latter involved explicit market-sharing agreements, the new order operated more subtly. It provided for constant consultation. If Texaco wanted to take more oil out of Saudi Arabia, it needed the approval of its Aramco partners, which in turn had to consider the impact of such a decision on their operations in Iraq, Venezuela, and elsewhere, where they had other partners with which they had to consult. No major change could occur without the approval of all the seven sisters. Yet there was no central accord or secretariat, as had existed in the "As Is" system, to offer an easy target for antitrust prosecution.

Nevertheless, in 1952, the Justice Department decided to challenge the petroleum cartel. The Antitrust Division had learned of the "As Is" agreements during its 1942 investigation of the ties between Standard Oil and IG Farben, and as part of the consent agreement terminating those arrangements Standard had promised to leave the "As Is." After the war, the division had briefly considered prosecuting the major oil companies, but it abandoned the plan because the assistant attorney general, Graham Morrison, considered the evidence inconclusive and believed that, as a regulated industry, petroleum had a special status.[29] Instead, the initiative came from the Federal Trade Commission, which as part of its study of international cartels prepared an extensive report on the operations of the oil industry.[30] The document appeared in 1952, and although the government had initially classified it to keep it confidential, Congress soon forced the Truman administration to publish the report. The Justice Department promptly concluded that the FTC had provided ample grounds for an antitrust suit.[31] The links among the seven sisters obviously limited competition, and American courts had proved willing in the *Timken* and *ICI* cases to break up cooperative ventures abroad.[32] The Antitrust Division planned a criminal suit against all seven major international oil companies.

This prospect horrified the national security establishment. As a joint report by the State and Defense Departments noted, "American and British oil companies . . . play a vital role in supplying one of the free world's most essential commodities. The maintenance of, and avoiding harmful interference with, an activity so crucial to the well-being and security of the United States and the rest of the free world must be a major objective of United States government policy." The State and Defense Departments were particularly concerned by the Justice Department's desire to pursue the case in the criminal courts rather than the civil ones. This would, they believed, create an aura of guilt that "harms the prestige of the [oil] companies in other countries, and can very well lead to an adverse effect upon the interests of the United States."[33]

These concerns were not speculative. The British and Dutch governments were furious about the impending actions against their companies.

London, which owned 51 percent of Anglo-Iranian, sharply limited the information that the firm could provide U.S. courts; the Dutch banned Royal Dutch from providing any documents at all.[34] The chief threat, however, involved the oil-producing countries. Many were politically unstable, with populations that resented the power that the large oil companies wielded in their nations. Iranians had vented these passions in 1951, when a nationalist regime had seized the country's oil fields, heretofore the property of Anglo-Iranian.[35] The British firm had responded by removing its personnel from Iran, which crippled production, and by organizing a boycott against Iranian crude. The other major firms went along with the boycott; they had enough oil on hand to meet demand, did not want to encourage nationalization, and knew that Anglo-Iranian would to sue anyone who bought oil from Iran for receiving stolen property.[36] By 1952, Iran was in economic chaos, with its central industry, petroleum, at a standstill. The U.S. government was trying to mediate a solution to the crisis and sought to avoid exacerbating tensions or encouraging similar events elsewhere.

Such considerations did not sway the Justice Department. It argued: "The Supreme Court had repeatedly rejected proof of public benefit and business necessity as justification for cartel operations and has emphasized the primacy of economic freedom as the highest value for our economy. . . . Our concern for an adequate future supply of petroleum is a concern ultimately for the preservation of freedom for ourselves and the free world. Free private enterprise can be preserved only by safeguarding it from excess of power, governmental and private. . . . The world petroleum cartel is authoritarian, dominating power over a great and vital world industry, in private hands. National security considerations dictate that the most expeditious method be employed to uncover the cartel's acts and effects and put an end to them."[37]

President Truman knew what he had to do. Although no friend of the oil companies—he had chaired the 1942 hearings that had pilloried Standard of New Jersey for its ties with IG Farben—he had to consider the precarious international situation. The nation was at war in Korea, an oil dispute had thrown Iran into confusion, and the Cold War was even more tense than usual. The secretaries of state and defense, as well as the joint chiefs of staff, all vigorously opposed prosecuting the petroleum cartel.[38] Washington could not afford the risks involved in restructuring the world oil industry. In January 1953, just before leaving the White House, Truman ordered the Antitrust Division to suspend the criminal investigation of the seven sisters.

The Justice Department did file a civil suit against the five American members of the cartel in the spring of 1953. Yet within two years, the administration of President Dwight D. Eisenhower had effectively neutralized the prosecution. In 1953, the Central Intelligence Agency engineered a coup in Iran that returned the pro-American Shah to power. The new regime needed oil revenue to survive. The economy remained severely depressed and only the renewed flow of crude could revive it. Unfortunately, Anglo-Iranian remained wildly unpopular in Iran; no government intent on survival could make a deal with the British firm, even on the best of terms. Washington concluded that only a consortium of leading producers, with their extensive marketing networks, could move Iranian oil fast enough to restore economic and political stability while avoiding a political backlash.

The prospect did not excite the American firms. As one of Standard of New Jersey's executives said, "We had a concession [Aramco] that was able to supply all of these requirements [for oil], and we knew when we went into the [Iranian] consortium that as a business deal, a straight business deal, it was for the birds. . . . We had to spend money for capacity and reserves we already had. . . . The point was that we went in there . . . to save the situation, and it was in the interests of the United States and Britain at the time."[39] The Justice Department's suit against the leading American oil companies for participating in similar ventures elsewhere also discouraged them from joining the Iranian syndicate. To get the U.S. firms to agree, President Eisenhower ordered the Justice Department to drop those parts of its case dealing with production agreements in the Middle East.[40] The American companies subsequently joined the Iranian consortium, which quickly restored production and, for the time being, stabilized Iran.[41]

Eisenhower's decision effectively crippled the oil case, but the Justice Department kept it alive for fourteen years. Although the government forced several companies to sign consent decrees that prohibited market-sharing accords, as a Justice Department official put it, "The decrees provided expressly that the companies are not prohibited . . . from participating in joint production operations, joint refining operations, joint pipeline operations or joint storage operations in foreign nations."[42] Such agreements dismantled some of the cartel accords that had survived from the 1930s, but they did not affect production arrangements, which were the nexus of the cartel's power. In 1968, Justice finally bowed to reality and suspended the prosecution.

The international oil cartel worked well. A Socony official spoke the truth when he said in the 1970s, "The performance in the post World War II era by the international petroleum industry of its function of meeting the Free World's petroleum needs with abundant supplies at stable and moderate prices must be judged excellent by any reasonable standard."[43] It was the collapse of this regime in the late 1960s and early 1970s, the victim of exploding demand and militant governments in producing countries, that sparked the oil shocks and the energy crisis. Few lamented the passing of the oil cartel, but none of the mechanisms subsequently devised to govern the industry have worked as well.

The history of the oil industry after 1945 demonstrates the complexity of the cartel issue. The production arrangements among the seven sisters probably did violate the antitrust laws, at least as interpreted by the American courts in the 1940s and 1950s. Yet it is hard to blame the Truman and Eisenhower administrations for ignoring these violations. The joint concessions in the Middle East and elsewhere that upset the sensibilities of trustbusters reflected political realities. Those in Iraq, Kuwait, and Iran emerged from tortuous international negotiations, and all the concessions reflected careful attempts to balance the interests of companies and producing nations. The Justice Department had nothing with which to replace these arrangements. Most of the oil pumped in Venezuela, Iran, Iraq, Kuwait, and Saudi Arabia went not to the United States but to Europe and Japan. Washington had no moral right to reorganize this trade without reference to the desires of all these nations. In addition to political questions, the scale of the tasks confronting oil companies operating in Third World countries often justified cooperation. These nations usually had very little in the way of modern infrastructure. The seven sisters not only had to drill wells and build pipelines, expensive operations in and of themselves, but had to construct ports, roads, and towns and to train the workforce. Cooperation allowed companies to spread these huge costs among themselves, making manageable tasks that might daunt a single firm. Nor did the United States itself tolerate a free market in oil. The Texas Railroad Commission and bodies like it regulated U.S. output with the sanction of the federal government, and Washington could not in good conscience enforce abroad something it did not accept at home.

Harold Ickes's Anglo-American Petroleum Agreement might have offered a way around these issues. It could have provided a framework for useful cooperation among firms while providing for government oversight to prevent abuses. Yet the American government's vocal stance against cartels, coupled with the popular prejudice against these organizations and the general distrust between government and business, precluded this option. Without such an organization, Washington either had to acquiesce to whatever arrangements the companies made or had to tear these apart and hope that the pieces fell into an acceptable pattern. Considering the importance of the oil industry, it is no surprise that the American government chose the first option.

Antitrust Abroad: Coal and Steel

Whereas the history of the oil industry demonstrated the limits of antitrust abroad, that of the European Coal and Steel Community suggested the possibilities. Before the war, cartels led by European producers had dominated world trade in steel. After the war, the industry, the largest in the developed countries, abandoned cartels. The change owed chiefly to the activities of the European Coal and Steel Community, which enjoyed strong support from Washington. The leader of the ECSC, Jean Monnet, believed that cartels had retarded the growth of Europe's steel industry and that progress required their elimination.

In dismantling cartels, Monnet and the ECSC had a difficult task. As one U.S. official noted, "The men who are responsible for the administration of the steel companies in these six countries [the ECSC] still have a low order of enthusiasm for competition, and are privately doing what they can to maintain cartel practices."[44] By the early 1950s, European steel producers had organized a cartel governing exports to non-ECSC countries, although this agreement only set prices, eschewing the sort of complex marketing controls developed during the 1930s. According to U.S. officials, "The High Authority [of the ECSC] does not like the cartel and in its public announcements has not hidden its disapproval. However, it can . . . take steps against the agreement only when this becomes justified under provisions of the [ECSC] treaty," which did not cover exports.[45] Yet U.S. officials feared that "export controls, thus operated, necessarily establish a high degree of control over domestic prices, without there being any overt acts of agreement."[46]

Nor was the export cartel the only problem. Under the ECSC, many German steel firms regained control of coal mines that they had lost during the Allied reorganization. More worrisome, the German coal cartel still operated. As American officials noted, "The continued existence of a centralized sales organization for Ruhr coal [the DKLB] is wholly inconsistent with the objectives of both the deconcentration program . . . and the basic concept of the Schuman plan [the ECSC]."[47] Addressing these objections, the Germans abolished the DKLB in 1953, replacing it with six sales organizations. Nevertheless, a central agency, the Gemeinschaftsorganisation, or Georg for short, continued to coordinate the activities of the six marketers. The new organization seemed only a little less powerful than the DKLB, and most U.S. officials believed that it ran counter to the ECSC agreement.[48] Finally, the ECSC allowed many of the steel companies created by the Allies in Germany to merge, permitting the resurrection of such venerable firms as Krupp and Thyssen. Considering the eagerness of the High Authority to maximize the considerable economies of scale inherent in steel production, this outcome was implicit in the ECSC accord. Nevertheless, the High Authority did not allow Germany's huge United Steelworks (Vereinigte Stahlwerke) to reappear. Thyssen, the largest firm in Europe, controlled only about 10 percent of the ECSC market, far less than U.S. Steel did in America.[49] In this area, at least, limits did exist.

Despite concerns, Washington strongly supported the Coal and Steel Community. As one State Department memo noted, "The H[igh] A[uthority of the ECSC] is the only agency in Europe armed with effective anti-cartel legislation."[50] "It was not expected," another source explained, "that the establishment of the [E]CSC would quickly lead to the abolition of all such arrangements [cartels] in view of the complexity of the problem; the long history of such arrangements in Europe; the limits on the High Authority's powers for dealing with restrictive arrangements outside the community; the pioneering character in Europe of the High Authority's efforts; and the long and careful preparation required in undertaking antitrust action."[51]

The U.S. contribution mainly involved taking, as one memo noted, "every opportunity to encourage the High Authority to use its powers firmly and expeditiously to develop a competitive common market for coal and steel."[52] Americans nagged the leaders of the High Authority incessantly about cartels.[53] Washington also conditioned a $100 million loan to the ECSC to finance industrial modernization on the money being used "in a manner consistent with the operations of a common market free from national barriers and private obstruction to competition."[54]

By the mid-1950s, the ECSC had scored important victories. It had persuaded the German government to break Georg into three separate organizations—perhaps not an ideal solution, but one that at least upheld the principle of competition and the High Authority's power.[55] It had also forced several smaller cartel organizations to disband or substantially reorganize themselves.[56] On the whole, Washington "concluded that the Coal and Steel Community is exercising the maximum influence practicable against restrictive practices in the light of the circumstances and the difficulties which confront it."[57]

What differentiated the oil industry from coal and steel? In the United States, the rule of capture distorted oil drilling so thoroughly as to justify regulation, but the laws of Third World petroleum producers operated differently, allowing companies to control entire fields and so avoid the problems they encountered in the United States. The key difference seems to have lain in the political realm. The governments of western Europe were stable democracies committed to open trade. Political risk was minimal. In contrast, the governments of most Third World oil producers were unstable autocracies in which the petroleum companies had to worry constantly about the security of their investments. The profits were large, but as Anglo-Iranian discovered in 1951, they were not secure. Even with a cartel, the risks of operating were quite high.

American attitudes toward the ECSC reflected a new approach to the cartel issue. During the late 1940s and the 1950s, the United States sought to underwrite democracy abroad with prosperity. The program had many facets—economic aid, reduction of trade barriers, currency stabilization— one of which was the elimination of cartels. Most U.S. officials believed that these organizations imposed rigidities that limited efficiency and thereby depressed living standards, and they urged other nations to emulate U.S. antitrust laws and ban cartels. Washington even included restrictions on international cartels among the few conditions it attached to Marshall Plan aid.[58] Antitrust constituted an important part of what historian Charles Maier has dubbed "the gospel of productivity," which conditioned U.S. economic policy in Europe.[59]

Three factors encouraged other governments to heed Washington's advice. First, American aid gave the United States a lot of leverage. At the same time this aid, particularly the Marshall Plan, convinced most of America's good intentions. Faced with generous infusions of money, recipients concluded that Washington was genuinely concerned about their economic well-being and that recommendations to limit or ban cartels were not subtle ploys to improve the competitive position of U.S. firms but well-meant advice. Finally, the U.S. economy was at this time undoubtedly the world's strongest, which inclined other nations to imitate its practices.

American officials believed that prosperity would further weaken cartels. One noted, "The only long range solution [to the cartel problem] will be found in healthy conditions of free and expanding economies."[60] This would create a sort of virtuous cycle, with prosperity weakening cartels and the decline of cartels reinforcing prosperity. Up to a point, events actually developed in this way. As the European economy improved and exports increased, continental steel makers were able to import cheap American coal; inexpensive oil from the Middle East replaced coal for other uses. The Ruhr's place in the European economy sharply declined, and by the 1960s coal was a "sick" industry, dependent in many cases on government subsidies. Although bad for coal miners, access to cheap sources of energy was a major factor in Europe's postwar prosperity. Of course, the international oil cartel provided much of this inexpensive fuel, but its success owed to effective competition against coal producers.

The combination of U.S. encouragement and the dazzling example of American prosperity led government after government to restrict cartels. In a 1965 survey, Corwin Edwards noted that in the previous twenty years, Sweden, Argentina, Britain, Denmark, Austria, France, Ireland, Norway, South Africa, the Netherlands, Finland, New Zealand, Israel, Colombia, Belgium, Brazil, Spain, Switzerland, and Australia had enacted measures directed against cartels. For the most part, these did not ban cartels outright but attacked perceived abuses: price fixing, market allocation, and the like. Nevertheless, they significantly impaired cartel operations.[61] For instance, Britain enacted a measure in 1956 that, although not categorically banning cartels, did force most of them to disband.[62] Perhaps most important of all, the 1957 agreement creating the European Community extended the ECSC's restrictions on cartels in the coal and steel industries to all of western Europe's businesses. In the 1981 update of his 1958 study, *Antitrust and American Business Abroad*, Kingman Brewster wrote, "America no longer has a monopoly on antitrust. Virtually all developed countries and many developing ones now have competition laws of their own, and many of these laws are being enforced with increasing diligence and sophistication."[63]

Americans played supporting rather than leading roles in these events. Governments abroad adopted and implemented suggestions from Washington as they saw fit. Nevertheless, the U.S. contribution was critical. Its efforts to restrict international cartels helped raise the issue in the first place. Before 1940, cartels were deeply entrenched in almost every industrial country. Without American encouragement and example, officials abroad probably would not even have thought to restrict cartels, and business, left to its own devices, no doubt would have continued to rely on them.

Conclusions

American antitrust policy abroad, despite its inconsistencies, developed within a broad economic and political context that gave it a certain coherence and that explains both its successes and failures. At the same time, the evolution of antitrust policy shaped this context, reinforcing certain tendencies and retarding others.

Washington's drive against international cartels coincided with the transformation of the United States from an inward-looking nation into the world's leading power. In the 1930s, most Americans sought to isolate themselves from troubles abroad. The Roosevelt administration's much-heralded "good neighbor" policy eschewed direct intervention in Latin America—long a staple of U.S. foreign policy—while the country prepared to grant independence to the Philippines, its chief possession in Asia. Washington had largely abandoned efforts to revive the international economy. Most important, Americans staunchly opposed involvement in the brewing war in Europe. The next twenty years saw an extraordinary change. By the 1950s, the United States was deeply involved in the affairs of Europe, East Asia, Latin America, and the Middle East, and it was maintaining huge military, diplomatic, and intelligence establishments to carry out its foreign policy. World War II and the Cold War explained the new state of affairs. The former taught Americans that events abroad could significantly affect them and even threaten the existence of the republic. The latter convinced them that the world remained a dangerous place in spite of the defeat of the Axis powers.

Cartel policy roughly mirrored these developments. In the 1930s, Americans showed little interest in how other countries managed their economic affairs. Although most disapproved of cartels at home (at least in principle), foreign cartels were not their problem. But the world war convinced many Americans that economic developments abroad could affect them. In particular, a substantial group that included many government officials saw the collapse of the world economy in the early 1930s, the Great Depression, as the key event propelling the Nazis to power in Germany and the militarists to office in Japan and, therefore, as the chief cause of the war. They blamed the Depression, in large part, on the industrial countries' ill-considered trade and monetary policies and advocated the reduction of trade barriers and the stabilization of currencies—liberalization—as the best way to avoid repeating these disasters. By the end of the war, Washington had formally embraced this program. As the United States assumed responsibility for the world economy, however, it encountered an uncomfortable contradiction. American law banned cartels, whereas most other countries allowed and even encouraged them. Still, a collision was not inevitable. In the midst of wars, both hot and cold, the subject might well have escaped notice. International cartels had proved adept at managing relations with American producers in the past, and left to their own devices they might well have continued to do so.

Thurman Arnold and his followers made the difference. With a few important exceptions, antitrust did not form a central part of the New Deal until the late 1930s. Even then interest did not guarantee action, as the history of the Temporary National Economic Committee demonstrated. But Arnold, after taking over the Antitrust Division of the Justice Department in 1938, expanded and energized it, giving the bureau a clear mission: to defend and encourage competition. Aggressive prosecutions forced business to pay attention. For perhaps the first time in U.S. history, the effort devoted to enforcing the antitrust laws matched the rhetorical and ideological importance attached to them. Despite some setbacks, these changes endured into the postwar era.

The outbreak of war in Europe in 1939 turned the attention of Arnold and his staff abroad. The crisis itself generated interest in foreign affairs, but self-interest played a part as well. The growing threat of war led the United States to mobilize, which created pressure for a relaxation of antitrust prosecutions. Suits distracted corporate executives from the vital task of filling military contracts, and just as important they irritated businessmen, whose

cooperation Washington needed. In response to these pressures, Arnold
latched onto international cartels, using them to relate the activities of his
bureau to mobilization. He argued that cartels, which often had ties to German companies, restricted American output and that by attacking them, the
Antitrust Division contributed to military readiness. The existence of these
organizations also demonstrated that the business community was not entirely trustworthy, casting doubt on the government's rapprochement with
industry, of which Arnold disapproved. Between 1940 and 1942, Thurman
Arnold and his lieutenants relentlessly pursued international cartels, not only
investigating and prosecuting them but also conducting a public-relations
campaign against them. The result was a series of exposés that culminated
in the spectacular allegations, aired in 1942, that an international cartel
involving Standard Oil had blocked the development in the United States
of desperately needed synthetic rubber. Although in this instance Arnold's
charges were dubious, the case defined the cartel issue for the rest of the
war, casting these organizations in a sinister light.

Despite this success, the drive against cartels stalled during the war. President Roosevelt sought the cooperation of business for mobilization, and in
accordance with this policy he gave the military power to delay antitrust
cases for the duration, which it did. When Arnold refused to go along with
this policy, FDR removed him from office.

The setback proved temporary. Arnold's staff remained intact and devoted
to the cause, and in 1944, President Roosevelt made it clear that antitrust
prosecutions would resume with peace. The Antitrust Division prepared a
brace of suits against international cartels that it would take up when the
war ended. At the same time, the American government incorporated antitrust into its broad drive to liberalize world trade. Arnold's publicity campaign had made it impossible to ignore these organizations, and most officials, although not necessarily accepting Arnold's most lurid charges, agreed
that cartels did indeed restrict commerce. In 1943, the State Department
organized the Cartel Committee to examine the subject and make recommendations. This body drew members from other agencies both to avail
itself of their expertise and to secure their support for its plans. Two of these
transplants, Edward Mason of the OSS and Corwin Edwards of the Antitrust
Division, dominated the committee, which recommended a hard line
against cartels that State adopted as its own. Meanwhile, plans for the occupation of Germany and Japan entailed restrictions on cartels and on big
business in general. The *Standard Oil* case had painted cartels as instru-

ments of economic aggression, and Washington was determined to deprive the former Axis powers of such tools. More important, many Americans considered cartels and big business in both Germany and Japan as part of an authoritarian economic system that bred political dictatorship.

These initiatives yielded mixed results. The attempt to negotiated restrictions on cartels with other countries failed. The 1948 charter of the International Trade Organization contained such provisions, but Congress refused to ratify it, largely for reasons unrelated to cartels. The General Agreement on Trade and Tariffs, which subsequently became the vehicle for liberalization, did not address the subject. But the judicial offensive triumphed. By 1945, Roosevelt appointees inclined to apply the antitrust laws strictly dominated the bench. After the defeat of Germany and Japan, antitrust prosecutions resumed, and the Justice Department won a string of critical decisions against international cartels. The federal courts overturned earlier precedents that had allowed U.S. companies to participate in restrictive patent agreements, to negotiate agreements with foreign cartels through Webb-Pomerene companies, and to work with rivals abroad through jointly owned subsidiaries, thereby closing the chief "back doors" through which American firms had cooperated with foreign cartels. Even before 1940, the U.S. economy had been the world's largest, and the devastation of East Asia and Europe during the war magnified its supremacy. In most industries, it was extremely difficult to organize an effective international cartel without the participation of American firms. Moreover, the courts applied restrictions on international cartels to all foreign firms operating in the United States, no matter how small their presence, creating further problems for these organizations. Unable to negotiate with American firms and liable to prosecution if their members had any U.S. presence, most international cartels shut down.

In Germany and Japan, reformers scored important victories, even though they fell short of their most ambitious goals. Occupation authorities in both countries disbanded most cartels and broke up some of the largest companies. Yet the same reformers who led the drive against cartels also devised measures to liquidate Germany's and Japan's biggest firms en masse. Not only did they blame German and Japanese business for those countries' aggression but they were deeply suspicious of big business in general, and at least some hoped that radical deconcentration abroad might set precedents at home. These initiatives encountered sharp opposition not only from the Germans and Japanese, who feared that dismantling so many firms would permanently weaken their economies, but also from many Americans who recognized that this program went beyond anything ever done in the United States. Washington's decision in 1948 to concentrate occupation policy on reviving German and Japanese industry put an end to radical deconcentration.

By the 1950s, the American government was encouraging other countries to enact antitrust laws. Officials in the United States argued that such legislation promoted competition and, thereby, efficiency. This initiative enjoyed considerable success in Europe, in part because of Washington's pressure and in part because American prosperity encouraged other nations to emulate its practices. Yet success was not universal. In Japan, the government backed away from the antitrust measures imposed by the occupation. The petroleum industry recreated its prewar cartel with Washington's acquiescence.

A relatively small group of people initiated these reforms. Although the large majority of Americans agreed that cartels were bad (at least in principle), few demonstrated much interest in doing anything about them. The lack of interest reflected the number of issues competing for attention. The progress of World War II and, after 1945, deteriorating relations with the Soviet Union took precedence over cartels. On the domestic side, securing full employment and deciding the future of New Deal programs dominated the agenda. Moreover, antitrust was losing its ability to excite the body politic. It had always drawn its strength from hostility to big business, which was waning in the 1940s. The impressive performance of large companies during the war did much to rehabilitate their reputation. Even on the left, attention focused not so much on breaking up big firms as on strengthening "countervailing" forces like organized labor. As historian Richard Hofstadter wrote, after 1945, antitrust became "one of the faded passions of American reformers."[1] This is not to say that Americans became indifferent to the antitrust laws. Most considered them useful regulations, like the food safely statutes. Yet few based their political philosophy on antitrust.

Top officials intervened only sporadically in the cartel issue. President Roosevelt seems to have paid attention only in 1944, when the DuPont/ICI case required a decision and when he thought that attacking cartels might help his reelection campaign. President Truman's only major initiative set into motion the Ferguson Committee investigation, which led nowhere. Dean Acheson neglected the subject even when he was chairman of the Cartel Committee. The export of antitrust was chiefly the work of middle-level officials operating on their own because responsibilities elsewhere occupied their superiors.

The anticartel program had a narrow bureaucratic base. Enthusiasm centered in the Antitrust Division of the Justice Department, which managed prosecutions, publicized the issue, and provided much of the staff for the decartelization agencies in occupied Germany and Japan. The career of the peripatetic Corwin Edwards demonstrates the reach of its personnel. He not only worked for the Antitrust Division for several years but also did much of the research for a Senate investigation of cartels, served with distinction on the State Department's Cartel Committee, and led the group that drafted Japan's deconcentration program. Outsiders did make contributions. Edward Mason of the OSS led the Cartel Committee effectively, and Senator Joseph O'Mahoney of Wyoming doggedly championed the cause in the upper house of Congress. Still, the number of government officials who devoted a major part of their time to the cartel issue probably numbered no more than a few hundred.

Politically, most of these men stood well to the left of center. They often drew political inspiration from Louis Brandeis and were on the whole deeply skeptical of big business. Large firms, many of them believed, were not only economically pernicious but a threat to political democracy. An unsigned memo, drafted in the Antitrust Division in 1942 and outlining a projected reorganization of business throughout the world, illuminates the scale of their ambitions: "Selling must largely be divorced from manufacture; manufacturing firms must become more narrowly specialized; needless industrial combination, whether vertical or horizontal, must be avoided; and the maximum permitted size in corporate units must approximate the minimum size required requisite to efficient, specialized production. Information about products (advertising) should be provided mainly by disinterested agencies, governmental and private."[2] Not everyone active against cartels would have embraced such a radical program, but many would have.

How did this relatively small group to the left of the political mainstream accomplish so much? First, they controlled the levers of power. The Antitrust Division of the Justice Department had the authority to file antitrust suits, which the judiciary, populated with Roosevelt appointees, was inclined to view sympathetically. Likewise, these people dominated the Cartel Committee and the deconcentration bureaus in occupied Germany and Japan. Moreover, the foes of cartels could count on public support, at least up to a point. Most Americans implicitly embraced the antitrust tradition—large companies were acceptable as long as they were efficient and stopped short of monopoly. Cartels fell outside this consensus, and even American businessmen who participated in them rarely defended the practice per se, arguing instead that some sort of exceptional circumstances justified their actions. Although antitrust was no longer a leading political issue, those enforcing it could still count on a substantial reservoir of public good will.

Yet the antitrust tradition could restrain as well as promote reform. Plans for the wholesale deconcentration of industry in Germany and Japan went well beyond anything ever done in the United States, falling outside the implicit compromise that had governed antitrust since the Progressive Era. These measures initially enjoyed some success because few Americans cared what happened to German and Japanese business. Reformers had the field to themselves. Once the Cold War had put these two countries back on the top of the nation's agenda, however, deconcentration foundered. Officials in Washington and, apparently, the public at large considered it too radical. Ultimately, preferences developed at home defined American antitrust policy abroad.

Why did so many other countries go along with the American campaign against cartels? The antitrust tradition was unique to the United States. Most other governments had tolerated and even encouraged cartels. Businessmen in other countries were accustomed to these organizations, and in industries like chemicals and electrical machinery, executives had never operated without them. Outside the United States, the immediate postwar years were very difficult, and hard times usually encouraged cooperation. Many wanted to rebuild cartels after the war. In early 1945, Baron Boel of Belgium's Solvay, a leading chemical firm, informed DuPont, "They [Solvay] still attach great importance to technical collaboration with ICI and, if possible, with Du-Pont. . . . and hope that it may be possible to work out an agreement which would make complete technical collaboration between the three parties possible."[3] DuPont did not follow up on this offer, presumably because the Justice Department was already suing to break its ties with ICI. European steel makers also wanted to rebuild their cartel after the war.[4] Pressure from Washington helped prevent a resurgence of cartels, but it was not decisive. After the war, no other country depended as heavily on the United States as Japan, but Tokyo abandoned many of the occupation's restrictions on cartels after regaining its sovereignty in 1953.

The American attack on cartels succeeded when it constituted part of a broader program of liberalization, and it failed where liberalization did not take hold. Japan lacked ready markets for its exports or guaranteed supplies of raw materials and so had little choice but to regulate trade strictly. In this context, antitrust made little sense. In contrast, antitrust became institutionalized in western Europe as governments moved to reduce trade restrictions and integrate their economies. Officials there promoted prosperity by expanding the size of markets, and by the 1950s, they had created what economists call a "virtuous cycle" in which freer trade spurred economic growth, which in turn allowed further liberalization. More broadly, after the war, all the industrial democracies reduced trade barriers and at least coordinated their currency policies, which led to a tremendous expansion of trade. Such an atmosphere is not congenial to cartels. As one historian noted, "A business approach based on competition and expansion was more suitable for a booming international economy than thinking in terms of caution, cooperation, and restriction."[5] Yet the retreat from cartels was not automatic. These organizations had deep roots in Europe, and prosperity and liberalization alone probably would not have eradicated them. Cartels formed during the last quarter of the nineteenth century, an economically turbulent period, did not vanish during the prosperous years of the early twentieth century. Speaking of Germany after World War II, the same historian has written, "The change . . . in favor of competition needed considerable time to be implemented. In fact, it occurred not before a new generation of managers took over."[6] Without American encouragement, it might not have happened at all.

Restrictions on cartels contributed to the "virtuous cycle" of growth and liberalization. Strong cartels changed the way business operated. Historian Alfred Chandler has gone so far as to argue that cartels constitute a key aspect of a distinct type of capitalism, which he calls "cooperative managerial capitalism."[7] Instead of competing to improve their position vis-à-vis competitors, firms cooperate to stabilize markets, setting prices and allocating sales and often coordinating the introduction of new products. Yet although stability has virtues, it exacts a price. Competition is the chief spur to innovation and efficiency, which are the keys to economic growth. Innovation is inherently disruptive—new products supersede old ones, and new plants render existing ones obsolete. It is no accident that economist Joseph Schumpeter described the activity of entrepreneurs as "creative destruction" or that John Maynard Keynes characterized the impulses behind investment as "animal spirits."

Cartels do not entirely eliminate competition. Even if these organizations set prices and allocate sales, the most efficient producers still earn higher profits. Likewise, cartels do not halt innovation—new products are still the best way to increase profits, and they can be valuable assets in negotiations with other firms. Factors other than the existence of cartels affect firms' behavior: the structure of markets, government policy, technology, and more. Despite its many cartel ties, DuPont compiled an impressive record of growth and innovation between the world wars. Although the German economy was in many ways the world's most cartelized before 1940, it was also the world's second largest and as technologically sophisticated as any.

Nevertheless, cartels do impede change. Simply because executives spend so much time on negotiations they have less time for the introduction of new products or the conquest of new markets. Strong cartels can distort investment. The German steel companies bought Ruhr coal mines not so much to improve efficiency or to earn a good return on capital but to gain a foothold in the coal cartel. Cartels deter innovations that might disrupt markets. Integrated steel plants had extraordinary economies of scale, limited as much by the size of the market as by technology. By fixing market share among members, steel cartels discouraged the construction of new, "best-practice" works that would, by their very size, reorder markets. During the 1920s and 1930s, everyone associated with the British steel industry agreed that it needed to construct larger, more cost-effective plants to compete internationally. Yet because industry and government refused to tolerate the disruption of markets entailed in opening such large works, the industry made limited progress. British steel makers had plenty of other problems: stagnant markets, weak management, and thin capital. But even firms able to overcome these obstacles, like the tube maker Stewarts & Lloyds, found that the fear of competition limited their ability to modernize and expand.[8] Jean Monnet had good reason to want the European Coal and Steel Community to dismantle cartels. Such considerations explain why relatively conservative figures like William Clayton and John McCloy embraced restrictions on cartels and why Lucius Clay took up the cause of reformers in this area even while blocking their plans for deconcentration.

In contrast, the petroleum companies retained their cartel largely because they operated in a distinctly illiberal atmosphere. They produced much of their oil in politically unstable, economically backward countries where they operated through concessions secured after difficult negotiations. Although the profits were large, they were not secure. A change in government could cost a firm its entire investment, as Anglo-Iranian discovered in 1951. The oil firms could ill afford the added risks of competition.

Antitrust policy forms part of a larger pattern. Although business always entails risks, these must be manageable. If the dangers of doing business become prohibitive, companies fail en masse, choking off investment and economic growth. During most of the interwar period, firms faced a catalogue of dangers: political instability, fluctuating currencies, and restrictive trade policies. In this atmosphere, many executives, government officials, and academics concluded that companies could not afford the added risks of competition and so embraced cartels. In the 1950s and 1960s, conditions were quite different, at least in North America and western Europe. Stable currencies, falling trade barriers, and a measure of political order gave companies the security they needed to compete. In this atmosphere, other governments willingly followed American recommendations for antitrust measures. Competition, particularly in the context of a buoyant economy, is one of the few forms of risk that actually improves economic performance, and so the retreat from cartels reinforced growth. The process was not automatic, however. Without American encouragement, countries with decades of experience with cartels probably would not have thought to restrict them. Yet at the same time, outside the context of liberalization, the most eloquent exhortations would have achieved little.

Since 1945, enthusiasm for antitrust has waxed and waned with that for liberalization. In Third World countries, support for free markets reached a nadir in the 1970s, as governments and intellectuals embraced "dependency theory," which held that the structure of international trade kept them economically subservient to the industrialized nations. They organized cartels — most notably the Organization of Petroleum Exporting Countries (OPEC) — to raise the prices for the commodities they exported to "just" levels. These efforts ultimately failed as high commodity prices choked off demand, leading to a collapse in the market for these products in the early 1980s. In the 1980s, Third World nations, beset by economic crisis, reversed themselves and began to liberalize their economies, reducing restrictions on trade and investment and trying to stabilize their currencies. These reforms often entailed enacting and enforcing strong antitrust laws.[9]

Roughly comparable events occurred in the industrial democracies. The economic crises of the 1970s initially led to an increase in government regulation. The Japanese government enforced a series of "rationalization" cartels on declining sectors like textiles and shipbuilding, the ECSC set prices for and allocated markets among European steel producers, and the U.S. government controlled the price and allocation of domestically produced oil. Since the 1980s, however, the developed nations have sought to increase competition by cutting regulation, privitizing government-owned firms, and further reducing trade barriers. As part of this shift, antitrust has received greater attention, particularly in the European Union.

Americans are too often ignorant of how and why their institutions work. Antitrust has improved the performance of the U.S. economy, largely by suppressing cartels. Yet it succeeded because a huge market, a stable government, and a strong currency made the risks of competition manageable. Thurman Arnold and many of his followers, who had little experience outside the United States, took these extraordinary conditions for granted, pursuing antitrust with little regard for anything else. The results could have been disastrous, particularly their plans to dismantle Germany's and Japan's large companies wholesale. The export of antitrust succeeded because people like Lucius Clay, John McCloy, Jean Monnet, and Ludwig Erhard modified it to fit within a broad framework of liberalization. Without Arnold, antitrust probably never would have traveled abroad, but without people like Clay, the attempt to export it probably would have failed.

The antitrust statutes rest on a paradox. They seek to preserve competition both to protect consumers and to provide incentive for innovation. To this end, the law regulates companies and punishes violations, at times severely. Yet the antitrust statutes can achieve their broader goals only in an atmosphere generally favorable to business. They will fail if economic or political instability crippled industry—the benefits of competition accrue only if firms can afford to compete. Reformers like Louis Brandeis and Thurman Arnold, who were deeply suspicious of big business, often accomplished less than more moderate figures such as Jean Monet and Lucius Clay, who grasped this reality. In the twenty-first century as in the twentieth, antitrust will advance or retreat with the growth and liberalization of national and international economies.

Notes

Introduction

1. Abe Fortas, Foreword to A. D. Neale, *The Antitrust Laws of the United States of America: A Study of Competition Enforced by Law* (Cambridge: Cambridge University Press, 1960), p. v.
2. Historian Alfred Chandler, Jr., has defined economies of scale as "those that result when the increased size of a single operating unit producing or distributing a single product reduces the unit cost of production or distribution." Economies of scope he describes as "those resulting from the use of processes within a single operating unit to produce or distribute more than one product" (*Scale and Scope: The Dynamics of Industrial Capitalism* [Cambridge, Mass.: Belknap Press, 1990], p. 17).
3. *Financial Times*, June 17–18, 2000, p. 5.

Chapter 1. The Cartel Ideal

1. Adam Smith, in one of many memorable passages in his classic, *The Wealth of Nations*, wrote, "People of the same trade seldom meet together, even for merriment and diversion, but the conversation ends in a conspiracy against the public, or in some contrivance to raise prices" (*An Inquiry into the Nature and Causes of the Wealth of Nations* [1776; reprint, London: William Allason, J. Maynard, and W. Blair, 1819], p. 177).
2. Robert Liefmann, *Cartels, Concerns and Trusts* (London: Methuen, 1932), pp. 16–24.

3.   Martin F. Parnell, *The German Tradition of Organized Capitalism: Self-Government in the Coal Industry* (Oxford: Clarendon Press, 1994), p. 164.

4.   Quoted in Jeffrey Fear, "German Capitalism" [teaching case] (Boston: Harvard Business School Press, 1996), p. 9.

5.   Harm Schröter, "Small European Nations: Cooperative Capitalism in the Twentieth Century," in Alfred Chandler, Franco Amatori, and Takashi Hinkino, eds., *Big Business and the Wealth of Nations* (Cambridge: Cambridge University Press, 1997); Alfred Chandler, Jr., *Scale and Scope: The Dynamics of Industrial Capitalism* (Cambridge, Mass.: Belknap Press, 1990), p. 588.

6.   W. J. Reader, *Imperial Chemical Industries: A History*, vol. 1, *The Forerunners, 1870–1926* (London: Oxford University Press, 1975); Ervin Hexner, *The International Steel Cartel* (Chapel Hill: University of North Carolina Press, 1943).

7.   Liefmann, *Cartels, Concerns and Trusts*, pp. 148–64.

8.   A. J. P. Taylor, *English History, 1914–1945* (Oxford: Clarendon Press, 1965), p. xxiv.

9.   For a brief discussion of the various systems of exchange controls in Europe, as well as the problem they could create for a firm, see Charles Wilson, *The History of Unilever: A Study in Economic Growth and Social Change* (New York: Praeger, 1968), vol. 2, pp. 66–73.

10. George W. Stocking and Myron W. Watkins, *Cartels in Action: Case Studies in International Business Diplomacy* (New York: Twentieth Century Fund, 1946), pp. 173–81.

11. W. J. Reader, *Imperial Chemical Industries: A History*, vol. 2, *The First Quarter-Century, 1926–1952* (London: Oxford University Press, 1975), pp. 109–15.

12. Ibid.; Hexner, *International Steel Cartel*, p. 89.

13. Experts argue over exactly how to measure the level of protection, which often varies considerably for different goods. During the 1920s and 1930s, many imports paid no duty, although in most cases they were goods like natural rubber that the United States did not produce itself. In 1920, the tariffs paid on dutiable imports totaled 16.40 percent of their value, a figure that increased to 38.07 percent by 1922. Tariffs remained in this vicinity until the Hawley-Smoot tariff of 1930, which by 1932 had raised payments to 59.06 percent of the value of dutiable imports (Bureau of the Census, *Historical Statistics of the United States, Colonial Times to 1970, Bicentennial Edition*, part 2 [Washington, D.C.: Government Printing Office, 1974], p. 888).

14. An essay that provides a good discussion of the ambiguity of American policy is Melvyn Leffler, "Herbert Hoover, the 'New Era,' and American Foreign Policy," in Ellis Hawley, ed., *Herbert Hoover as Secretary of Commerce: Studies in New Era Thought and Practice* (Iowa City: University of Iowa Press, 1981), pp. 148–84.

15. Otis L. Graham, Jr., "The Planning Ideal and American Reality: The 1930s," in Stanley Elkins and Erik McKitrick, eds., *The Hofstadter Aegis: A Memorial* (New York: Knopf, 1974), p. 259.

16. J. George Frederick, "General Summing Up by the Editor," in J. George Frederick, ed., *The Swope Plan: Details, Criticisms, Analysis* (New York: Business Bourse, 1931), pp. 212–13.

17. Karl Pribram, *Cartel Problems: An Analysis of Collective Monopolies in Europe with American Applications* (Buffalo, N.Y.: Hein, 1937), p. 5.

18. Quoted in Reader, *Imperial Chemical Industries*, vol. 2, p. 425.

19. Quoted in Hexner, *International Steel Cartel*, p. 243.

20. Liefmann, *Cartels, Concerns and Trusts*, p. 153.

21. Edouard Herriot, *The United States of Europe* (New York: Viking Press, 1930), pp. 122, 169–70.

22. League of Nations World Economic Conference, *Final Report* (C.E.I. 44), June 3, 1927, pp. 40–41.

23. Tony Freyer, *Regulating Big Business: Antitrust in Great Britain and America, 1880–1990* (Cambridge: Cambridge University Press, 1992), pp. 213–17.

24. Ervin Hexner gives brief histories of these cartels in *International Cartels* (Chapel Hill: University of North Carolina Press, 1946).

25. Schröter, "Small European Nations," p. 193.

26. Hexner, *International Cartels*, pp. 402–4.

27. The previous year at the Munich Conference, the great powers of Europe had, at Hitler's behest, partitioned Czechoslovakia, hoping thereby to appease the Nazis and avoid war. Hitler's occupation of the rump of Czechoslovakia in 1939, perhaps more than any other event, convinced the people of Britain and France that war with Germany was inevitable.

28. Quoted in Reader, *Imperial Chemical Industries*, vol. 2, p. 7.

29. Debora L. Spar provides a good discussion of the sacrifices involved in making a cartel work in *The Cooperative Edge: The Internal Politics of International Cartels* (Ithaca, N.Y.: Cornell University Press, 1994).

30. Edwin Mansfield, *Microeconomics: Theory and Applications*, 4th ed. (New York: Norton, 1982), p. 345. Similar sentiments appear in Alan S. Blinder and William J. Baumol, *Economics: Principles and Policy*, 7th ed. (Fort Worth, Tex.: Dryden Press, 1997), p. 284.

31. D. K. Osborne, "Cartel Problems," *American Economic Review* 66 (1976): 836.

32. George J. Stigler, "A Theory of Oligopoly," *Journal of Political Economy* 72 (1964): 46.

33. William A. Brock and Jose A. Scheinkman, "Price Setting and Supergames with Capacity Constraints," *Review of Economic Studies* 52 (1985): 371.

34. Liefmann, *Cartels, Concerns and Trusts*, pp. 8–9.

35. Osborne, "Cartel Problems," p. 843.

36. The account of the steel cartel draws largely from Hexner, *International Steel Cartel*.

37. The Saar, which had been part of Germany before the war, had in 1920 been put under French administration for fifteen years, after which a referendum would decide its future. Until that time, this coal-rich region was treated as a separate country in cartel negotiations. In 1935, the region reverted to Germany after the inhabitants voted for that course.

38. Stocking and Watkins, *Cartels in Action*, p. 204. These prices are in the old system, in which the pound was divided not into 100 pence but into 20 shillings. Therefore, £6 10s was six and a half pounds.

39. Interestingly, the power of the French cartel within France was apparently quite limited—its chief utility was its ability to regulate the export trade (Daniel Barbezat, "Comptoir Sidérurgique de France, 1930–1939," *Business History Review* 70 [1996]: 517–40).

40. Sweden was the only substantial European exporter outside the cartel. Most of its foreign sales, however, consisted of specialty steel, a high-value product whose sales hinged more on quality than price. The cartel never tried to regulate this trade. The failure of Swedish producers to adhere to the cartel, therefore, created no major difficulties for it.

41. Hexner, *International Steel Cartel*, pp. 326–27.

42. Steel mills are very expensive, entailing substantial fixed changes for depreciation as well as interest and dividends. With lower output a steel company has few units over which to spread these costs, and so the cost per ton of steel increases.

43. See chapter 2.

44. Richard A. Lauderbaugh, *American Steelmakers and the Coming of the Second World War* (Ann Arbor, Mich.: UMI Research Press, 1980), pp. 121–96.

45. Stocking and Watkins, *Cartels in Action*, p. 204.

46. Hexner, *International Steel Cartel*, p. 240.

47. The term "heavy" applies not to the weight of the chemicals themselves but to the vast quantities in which they were produced.

48. This account draws chiefly on Leonard S. Reich, "General Electric and the World Cartelization of Electric Lamps," in Akira Kudo and Terushi Hara, eds., *International Cartels in Business History: International Conference of Business History 18, Proceedings of the Fuji Conference* (Tokyo: University of Tokyo Press, 1992), pp. 213–31; Stocking and Watkins, *Cartels in Action*, pp. 304–62; U.S. Congress, Temporary National Economic Committee (TNEC), *Investigation of Concentration of Economic Power: Monograph No. 31, Patents and Free Enterprise*, 76th Cong., 3rd sess., 1940, pp. 93–103; and Leonard S. Reich, "Lighting the Path to Profit: GE's Control of the Electric Lamp Industry, 1892–1941," *Business History Review* 66 (1992): 305–34.

49. *United States* v. *General Electric Company et al.*, 272 U.S. 476, 477.

50. At the turn of the century, GE relied on many devices to control competition in light bulbs, but antitrust prosecution led it to abandon all save those involving patents.

51. Stocking and Watkins, *Cartels in Action*, pp. 308–9.

52. *United States* v. *General Electric Co. et al.*, 82 F. Supp. 753.

53. Reich, "General Electric and World Cartelization," p. 231.

54. Chandler, *Scale and Scope*, p. 542.

55. "Fine" chemicals were those of high value produced in relatively small batches.

56. Crawford H. Greenwalt, "Bigness Is a Result," Bruce Barton Papers, DuPont Correspondence, Wisconsin State Historical Society, Madison.

57. Reader, *Imperial Chemical Industries*, vol. 2, pp. 193–94.

58. The account of the rubber cartel draws largely on Stocking and Watkins, *Cartels in Action*, pp. 56–117, and Hexner, *International Cartels*, pp. 280–93.

59. Hexner, *International Cartels*, p. 282.

60. Ibid., p. 285.

61. National Association of Manufacturers, *NAM Looks at Cartels: Positions Formulated by the Committee on International Economic Relations and Approved by the Board of Directors Together with an Analysis of the Economic Aspects of Cartels Prepared by the Research Department* (New York: National Association of Manufacturers, 1946).

62. Hexner, *International Cartels*, pp. 398–401. These pages contain a list of various internationally traded goods and how much of world trade they accounted for.

63. Liefmann, *Cartels, Concerns and Trusts*, p. 4.

64. Graham D. Taylor and Patricia E. Sudnik, *DuPont and the International Chemical Industry* (Boston: Twayne, 1984), p. 92.

Chapter 2. The Context of Antitrust

1. The best account of this process remains Alfred D. Chandler, Jr., *The Visible Hand: The Managerial Revolution in American Business* (Cambridge, Mass.: Belknap Press, 1977); Robert H. Wiebe explored the social consequences of these economic changes in *The Search for Order, 1877–1920* (New York: Hill & Wang, 1967).

2. Matthew Josephson, *The Robber Barons: The Great American Capitalists* (New York: Harcourt, Brace, 1934), p. 29.

3. Quoted in Ellis Hawley, *The New Deal and the Problem of Monopoly: A Study in Economic Ambivalence* (Princeton, N.J.: Princeton University Press, 1966), p. 472.

4.   Predatory pricing allows large firms active in many markets to destroy smaller
      rivals doing business in only a few. The large company cuts prices to ruinously
      low levels in competitive markets, driving its smaller rival into bankruptcy,
      while maintaining charges in other markets in which it does not have to com-
      pete. Large firms could also secure rebates from railroads, which in the late
      nineteenth century competed fiercely for long-distance traffic between major
      centers (as opposed to more isolated areas where they enjoyed monopolies).
      The railroads gave rebates because large firms could supply a lot of traffic, and
      sustained volume was the key to keeping railroads profitable. Smaller firms,
      however, could not provide the volume to command such terms. Finally, a
      large firm with ties to a major banker like J. P. Morgan & Co. might be able
      to survive and expand even if it was not as efficient as smaller rivals. In this
      period, the American financial system was not as sophisticated as the country's
      transportation and manufacturing sectors—capital was often hard to come by,
      and credit crunches were a recurring feature of economic life. A large firm
      with guaranteed financing could ride out these crises, whereas smaller rivals
      might fail.

5.   Quoted in Thomas McCraw, *Prophets of Regulation: Charles Francis Adams,
      Louis D. Brandeis, James M. Landis, Alfred Kahn* (Cambridge, Mass.: Belknap
      Press, 1984), p. 108.

6.   Woodrow Wilson, *The New Freedom: A Call for the Emancipation of the
      Generous Energies of a People* (Englewood Cliffs, N.J.: Prentice-Hall, 1961),
      p. 20.

7.   Theodore Roosevelt, *The New Nationalism* (New York: Outlook, 1911),
      pp. 12, 15.

8.   Ibid.

9.   Herbert Croly, *The Promise of American Life* (New York: Macmillan, 1909),
      p. 27.

10.   Chandler, *Visible Hand*, pp. 333–34.

11.   Standard Oil was broken into several firms, the largest of which was Standard
      Oil of New Jersey (Exxon). Other important successor companies were Stan-
      dard Oil of New York (Mobile), Standard Oil of Ohio, Standard Oil of Indiana
      (Amoco), and Standard Oil of California (Chevron).

12.   Tony Freyer, *Regulating Big Business: Antitrust in Great Britain and America,
      1880–1990* (Cambridge: Cambridge University Press, 1992), pp. 132–41.

13.   Some historians like Josephson see the antitrust movement as a heroic cam-
      paign against big business (*Robber Barons*), whereas others like Gabriel Kolko
      consider it a sell-out to big business because it did not really change that much
      (*The Triumph of Conservatism: A Reinterpretation of American History* , 1900–
      1916 [New York: Free Press], 1963). Both miss the point. Americans on the
      whole wanted to contain big business, not eliminate it, and judging antitrust
      on the damage it did large firms is inappropriate.

14. In the first half of the twentieth century, Britain probably had the most favorable environment for business outside the United States, with a currency that was generally strong and a political system as stable as any in the world. The British population, however, numbered only about 40 percent that of the United States, and its per capita income was lower. The vast British Empire only partly offset this disadvantage. Most of its subjects were quite poor, and the wealthy dominions (Canada, Australia, South Africa) protected their own domestic producers against foreign competition, including that from the mother country. Moreover, the world wars severely taxed Britain's economic resources, imposing immense strains on the business structure. The world's second largest economy, Germany, presented a far more difficult landscape to businessmen. In the first half of the twentieth century, Germany had four governments: an erratic monarchy, a weak republic, a totalitarian dictatorship, and an alien occupation. Germany lost two disastrous wars, the second of which led to the country's division. Its currency became worthless, twice. As for its domestic market, although its population was about 60 percent that of the United States, living standards were considerably lower than those of Americans or, for that matter, Britons.

15. Herbert Hoover, *Public Papers of the Presidents of the United States, Herbert Hoover, 1929* (Washington, D.C.: Government Printing Office, 1974), p. 507.

16. Joseph Brandes, "Product Diplomacy: Herbert Hoover's Anti-Monopoly Campaign at Home and Abroad," in Ellis Hawley, ed., *Herbert Hoover as Secretary of Commerce: Studies in New Era Thought and Practice* (Iowa City: University of Iowa Press, 1981), pp. 185–216; Robert F. Himmelberg, *The Origins of the National Recovery Administration: Business, Government, and the Trade Association Issue, 1921–1933* (New York: Fordham University Press, 1993).

17. Quoted in U.S. Congress, TNEC, *Investigation of Concentration of Economic Power: Monograph No. 6, Export Prices and Export Cartels*, 76th Cong., 3rd sess., 1940, p. 126.

18. U.S. Congress, TNEC, *Investigation of Concentration of Economic Power: Part 25, Cartels*, 76th Cong., 3rd sess., 1940, p. 13172. The executive was talking about the situation in the 1920s. In the 1930s, as new low-cost mines drove American exporters from world markets and the U.S. Congress enacted a prohibitive tariff on imports, the American copper market did, in fact, become more or less separate from that of the rest of the world.

19. Hoover had some success encouraging the development of potash deposits in the American Southwest, but little in finding new sources of rubber.

20. Brandes, "Product Diplomacy," pp. 185–216.

21. Arthur M. Schlesinger, Jr., *The Coming of the New Deal* (Boston: Houghton Mifflin, 1959), p. 424.

22. Franklin D. Roosevelt, *The Public Papers and Addresses of Franklin D. Roosevelt, 1936* (New York: Random House, 1938), pp. 233–36.

23. *New York Times*, December 31, 1937, p. 2.

24. Hawley, *New Deal and the Problem of Monopoly*, p. 14.

25. Gerard Swope, "The Swope Plan—Details," in J. George Frederick, ed., *The Swope Plan: Details, Criticisms, Analysis* (New York: Business Bourse, 1931), p. 23; see also Louis Domerstzky, "Cartels and the Business Crisis," *Foreign Affairs*, October 1931, pp. 35–36.

26. Whether the NRA codes could set minimum prices was not entirely clear from the language of the act, and it was one of the most controversial issues involved in these codes. But cleverly drafted codes could effectively support prices by limiting output.

27. Hawley, *New Deal and the Problem of Monopoly*, p. 477.

28. Ibid., p. 480.

29. For a good example of a market imperfection, see chapter 6, which discusses the "rule of capture" in oil drilling.

30. Kingman Brewster, Jr., *Antitrust and American Business Abroad* (New York: McGraw-Hill, 1958), p. 26.

31. Alan Brinkley, *End of Reform: New Deal Liberalism in Recession and War* (New York: Vintage Books, 1995), pp. 56–58.

32. Thurman W. Arnold, *The Bottlenecks of Business* (New York: Reynal & Hitchcock, 1940), pp. 11, 13–14.

33. Franklin D. Roosevelt, *Public Papers and Addresses of Franklin D. Roosevelt, 1938* (New York: Macmillan, 1941), p. 310.

34. Ibid., p. 308.

35. U.S. Congress, TNEC, *Investigation of Concentration of Economic Power: Final Report of the Executive Secretary*, 77th Cong., 1st sess., 1941, p. 102.

36. U.S. Congress, TNEC, *Monograph No. 6*, p. 110.

37. U.S. Congress, TNEC, *Investigation of Concentration of Economic Power: Monograph No. 31, Patents and Free Enterprise*, 76th Cong., 3rd sess., 1940, pp. 45–46, 71, 165.

38. Ibid., pp. 145–58.

39. U.S. Congress, TNEC, *Final Report*, p. 36.

40. Alan Brinkley, "The Antimonopoly Ideal and the Liberal State: The Case of Thurman Arnold," *Journal of American History* 80 (1993): 565.

41. See the list of cases in U.S. Congress, TNEC, *Monograph No. 16: Antitrust in Action*, 76th Cong., 3rd sess., 1940, pp. 142–43.

42. Thurman Arnold, *The Folklore of Capitalism* (New Haven, Conn.: Yale University Press, 1937), pp. 3–4, 207–11.

43. Arnold, *Bottlenecks of Business*, pp. 3–4, 116.

44. Gene M. Gressley, ed., *Voltaire and the Cowboy: The Letters of Thurman Arnold* (Boulder: Colorado Associated University Press, 1977), p. 21.

45. In a letter to Robert Lasch, April 22, 1946, Wendell Berge wrote, "The success of industrial development in the west during the postwar period depends upon

giving independent local and regional groups a chance to develop new industries, and keeping eastern monopoly controls out" (Wendell Berge Papers, Box
17, Lasch correspondence, Library of Congress, Washington, D.C.).

Chapter 3. Reform versus Mobilization

1. W. J. Reader, *Imperial Chemical Industries: A History*, vol. 2, *The First Quarter-Century, 1926–1952* (London: Oxford University Press, 1975), p. 413.

2. For the history of the relations between DuPont and ICI, see ibid., and Graham D. Taylor and Patricia E. Sudnik, *DuPont and the International Chemical Industry* (Boston: Twayne, 1984).

3. Memorandum for Herbert A. Berman, June 23, 1941, and "The Standard Oil-I.G. Farbenindustrie Partnership and Its Consequences," January 2, 1942, both in Roy A. Pewitt Files, Box 14, Rubber, Record Group 112, National Archives, Washington, D.C.; Peter Hayes, *Industry and Ideology: IG Farben and the Nazi Era* (Cambridge: Cambridge University Press, 1987), pp. 37–38. The Nazi regime did indeed heavily subsidize oil from coal, and hydrogenation plants supplied much of Germany's petroleum needs during World War II.

4. Daniel Yergin, *The Prize: The Epic Quest for Oil, Money, and Power* (New York: Touchstone Books, 1991), p. 331.

5. Henrietta M. Larson, Evelyn H. Knowleton, and Charles S. Popple, *New Horizons: History of Standard Oil Company (New Jersey), 1927–1950* (New York: Harper & Row, 1971), p. 156.

6. Memorandum for Berman, June 23, 1941.

7. Memorandum for the Files, August 18, 1941, Pewitt Files, Box 14, Rubber.

8. U.S. Senate, Special Committee Investigating the National Defense Program, *Investigation of the National Defense Program: Part 11, Rubber*, 77th Cong., 1st sess., 1942, pp. 4376, 4585.

9. Jasper E. Crane to Eduard Weber-Andreae, September 7, 1939, DuPont Records, S2P2, Jasper E. Crane Papers, Box 1038, IG Farben 1936–41, Hagley Museum and Library, Wilmington, Del.

10. Jasper E. Crane to Eduard Weber-Andreae, October 27, 1939, Crane Papers, Box 1038, IG Farben 1936–41.

11. Ibid.

12. E. I. DuPont De Nemours & Company to Fritz Ter Meer, April 18, 1941, Crane Papers, Box 1038, IG Farben 1936–41.

13. Fritz Ter Meer to E. I. DuPont de Nemours & Company, June 25, 1941, Crane Papers, Box 1038, IG Farben 1936–41.

14. Wendell Berge, *Cartels: Challenge to a Free World* (Washington, D.C.: Public Affairs Press, 1944), p. 217.

15. *Click*, June 1941, pp. 3–6.

16. U.S. Senate, Committee on Patents, *Patents*, 77th Cong., 2nd sess., 1942, pp. 878–79.

17. *Congressional Record*, 1941, p. A3845.

18. George W. Stocking and Myron W. Watkins, *Cartels in Action: Case Studies in International Business Diplomacy* (New York: Twentieth Century Fund, 1946), p. 473; Hayes, *Industry and Ideology*, p. 334.

19. Clipping, *Democrat & Chronicle* (Rochester, N.Y.), September 8, 1944, Wendell Berge Papers, Box 57, Library of Congress, Washington, D.C.

20. Quoted in Berge, *Cartels*, pp. 166–67.

21. *Democrat & Chronicle*, September 8, 1944.

22. Quoted in Lawrence Langner, "We Depend on Invention: An Answer to Thurman Arnold," *Atlantic Monthly*, July 1942, p. 25.

23. U.S. House, Committee on Patents, *Preventing Publication of Inventions and Prohibiting Injunctions on Patents*, 77th Cong., 1st sess., 1941, pp. 120–21.

24. Thurman Arnold to Robert Jackson, May 16, 1940, Thurman Arnold Papers, Box 20, Correspondence, May 1940, American Heritage Center, University of Wyoming, Laramie.

25. Such action would have raised questions concerning the constitutional prohibition against infringing on contracts. In a national emergency, however, the courts have generally allowed the government considerable latitude.

26. Arthur M. Schlesinger, Jr., *The Coming of the New Deal* (Boston: Houghton Mifflin, 1959), pp. 533–52.

27. William L. O'Neill, *A Democracy at War: America's Fight at Home and Abroad in World War II* (New York: Free Press, 1993), pp. 77–85; Bruce Catton, *The War Lords of Washington* (New York: Harcourt, Brace, 1948), pp. 51–55.

28. Stimson, a lawyer, had served as secretary of war under President William Howard Taft and secretary of state under President Hoover. Knox, a newspaper publisher, had been the Republican Party's vice-presidential candidate in 1936.

29. Catton, *War Lords of Washington*, pp. 29–30.

30. *New York Times*, May 26, 1940, sec. 3, p. 7.

31. Thurman Arnold to Bruce Bliven, August 10, 1940, Arnold Papers, Box 21, Correspondence, August 6–30, 1940.

32. *Business Week*, September 14, 1941, p. 15.

33. Arnold to Bliven, August 10, 1940.

34. Thurman W. Arnold, *The Bottlenecks of Business* (New York: Reynal & Hitchcock, 1940), pp. 67–68.

35. *Business Week*, September 14, 1941, p. 15.

36. Alan Brinkley, *End of Reform: New Deal Liberalism in Recession and War* (New York: Vintage Books, 1995), pp. 118–20.

37. Robert A. Brady, *The Spirit and Structure of German Fascism* (London: Gollancz, 1937), p. 33.

38. Ibid., pp. 11–12; Arthur M. Schlesinger, Jr., *The Politics of Upheaval* (Boston: Houghton Mifflin, 1960), p. 170.

39. Franz Neuman, *Behemoth: The Structure and Practice of National Socialism* (London: Gollancz, 1942), p. 295.

40. Ibid., p. 225.

41. *New York Times Book Review*, June 27, 1937, p. 1.

42. *The Nation*, July 10, 1937, p. 50.

43. Robert Jackson, "The Philosophy of Big Business," *Vital Speeches of the Day*, January 15, 1938, p. 209.

44. *New York Times*, December 31, 1937, p. 2.

45. Arnold, *Bottlenecks of Business*, pp. 11, 114–15.

46. Ibid., pp. 16, 18.

47. *New York Times*, August 10, 1940, p. 2.

48. *New York Times*, November 10, 1941, p. 11.

49. *New York Times*, October 7, 1941, p. 7.

50. Richard Polenberg, *War and Society: The United States, 1941–45* (New York: Lippincott, 1972), p. 10.

51. Richard A. Lauderbaugh, *American Steelmakers and the Coming of the Second World War* (Ann Arbor, Mich.: UMI Research Press, 1980), pp. 70–71.

52. Thurman Arnold to Preston Slosson, October 26, 1939, Arnold Papers, Box 18, Correspondence, October 1939.

53. Thurman Arnold, "How Monopolies Have Hobbled Defense," *Reader's Digest*, July 1941, p. 51.

54. DuPont also owned mines producing natural nitrates in Chile, whose output fell under the authority of the Chilean national cartel.

55. "United States of America v. Chilean Nitrate Sales Corporation, et al.," Arnold Papers, Box 65, Fertilizer Industry; "United States of America v. E. I. Du Pont de Nemours & Company, et al.," Arnold Papers, Box 63, E. I. DuPont.

56. Public statement, May 29, 1941, Arnold Papers, Box 59, Allied Chemical Company.

57. George David Smith, *From Monopoly to Competition: The Transformation of Alcoa, 1888–1986* (Cambridge: Cambridge University Press, 1988), pp. 204–5.

58. O'Neill, *Democracy at War*, p. 83.

59. *New York Times*, December 29, 1940, p. 18.

60. *Time*, May 26, 1941, p. 21.

61. *New Republic*, May 26, 1941, pp. 723–24.

62. Arnold, "How Monopolies Have Hobbled Defense," p. 54.

63. C. C. Carr to Kenneth W. Payne, July 18, 1941, Arnold Papers, Box 23, Correspondence, February 19–28, March 1–18, 1941.

64. Memorandum, Walter Hick to Thurman Arnold, January 9, 1941, Joseph O'Mahoney Papers, Box 56, Aluminum, American Heritage Center, University of Wyoming.

65. Bureau of the Census, *Historical Statistics of the United States, Colonial Times to 1970, Bicentennial Edition*, part 2 [Washington, D.C.: Government Printing Office, 1974], p. 698.

66. Ervin Hexner, *International Cartels* (Chapel Hill: University of North Carolina Press, 1946), p. 220; *New Republic*, May 26, 1941, p. 725.

67. *New York Times*, October 7, pp. 1, 39, and October 10, 1941, p. 25.

68. I. F. Stone, "Making Defense Safe for Alcoa," *The Nation*, September 27, October 4 and 18, 1941, pp. 271–73, 299–301, 363–64; Harold Ickes to Franklin D. Roosevelt, September 3, 1941, Office Files (OFF) 1050, Box 1, Franklin D. Roosevelt Library, Hyde Park, N.Y.

69. Smith, *From Monopoly to Competition*, pp. 191–214. Hand and two other federal appeals judges delivered the final decision because so many members of the Supreme Court had been involved in the Alcoa case over the years and had to recuse themselves that the High Court could not muster a quorum. A special act of Congress created an ad hoc bench to decide the matter.

70. Smith, *From Monopoly to Competition*, pp. 270–74.

71. *Ethyl Gasoline Corporation et al. v. United States*, 309 U.S. 453.

72. Ibid.

73. Thurman Arnold to Robert H. Jackson, May 18, 1940, Arnold Papers, Box 20, Correspondence, May 1940; Gene M. Gressley, ed., *Voltaire and the Cowboy: The Letters of Thurman Arnold* (Boulder: Colorado Associated University Press, 1977), pp. 305–6.

74. Gressley, ed., *Voltaire and the Cowboy*, pp. 305–6.

75. Department of Justice, press release, September 25, 1941, DuPont Records, S2P2, Walter S. Carpenter Papers, Box 833, Correspondence—Legal Department, 1940–47, Hagley Museum and Library; Thurman Arnold to parents, October 15, 1941, Arnold Papers, Box 25, Correspondence 1941, October 14–31.

76. *United States v. General Electric Co. et al.*, 80 F. Supp. 989.

77. "Tungsten Carbide," n.d., Francis Biddle Papers, Box 1, Antitrust, Roosevelt Library; Joseph Borkin and Charles A. Welsh, *Germany's Master Plan: The Story of Industrial Offensive* (New York: Duell, Sloan and Pearce, 1943), pp. 260–70; U.S. Senate, Subcommittee on War Mobilization of the Committee on Military Affairs, *Economic and Political Aspects of Cartels*, 78th Cong., 2nd sess., 1944, p. 13. This outcome was fortunate for the Antitrust Division because the case was suspended for the duration after the attack on Pearl Harbor.

78. Public statement, January 30, 1941, Arnold Papers, Box 59, Aluminum Company.

79. Department of Justice, press release, April 15, 1942, Arnold Papers, Box 59, Aluminum Company.

80. *New York Times*, August 10, 1940, p. 12.

81. *Time*, February 10, 1941, p. 66.

82. Polenberg, *War and Society*, p. 73.

83. In 1942 and 1943, Congress disbanded the Civilian Conservation Corps, the Works Progress Administration, and the National Youth Administration, all New Deal relief organizations, as well as the National Resources Planning Board, an organization charged with economic planning (John Morton Blum, *V Was for Victory: Politics and American Culture During World War II* [New York: Harvest, 1976], pp. 234–40).

84. O'Neill, *Democracy at War*, pp. 90–91, 97–98; Catton, *War Lords of Washington*, pp. 106–8.

85. They were known as "dollar-a-year-men" because their companies kept them on the payroll while they worked for the government, which paid them only $1 a year.

86. Peter F. Drucker, *The Concept of the Corporation* (New Brunswick, N.J.: Transaction, 1993), p. 117.

87. Smith, *From Monopoly to Competition*, p. 222; Charles W. Cheape, *Strictly Business: Walter Carpenter at DuPont and General Motors* (Baltimore: Johns Hopkins University Press, 1995), p. 186.

88. Quoted in Harley Notter, *Postwar Foreign Policy Preparation, 1939–1945*, General Foreign Policy Series, no. 15 (Washington, D.C.: Department of State, 1949), pp. 34–35.

89. Department of State, memorandum of conversation, February 6, 1947, Clayton-Thorp Papers, Box 4, Commodity Agreements—Coffee, Harry S. Truman Library, Independence, Mo.; Hexner, *International Cartels*, pp. 186–87; Department of State, memorandum of conversation, February 6, 1947; Analysis and Report Division, Foreign Trade Technical Services Branch, September 12, 1943; "Commodity Agreements Between United States and Foreign Countries, Commodity by Country Analysis as of September 15, 1943," all in O'Mahoney Papers, Box 227, Legislation 1943, Cartels.

90. "Editorial Notes," in Department of State, *Foreign Relations of the United States, Diplomatic Papers, 1942*, vol. 1, *General: The British Commonwealth; The Far East* (Washington, D.C.: Government Printing Office, 1960), pp. 512–13; "Secretary of State to the Ambassador in the United Kingdom," August 28, 1944, in Department of State, *Foreign Relations of the United States, Diplomatic Papers, 1944*, vol. 2, *General: Economic and Social Matters* (Washington, D.C.: Government Printing Office, 1967), pp. 1005–6.

91. Cartel accords invariably had a provision providing for the suspension of the agreement if members' governments went to war. Implicit in these clauses was the expectation that firms would resume cooperation when peace returned, although wartime events might alter the balance of power between them and require renegotiation of the cartel.

92. Memorandum, Wendell Berge to Attorney General, April 17, 1944, Berge Papers, Box 28, General Correspondence.

93. Indictment of General Dyestuff Corporation et al., December 19, 1941, Arnold Papers, Box 59, Allied Chemical Company.

94. Memorandum of Meeting with I.G. Officials, October 23, 1935, Crane Papers, Box 1038, IG Farben 1935–41. The behavior of the IG in this situation indicates one of the reasons why American and British firms were reluctant to enter into wide-ranging cartel agreements with the Germans. How could anyone trust a company that would lie about such an important matter? Such concerns did not preclude cooperation on specific matters, but they did bar the sort of open-ended alliance that DuPont and ICI had.

95. E. H. Foley, Jr., to Secretary Morgenthau, January 7, 1942, Personal Secretary's File (PSF), Departmental Files, Treasury, Box 78, Roosevelt Library.

96. Department of Justice, press release, December 19, 1941, Arnold Papers, Box 59, Allied Chemical Company.

97. Memorandum, Heinrich Kronstein to Thurman Arnold, March 16, 1942, Arnold Papers, Box 27, Correspondence, March 12–24, 1942. Presumably, the reference to ties between oil companies and the IG involved hydrogenation technology, which most U.S. petroleum refiners licensed from the Standard/IG company.

98. Though altered throughout the first months of war, a final picture of the synthetic rubber program can be found in James B. Conant, Karl T. Compton, and Bernard M. Baruch, "Report of the Rubber Survey Committee," September 10, 1942, Carpenter Papers, Box 831, Correspondence: Synthetic Rubber.

99. Larson, Knowleton, and Popple, *New Horizons*, p. 431.

100. Department of Justice, press release, March 25, 1942, Arnold Papers, Box 70, Standard Oil.

101. U.S. Senate, *Investigation of the National Defense Program*, p. 4307.

102. Ibid., pp. 4308, 4312–15.

103. Under the Jasco agreement, Standard would usually have controlling interest in anything it discovered. Butyl, however, represented an improvement on vistanex, a polymer developed by Farben, which apparently gave the IG control over butyl too.

104. U.S. Senate, *Investigation of the National Defense Program*, pp. 4309, 4312, 4317.

105. Ibid., p. 4308.

106. *Time*, April 6, 1942, p. 16.

107. *Wall Street Journal*, April 3, 1942, p. 3.

108. *New Republic*, April 6, 1942, p. 460.

109. U.S. Senate, Special Committee Investigating the National Defense Program, *Additional Report of the Special Committee Investigating the National Defense Program: Rubber*, 77th Cong., 2nd sess., 1942, p. 40.

110. U.S. Senate, *Investigation of the National Defense Program*, pp. 4360, 4383–84, 4388.

111. Ibid., p. 4433.

112. Memorandum on Synthetic Rubber, January 2, 1940, in ibid., pp. 4605–8.

113. U.S. Senate, *Investigation of the National Defense Program*, pp. 4433–51.

114. Larson, Knowleton, and Popple, *New Horizons*, pp. 415–18.

115. U.S. Senate, *Additional Report of the Special Committee*, p. 22.

116. Larson, Knowleton, and Popple, *New Horizons*, p. 435.

117. U.S. Senate, Subcommittee on Rubber of Senate Special Committee Investigating the Defense Program (closed hearings), March 23, 1942, pp. 12, 15–16, 30, 53, Harry S. Truman Papers, Senatorial File, Box 117, National Defense—Rubber Situation, Truman Library.

118. U.S. Senate, *Investigation of the National Defense Program*, pp. 4383–84.

119. Ibid., p. 4404.

120. Ibid., pp. 4461–62.

121. In the fall of 1942, the federal government did impose a national speed limit of 35 miles per hour to conserve rubber.

122. O'Neill, *Democracy at War*, p. 92.

123. *New York Times*, April 2, 1942, p. 20.

124. *Wall Street Journal*, April 4, 1942, p. 4.

125. *New York Times*, September 14, 1943, p. 16.

126. Blum, *V Was for Victory*, pp. 132–33.

127. Brinkley, *End of Reform*, pp. 120–21.

128. Clipping, *Capital Times* (Madison, Wis.), June 28, 1945, Berge Papers, Box 57.

129. Larson, Knowleton, and Popple, *New Horizons*, p. 441.

130. Quoted in *The Nation*, June 12, 1943, pp. 826–27. Emphasis in original.

131. Quoted in Blum, *V Was for Victory*, p. 133.

132. Francis Biddle, Henry L. Stimson, Frank Knox, and Thurman Arnold to the President, March 20, 1942, OFF 277, Box 3, Roosevelt Library.

133. Press releases, September 10 and 30, 1942, Arnold Papers, Box 105, Professional File, 1942–43, General-Business Policy, Antitrust Law, and Defense; press release, February 10, 1943, Arnold Papers, Box 66, General Electric (1).

134. Blum, *V Was for Victory*, p. 135.

135. Memorandum, Thurman Arnold to Francis Biddle, September 11, 1942, Arnold Papers, Box 29, Correspondence, September 1942.

136. Cabinet notes, September 11, 1942, Biddle Papers, Box 1, Cabinet Meetings, July–December 1942.

137. Donald Nelson to Francis Biddle, September 5, 1942, Arnold Papers, Box 29, Correspondence, September 1942.

138. Thurman Arnold to Francis Biddle, September 9, 1942, Arnold Papers, Box 29, Correspondence, September 1942.

139. Ibid.

140. Donald Nelson to Francis Biddle, September 19, 1942, Arnold Papers, Box 29, Correspondence, September, 1942.

141. Quoted in Brinkley, *End of Reform*, p. 121.

142. Gressley, ed., *Voltaire and the Cowboy*, p. 49.

143. Joseph O'Mahoney, S. 1476, October 25, 1943, O'Mahoney Papers, Box 132, Legislation 1944.

144. Ralph W. Gallagher, statement, May 23, 1944, Crane Papers, Box 1052, Tariffs and Foreign Relations, 1942–44.

145. Francis Biddle to Joseph O'Mahoney, November 30, 1943, O'Mahoney Papers, Box 227, Legislation 1943, Cartels.

146. Memorandum, Mr. Terrill to Mr. Haley, May 4, 1945, Record Group 59, 800.602/5-445, National Archives.

147. Gallagher statement, May 23, 1944.

148. *Time*, February 19, 1945, pp. 78–80.

149. Cartel Memo 85a, [1945], Harley Notter Papers, Record Group 59, National Archives. Standard Oil's president, Ralph Gallagher, offered comparable suggestions in his statement of May 23, 1944. To a degree, this measure resembled the Webb-Pomerene Act, but it allowed individual companies to join foreign cartels, not just special, combined firms. Moreover, it explicitly permitted firms to join cartels, whereas the Webb Act's permission was implicit—if that.

150. Terrill to Haley, May 4, 1945.

151. National Association of Manufacturers, *NAM Looks at Cartels: Positions Formulated by the Committee on International Economic Relations and Approved by the Board of Directors Together with an Analysis of the Economic Aspects of Cartels Prepared by the Research Department* (New York: National Association of Manufacturers, 1946).

152. Cartel Memo 98, November 18, 1944, Notter Papers.

153. Memorandum from Elvin H. Killheffer, August 3, 1944, Crane Papers, Box 1052, Tariffs and Foreign Policy, 1944–45.

154. Kingman Brewster, Jr., *Antitrust and American Business Abroad* (New York: McGraw-Hill, 1958), pp. 26–27.

155. Thurman Arnold, "The Abuse of Patents," *Atlantic Monthly*, July 1942, p. 16.

156. Berge, *Cartels*, pp. 37, 45.

157. Ibid., pp. 43, 48.

158. Thurman Arnold to John K. Jessup, April 21, 1942, Arnold Papers, Box 24, Correspondence, August 1942.

159. Arnold, "Abuse of Patents," p. 20.

160. Joseph O'Mahoney, "Don't Fence Me In," manuscript, O'Mahoney Papers.

161. Charles F. Kettering, Chester C. Davis, Francis P. Gaines, Edward F. McGrady, and Owen D. Young, *The American Patent System* (Washington, D.C., 1943), pp. 8, 25.

162. Joseph O'Mahoney, Homer Bone, and Robert LaFollette, Jr., S. 2491, April 28, 1942, Arnold Papers, Box 106, Professional File, 1942, General—Patent Abuses (2 of 3).

163. Memorandum, Ernest S. Meyers to Assistant Attorney General Arnold, February 9, 1943, Pewitt Files, Box 23, Patents—Proposed Legislation.

164. Cartel Memo 110, January 3, 1945, Notter Papers.

165. Langner, "We Depend on Invention," p. 22.

166. Hugh Sanford to Thurman Arnold, September 14, 1942, Arnold Papers, Box 29, Correspondence, September 1942.

167. Edward R. Weidlein, "Industrial Research and the Patent System," in *Industrial Research and Patents* (New York: National Association of Manufacturers, 1946), p. 34. It is extremely difficult to determine whether anyone has successfully suppressed an important new invention because an effective effort would presumably conceal the existence of a development permanently.

168. Ibid., p. 35.

169. National Association of Manufacturers, "The Need for Emphasizing the Fundamentals of Our Patent System," [1943], National Association of Manufacturers Papers, Series I, Box 287, Committee: Patents, 1943, Hagley Museum and Library.

170. Sanford to Arnold, September 14, 1942.

171. U.S. Senate, *Patents*, pp. 1283–84.

172. Cartel Meeting 33, May 19, 1944, Notter Papers.

173. J. King Harness, "Patent Pool Monopolies?" *The Rotarian*, August 1945, p. 57.

174. NAM, "The Need for Emphasizing the Fundamentals of Our Patent System."

Chapter 4. Making the World Safe for Competition

1.   Wendell Berge, *Cartels: Challenge to a Free World* (Washington, D.C.: Public Affairs Press, 1944); U.S. Senate, Subcommittee on War Mobilization of the Committee on Military Affairs, *Economic and Political Aspects of International Cartels*, 78th Cong., 2nd sess., 1944; Joseph Borkin and Charles A. Welsh, *Germany's Master Plan: The Story of Industrial Offensive* (New York: Duell, Sloan and Pearce, 1943).

2.   U.S. Senate, Subcommittee on Scientific and Technical Mobilization of the Committee on Technical Mobilization, *Scientific and Technical Mobilization*, 78th Cong., 1st sess., 1943; U.S. Senate, Subcommittee on Scientific and Technical Mobilization of the Committee on Technical Mobilization, *Scientific and Technical Mobilization*, 78th Cong., 2nd sess., 1944 (these were part of a sequence that spanned two sessions of the Seventy-eighth Congress); U.S. Senate, Committee on Patents, *Patents*, 77th Cong., 2nd sess., 1942.

3.   Borkin and Welsh, *Germany's Master Plan*, p. 14.

4. *New Republic*, April 6, 1942, pp. 450–51.

5. *New Republic*, February 14, 1944, pp. 199–200.

6. Henry Wallace, "What We Fight For," *Vital Speeches*, October 1, 1943, pp. 754–57.

7. I. F. Stone, "The Cartel Cancer," *The Nation*, February 2, 1944, pp. 178–79.

8. Clipping, *Boston Globe*, December 18, 1944, Wendell Berge Papers, Box 57, Library of Congress, Washington, D.C.

9. Josephus Daniels to Franklin Roosevelt, September 4, 1944, OFF 277, Box 3, Franklin D. Roosevelt Library, Hyde Park, N.Y.

10. Clipping, *Capital Times* (Madison, Wis.), June 28, 1945, Berge Papers, Box 57.

11. Corwin Edwards, *Economic and Political Aspects of International Cartels* (New York: Arno Press, 1976), p. 24. For the price policies of some cartels, see chapter 1.

12. National Association of Manufacturers, *NAM Looks at Cartels: Positions Formulated by the Committee on International Economic Relations and Approved by the Board of Directors Together with an Analysis of the Economic Aspects of Cartels Prepared by the Research Department* (New York: National Association of Manufacturers, 1946), p. 3. NAM's board of directors approved the statement quoted in April 1945.

13. NAM, 1945 Annual Report, National Association of Manufacturers Papers, Series I, Box 40, Corporate Records, Annual Reports, Hagley Museum and Library, Wilmington, Del.

14. Jasper Crane, "International Cartels: Their Effects on DuPont's Business Policies," August 2, 1945, Walter S. Carpenter Papers, Box 829, Correspondence: Miscellaneous, 7/45–12/45, Hagley Museum and Library.

15. "Final Declaration of the Thirty-first National Foreign Trade Convention, October 9, 10, and 11," NAM Papers, Series I, Box 859, National Postwar Conference, Spring Lake, N.J., September 1944.

16. Thurman W. Arnold, *The Bottlenecks of Business* (New York: Reynal & Hitchcock, 1940), p. 97.

17. Ervin Hexner, *The International Steel Cartel* (Chapel Hill: University of North Carolina Press, 1943), and *International Cartels* (Chapel Hill: University of North Carolina Press, 1946).

18. Anton de Haas, *International Cartels in the Postwar World* (Washington, D.C.: American Enterprise Association, 1945).

19. Clipping, *Washington Post*, May 1, 1944, Berge Papers, Box 57.

20. Department of State, "Post-War Implications of the Trend Toward Monopoly in Great Britain," August 6, 1943, Joseph O'Mahoney Papers, Box 227, Legislation 1943, Cartels, American Heritage Center, University of Wyoming, Laramie.

21. Report on Conversations with British Officials, March 1945, April 24, 1945, Clayton-Thorp Papers, Box 1, Commercial Policy, Harry S. Truman Library, Independence, Mo.

22. Notes for Discussion with the President on Conversations in London, April 7–29, 1944, PSF, Department Files: State, Edward R. Stettinius, Box 75, Roosevelt Library.

23. Memorandum, Washington to Foreign Office, March 5, 1945, Foreign Office (FO), 371/44590, Public Records Office, Kew, England.

24. "A National Policy for Industry," NAM Papers, Series I, Box 290, Postwar—"A National Policy for Industry."

25. Harry McGowan, "Combines and Cartels," *Sunday Times* (London), July 25, 1943, reprint, Carpenter Papers, Box 836, Correspondence, ICI 1943–45. Emphasis in original.

26. Clipping, *Post-Dispatch* (St. Louis), January 1, 1944, Berge Papers, Box 57.

27. *New York Times*, August 19, 1943, p. 7.

28. Walter Carpenter to Harry McGowan, January 6, 1943, Carpenter Papers, Box 836, Correspondence, ICI 1943–45.

29. Franklin D. Roosevelt, *The Public Papers and Addresses of Franklin D. Roosevelt*, vol. 13, *Victory and the Threshold of Peace, 1944–45* (New York: Russell & Russell, 1950), p. 41.

30. Ibid., pp. 255–56.

31. Ibid., p. 377.

32. The chief exceptions to this agreement were alkali and rayon. DuPont avoided the alkali business, which it deemed insufficiently profitable, and ICI did not engage in the rayon business out of deference to Courtaulds, the leading British producer and one of its largest customers. The agreement also allowed each firm to make special arrangements for particularly important discoveries. DuPont put nylon in this category; ICI did the same for polythene.

33. Borkin and Welsh, *Germany's Master Plan*, p. 91.

34. Memorandum, Corwin Edwards to Thurman Arnold, September 8, 1942, Thurman Arnold Papers, Box 59, DuPont, American Heritage Center, University of Wyoming.

35. Memorandum, Tom Clark to the Attorney General, August 11, 1943, Roy A. Pewitt Files, Box 9, DuPont, Record Group 112, National Archives, Washington, D.C.; W. J. Reader, *Imperial Chemical Industries: A History*, vol. 2, *The First Quarter-Century, 1926–1952* (London: Oxford University Press, 1975), p. 413.

36. Mr. Berge, statement, January 6, 1944, Jasper E. Crane Papers, Box 1036, Department of Justice—Complaint Against DuPont, Remington Arms, and ICI, Hagley Museum and Library.

37. W. S. Carpenter, statement, January 6, 1944, Crane Papers, Box 1036, Department of Justice—Complaint Against DuPont, Remington Arms, and ICI.

38. Harry McGowan to Walter Carpenter, January 7, 1944, Carpenter Papers, Box 833, Correspondence: Indictments.

39. Reader, *Imperial Chemical Industries*, vol. 2, p. 430.

40. Wendell Berge to Russell and Eleanor Catron, January 8, 1944, Berge Papers, Box 16, Catron letters.

41. Clipping, *Philadelphia Inquirer*, January 8, 1944, FO 371/38583.

42. Clipping, *Lincoln Star*, February 1944, Berge Papers, Box 57.

43. Foreign Office to Washington, January 9, 1944, FO 371/38583.

44. Washington to Foreign Office, January 31, 1944, FO 371/38583.

45. Quoted in memorandum from Lord Halifax, April 18, 1944, FO 371/38584.

46. Lord Halifax to Cordell Hull, April 27, 1944, OFF 277, Box 3, Antitrust Laws, 1944–45, Roosevelt Library; see also Lord Halifax to E. R. Stettinius, February 21, 1944, FO 371/38584; memorandum from Lord Halifax, April 25, 1944, FO 371/38585.

47. Henry Stimson to Francis Biddle, April 25, 1944, OFF 277, Box 3, Antitrust Laws, 1944–45, Roosevelt Library.

48. James Forrestal to Francis Biddle, May 8, 1944, OFF 277, Box 3, Antitrust Laws, 1944–45, Roosevelt Library.

49. For the agreement between the service departments and Justice, see chapter 3.

50. Interview with Julius Amberg, Major Gallagher, and Robert Miller, March 18, 1944, FO 371/38584.

51. Francis Biddle to Henry Stimson, May 4, 1944, OFF 277, Box 3, Antitrust Laws, 1944–45, Roosevelt Library.

52. Francis Biddle to Franklin Roosevelt, May 12, 1944, OFF 277, Box 3, Antitrust Laws, 1944–45, Roosevelt Library.

53. Francis Biddle to Franklin Roosevelt, June 3, 1944, PSF, Box 56, Justice Department—Francis Biddle, Roosevelt Library.

54. Halifax to Hull, April 27, 1944; Halifax memo, April 25, 1944.

55. James Byrnes to the President, May 22, 1944, OFF 277, Box 3, Antitrust Laws, 1944–45, Roosevelt Library.

56. Memorandum, James Byrnes to the President, May 26, 1944, PSF, Box 56, Justice Department—Francis Biddle, Roosevelt Library.

57. Unsigned memorandum, May 22, 1944, PSF, Box 56, Justice Department—Francis Biddle, Roosevelt Library.

58. Franklin Roosevelt to Lord Halifax, June 19, 1944, PSF, Box 56, Justice Department—Francis Biddle, Roosevelt Library.

59. Francis Biddle to Franklin Roosevelt, June 23, 1944 (2 letters), OFF 277, Box 3, Antitrust Laws, 1944–45, Roosevelt Library; John Morton Blum, *V Was for Victory: Politics and American Culture During World War II* (New York: Harvest, 1976), pp. 138–39.

60. Charles W. Cheape, *Strictly Business: Walter Carpenter at DuPont and General Motors* (Baltimore: Johns Hopkins University Press, 1995), p. 221.

61. For Webb-Pomerene companies and the "silver letter," see chapters 1 and 2.

62. J. W. Adams, "Alkali Export Associations and Domestic Trade," September 15, 1943, Prewitt Files, Box 1, Alkali Industry.

63. Wendell Berge, "Export Associations and the Sherman Act," *Vital Speeches*, May 15, 1944, p. 477.

64. Memorandum, Aute L. Carr to Mr. Berman, December 20, 1943, Berge Papers, Box 46, Webb-Pomerene.

65. Berge, "Export Associations and the Sherman Act," p. 479.

66. *Wall Street Journal*, September 1, 1944, pp. 1, 4.

67. Memorandum of Meeting, June 22, 1944, Record Group 59, 800.602/6-2244, National Archives. The most notable of the studies that emerged from this effort was Federal Trade Commission, *The International Petroleum Cartel* (Washington, D.C.: Government Printing Office, 1952). For the policy implications of this report, see chapter 6.

68. For a general overview of the factors guiding postwar economic planning, see Richard N. Gardner, *Sterling–Dollar Diplomacy: Anglo-American Collaboration in the Reconstruction of Multilateral Trade* (Oxford: Clarendon Press, 1956), pp. 1–40.

69. Traditionally when confronted with a balance-of-payments deficit, nations raised interest rates and took other steps to deflate their economies, which usually created unemployment. Direct controls over foreign exchange and trade can make such steps unnecessary.

70. R. F. Harrod, *The Life of John Maynard Keynes* (New York: Discus Books, 1951), p. 584.

71. "Article VII of the Mutual Aid Agreement Between the Governments of the United States and the United Kingdom," February 23, 1942, in Harley Notter, *Postwar Foreign Policy Preparation, 1939–1945*, General Foreign Policy Series, no. 15 (Washington, D.C.: Department of State, 1949), p. 463.

72. Department of Justice, "Cartels and General Post-War Policy," Arnold Papers, Box 29, Correspondence, November 1942.

73. D. H. MacGregor, Introduction to Robert Liefmann, *Cartels, Concerns and Trusts* (London: Methuen, 1932), pp. ix–x.

74. Department of State, "Proposal for the Organization of World for the Formulation of Post-War Foreign Policies," September 12, 1941, in Notter, *Postwar Foreign Policy Preparation*, p. 465.

75. "The Twelve Special Economic Committees of the Interdepartmental Committee on Post-War Foreign Economic Policy," 1943, in Notter, *Postwar Foreign Policy Preparation*, p. 538.

76. J. A. Maxwell to Mr. Brown, August 22, 1944, Record Group 59, 800.60/8-2244, National Archives.

77. Franklin D. Roosevelt to Cordell Hull, September 6, 1944, in Franklin D. Roosevelt, *The Public Papers and Addresses of Franklin D. Roosevelt*, vol. 13, *Victory and the Threshold of Peace, 1944–45* (New York: Russell & Russell, 1950), pp. 255–56.

78. See chapter 3.

79. Dean Acheson, "Post-War International Economic Problems," *Department of State Bulletin*, December 3, 1944, p. 660.

80. Dean Acheson, *Present at the Creation: My Years in the State Department* (New York: Norton, 1969).

81. Edward S. Mason, "The Future of International Cartels," *Foreign Relations* 22 (1944): 604, 608, 613, 615.

82. Memorandum for Mr. Stettinius, October 16, 1944, Record Group 59, 800.602/9-3044, National Archives.

83. Cartel Memo 119, February 20, 1945, Harley Notter Papers, Record Group 59, National Archives.

84. Arnold, *Bottlenecks of Business*, pp. 213–14.

85. "Ambassador in the United Kingdom to the Secretary of State," December 19, 1942, in Department of State, *Foreign Relations of the United States, Diplomatic Papers, 1942*, vol. 1, *General: The British Commonwealth; The Far East* (Washington, D.C.: Government Printing Office, 1960), p. 241.

86. Memorandum for Mr. Berle, October 23, 1943, Record Group 59, 800.602/26 1/2, National Archives.

87. Ibid.

88. Quoted in Harrod, *Life of John Maynard Keynes*, p. 646.

89. Cartels Paper No. 4, October 14, 1943, Prewitt Files, Box 5, Cartels Policy—British Discussions.

90. Commodities, first meeting, September 22, 1943, Prewitt Files, Box 7, Commodity Policy—British Discussions.

91. Harrod, *Life of John Maynard Keynes*, p. 644.

92. Commodities, first meeting, September 22, 1943.

93. "Joint Statement on International Commodity Policy," Prewitt Files, Box 7, Commodity Policy—British Discussions.

94. Ibid.

95. Cartel Committee, "Tentative Program for Dealing with International Cartels," May 29, 1944, in Notter, *Postwar Foreign Policy Preparation*, p. 625.

96. Cartel Memo 38a, March 1, 1944, Notter Papers.

97. Commodity Agreements Committee, "Summary of the Report on International Commodity Arrangements," September 19, 1944, PSF, Departmental Files, State, Hull, Cordell, Box 75, Roosevelt Library.

98. Cartel Meeting 66, February 9, 1945, Notter Papers.

99. "To All Members of the House of Commons," FO 371/38585; in the upper house at this time, Lord McGowan made his most comprehensive public defense of the system of cartels.

100. Helen Mercer, *Construction a Competitive Order: The Hidden History of British Antitrust Policies* (Cambridge: Cambridge University Press, 1995), p. 74; Guenter Reimann, *Patents for Hitler* (London: Gollancz, 1945).

101. War Cabinet Reconstruction Committee, joint memorandum, March 29, 1944, FO 371/45683.

102. Foreign Office, "Draft Brief for Possible Discussion with American Officials on Cartels," January 16, 1945, FO 371/45683.

103. Cartel Meeting 66, February 9, 1945.

104. Cartel Memo 158, September 8, 1945, Notter Papers.

105. Richard N. Gardner, *Sterling–Dollar Diplomacy: Anglo-American Collaboration in the Reconstruction of Multilateral Trade* (Oxford: Clarendon Press, 1956), pp. 145–46.

106. Cartel Committee, "Proposals for Consideration by an International Conference on Trade and Employment," November 1945, in Notter, *Postwar Foreign Policy Preparation*, p. 634.

107. "Department of State to Certain Diplomatic Missions," April 2, 1946, in Department of State, *Foreign Relations of the United States, 1946*, vol. 1, *General: The United Nations* (Washington, D.C.: Government Printing Office, 1972), pp. 1261–62. For these agreements, see chapter 3.

108. Cartel Committee, "Proposals for Consideration by an International Conference on Trade an Employment," November 1945, p. 632.

109. Ray Atherton to the Secretary of State, January 3, 1946, Record Group 59, 800.602/1-346, National Archives.

110. *New York Times*, November 14, 1944, p. 29.

111. Edwards, *Economic and Political Aspects of International Cartels*, p. 47.

112. "Director of the Office of International Trade Policy to the Secretary of State," December 27, 1946, in Department of State, *Foreign Relations of the United States, 1946*, vol. 1, p. 1362.

113. "Ambassador in the Soviet Union to the Secretary of State," November 23, 1946, in Department of State, *Foreign Relations of the United States, 1946*, vol. 1, p. 1356.

114. For examples of Soviet statements on cartels, see Telegram from George Kennan, April 18, 1945, Record Group 56, 800.602/4-1845, National Archives. With respect to participation in cartels, the Soviet Union had accepted payments from the alkali cartel to abstain from exporting.

115. The participants were the United States, Great Britain, Canada, Cuba, Norway, Belgium, the Netherlands, France, India, Australia, and Czechoslovakia.

116. "Confidential Report for an International Conference," December 27, 1946, in Department of State, *Foreign Relations of the United States, 1946*, vol. 1, p. 1363.

117. Ibid., p. 1364.

118. "Ambassador in the United Kingdom to Secretary of State," September 4, 1946, in Department of State, *Foreign Relations of the United States, 1946*, vol. 1, pp. 1347–48.

119. "Confidential Report," December 27, 1946, p. 1361.

120. Department of State, "Memorandum Prepared in the Division of Commercial Policy," February 6, 1946, in Department of State, *Foreign Relations of the United States, 1946*, vol. 1, p. 1281.

121. "Confidential Report," December 27, 1946, p. 1362.

122. Havana to Foreign Office, November 27, 1947, FO 371/62761.

123. Havana to Foreign Office, December 15, 1947, FO 371/62763.

124. Ibid.

125. Havana to Foreign Office, December 29, 1947, FO 371/62765.

126. For instance, the British government controlled British Petroleum, and in the 1940s it took ownership of the coal and steel industries. The French government, if anything, was more active in industry. Even in West Germany, where the government intervened less in the economy than in most other European countries, Bonn controlled several large companies, including Deutsch Telekom.

127. *New York Times*, March 25, 1948, p. 2.

128. Gardner, *Sterling–Dollar Diplomacy*, p. 375.

129. International Chamber of Commerce, "Report on the United States 'Proposals for the Expansion of World Trade and Employment,'" NAM Papers, Series I, Box 16, Chamber of Commerce.

130. NAM, "Statement on the ITO Charter," March 30, 1949, NAM Papers, Series I, Box 104, Positions: ITO.

131. NAM, "Position on Inter-Governmental Commodity Agreements," March 1946, reprinted February 2, 1949, NAM Papers, Series 1, Box 104, Positions: ITO.

132. James G. Fulton and Jacob K. Javits, *The International Trade Organization*, 80th Cong., 2nd sess., 1948, pp. 40–43.

133. For the ITO debate, see Susan A. Aaronson, *Trade and the American Dream: A Social History of Postwar Trade Policy* (Lexington: University Press of Kentucky, 1996), pp. 13–132.

134. *Wall Street Journal*, September 1, 1944, pp. 1, 4. The suits covered dyestuffs, magnesium, aluminum, news services, military optics, matches, plastics, quebracho (substance used in tanning), photographic chemicals, tungsten carbide, incandescent lamps, fluorescent lamps, magnesium brick, chemicals, phar-

maceuticals, titanium compounds, alkali, and grain disk separators (devices used to mill grain).

135. For the 1926 GE case, see chapter 1.

136. *United States v. National Lead Co. et al.*, 63 F. Supp. 513.

137. Berge, *Cartels*, p. 141.

138. *United States v. National Lead Co. et al.*, 63 F. Supp. 513.

139. Ibid.

140. Ibid.

141. *United States v. National Lead Co. et al.*, 332 U.S. 319.

142. *United States v. United States Gypsum Co. et al.*, 333 U.S. 364.

143. *United States v. Line Material Co. et al.*, 333 U.S. 287.

144. *United States v. United States Gypsum Co. et al.*, 333 U.S. 364.

145. *United States v. Line Material Co. et al.*, 333 U.S. 287.

146. See chapter 3.

147. A. D. Neale, *The Antitrust Laws of the United States of America: A Study of Competition Enforced by Law* (Cambridge: Cambridge University Press, 1960), p. 355.

148. Lord McGowan, address, November 1, 1946, Carpenter Papers, Box 836, Correspondence, ICI 1946–48.

149. Draft of consent decree, December 11, 1946, Carpenter Papers, Box 836, Correspondence, ICI 1946–48; Cheape, *Strictly Business*, p. 222.

150. D. C. Coleman, *Courtaulds: An Economic and Social History*, vol. 3, *Crisis and Change, 1940–1965* (Oxford: Clarendon Press, 1980), p. 79.

151. Memorandum, Foreign Relations Department to General Managers and Presidents of Subsidiary Companies, June 29, 1948, DuPont Records, Series II, Part 2, Foreign Relations Committee, Box 530, ICI Commercial Policy, 1939–1948, Hagley Museum and Library.

152. Reader, *Imperial Chemical Industries*, vol. 2, pp. 435–39.

153. *United States v. Imperial Chemical Industries Limited et al.*, 100 F. Supp. 504; *United States v. Imperial Chemical Industries Limited et al.*, 105 F. Supp. 215.

154. *United States v. Imperial Chemical Industries Limited et al.*, 100 F. Supp. 504; *United States v. Imperial Chemical Industries Limited et al.*, 105 F. Supp. 215; Kingman Brewster, Jr., *Antitrust and American Business Abroad* (New York: McGraw-Hill, 1958), p. 92; Neale, *Antitrust Laws of the United States*, p. 333.

155. *United States v. General Electric Co. et al.*, 80 F. Supp. 989. For the tungsten carbide cartel, see chapter 3.

156. *United States v. General Electric Co. et al.*, 82 F. Supp. 753.

157. Ibid. For the Phoebus cartel, see chapters 1 and 2.

158. Mira Wilkins, *The Maturing of Multinational Enterprise: American Business Abroad from 1914 to 1970* (Cambridge, Mass.: Harvard University Press, 1974), pp. 294–96; *United States v. General Electric Co. et al.*, 115 F. Supp. 835.

159. *United States* v. *United States Alkali Export Association, Inc., et al.,* 86 F. Supp. 59. For the "silver letter," see chapter 1.

160. Brewster, *Antitrust Abroad,* pp. 116–20.

161. *United States* v. *Minnesota Mining & Manufacturing Co. et al.,* 92 F. Supp. 947.

162. *United States* v. *Timken Roller Bearing Co.,* 83 F. Supp. 284.

163. Ibid.

164. *Timken Roller Bearing Co.* v. *United States,* 341 U.S. 593. Timken acquired complete ownership of its British and French subsidiaries in the late 1950s. The language of the company's agreement with the Antitrust Division, however, forced the American firm to continue competing against its foreign subsidiaries. Only in the 1980s, when the Justice Department agreed to change the accord, were these three organizations able to entirely coordinate their activities.

165. Brewster, *Antitrust Abroad,* pp. 74–75.

166. In particular, the chemical and petroleum cartels made use of joint subsidiaries. ICI and DuPont had numerous joint enterprises, which, in turn, often entered into joint ventures with IG Farben. The international petroleum cartel used joint enterprises both for controlling production and for marketing.

167. Brewster, *Antitrust Abroad,* pp. 74–75.

Chapter 5. Among Unbelievers: Antitrust in Germany and Japan

1. Cartel Memo 8, [1944], Harley Notter Papers, Record Group 59, National Archives, Washington, D.C.

2. U.S. Senate, Subcommittee in War Mobilization to the Committee on Military Affairs, *Cartels and National Security,* 79th Cong., 2nd sess., 1944, p. 5.

3. Cartel Memo 8, [1944].

4. U.S. Senate, *Cartels and National Security,* pp. 6–7.

5. Fritz Thyssen, *I Paid Hitler* (New York: Farrar & Rinehart, 1941).

6. Cartel Memo 8, [1944].

7. U.S. Senate, *Cartels and National Security,* pp. 6–7.

8. Ibid., p. 8.

9. Ibid., p. 9.

10. Henry A. Turner attacks the idea that German big business contributed to Hitler's rise to power in a vital way in *German Big Business and the Rise of Hitler* (New York: Oxford University Press, 1985).

11. This purge, known as the "Night of the Long Knives," eliminated potential threats to Hitler's dominance of the Nazi Party.

12. Peter Hayes provides a thorough history of the often unhappy relationship between Germany's largest company and the Nazis in *Industry and Ideology: IG Farben and the Nazi Era* (Cambridge: Cambridge University Press, 1987).

13. "JSC 1067," April 1945, in Department of State, *Germany, 1947–49: The Story in Documents* (Washington, D.C.: Government Printing Office, 1950), pp. 29–30.

14. "Protocol of the Potsdam Conference," August 1, 1945, in Department of State, *Germany, 1947–49*, p. 49.

15. Eleanor M. Hadley, *Antitrust in Japan* (Princeton, N.J.: Princeton University Press, 1970), p. 9. The most prominent businessman assassinated was Baron Dan, the head of the Mitsui combine, the country's largest.

16. Institute of Pacific Relations, *Security in the Pacific* (New York: International Secretariat of the Institute of Pacific Relations, 1945), p. 41.

17. Cartel Memo 168, November 15, 1945, Notter Papers.

18. Hadley, *Antitrust in Japan*, p. 47.

19. Cartel Memo 168, November 15, 1945.

20. Michael Schaller, *The American Occupation of Japan: The Origins of the Cold War in Asia* (New York: Oxford University Press, 1985), pp. 31–32.

21. Quoted in Hadley, *Antitrust in Japan*, pp. 6–8.

22. Cartel Meeting 19, January 28, 1944, Notter Papers.

23. For a lengthier discussion of this subject, see John Lewis Gaddis, *The United States and the Origins of the Cold War, 1941–1947* (New York: Columbia University Press, 1972), pp. 95–132.

24. "JSC 1067," April 1945.

25. Howard B. Schonberger, *Aftermath of War: Americans and the Remaking of Japan, 1945–1952* (Kent, Ohio: Kent State University Press, 1989), pp. 11–39.

26. J. F. J. Gillen, "Deconcentration and Decartelization in West Germany, 1945–1953," 1953, Office of High Commissioner Records (HICOG), Decartelization Division, Box 6, Reports, pp. 13–16, Record Group 466, National Archives.

27. Carolyn Woods Eisenberg, *Drawing the Line: The American Decision to Divide Germany, 1944–1949* (Cambridge: Cambridge University Press, 1996), pp. 139–51.

28. Quoted in Gillen, "Deconcentration and Decartelization in West Germany, 1945–1953," p. 42.

29. Minutes of U.S./German Decartelization Conference, October 2, 1951, HICOG, Decartelization Division, Box 3, Conferences AMDAG/GEDAG.

30. "Decartelization and Deconcentration," November 1, 1950, FO 1036/176, Public Records Office, Kew, England.

31. The New Military Government Decartelization Law for Germany, June 10, 1947, HICOG, Decartelization Branch, Box 8, Law 56; "Manual for Enforcement," February 26, 1947, HICOG, Decartelization Branch, Box 5, Decartelization Main File.

32. Gillen, "Deconcentration and Decartelization in West Germany, 1945–1953," pp. 16–19. The reports in question take up dozens of boxes in the Office of

Military Government (U.S.) (OMGUS), Records of the Economics Division, Decartelization Branch, Record Group 260, National Archives.

33. Memorandum, "Draft of Monthly Report," November 15, [1945], OMGUS, Records of the Economics Division, Decartelization Branch, Farben Control, Box 96, Rohm and Haas.

34. Gillen, "Deconcentration and Decartelization in West Germany, 1945–1953," p. 20.

35. "Report of the Committee Appointed to Review the Decartelization Program in Germany," [April 1949], pp. 13, 92, Joseph O'Mahoney Papers, Box 341, Resource File, 1949, Decartelization Program in Germany, American Heritage Center, University of Wyoming, Laramie.

36. Outgoing message, Keating to Co. Dawson, November 30, 1946, OMGUS, Records of the Economics Division, Decartelization Branch, Box 88, 1947 Study.

37. Control Council, [August 1945], OMGUS, Records of the Economic Directorate, Box 254, DECO 1–35.

38. Allied Control Authority, Economic Directorate, Working Party on Decartelization, October 8, 1946, FO 1039/290. The Allies had to calculate the turnover and capital of firms in 1938 Reichmarks because wartime inflation had rendered the German currency almost worthless.

39. Eisenberg, *Drawing the Line*, p. 147.

40. Allied Control Authority, Economic Directorate, Decartelization Law, November 5, 1946, FO 1039/290; Allied Control Authority, Economic Directorate, Working Party on Decartelization, October 8, 1946.

41. James Stewart Martin, *All Honorable Men* (Boston: Little, Brown, 1950), pp. 169–71.

42. Review, [July 1951], HICOG, Subject Files, Tripartite IG Farben Control Organization (TRIFCOG), Box 39, Successor Companies (1 of 3).

43. Allied Control Authority, IG Farbenindustrie Control Committee, October 15, 1946; Allied Control Authority, Economic Directorate, IG Farben Control Committee, March 1, 1947; Allied Control Authority, Economic Directorate, February 14, 1947, all in OMGUS, Records of the Economics Division, Decartelization Branch, Box 130, Decartelization, IG Farben, 1947.

44. James S. Martin to Miriam Stuart, August 9, 1946, OMGUS, Records of the Economics Division, Decartelization Branch, Box 145, Feb.–Oct. 1946.

45. Decartelization, [December 1946], OMGUS, Records of the Economics Division, Decartelization Branch, Box 140, Progress Report for six months ending 31 Dec. 1946; "Report of the Committee Appointed to Review the Decartelization Program in Germany," [April 1949].

46. P. Hawkins to Mr. McCloy, July 29, 1949, HICOG, Decartelization Division, Box 5, Decartelization.

47. Phillip Hawkins to George Hays, March 3, 1948, OMGUS, Records of the Economics Division, Decartelization Branch, Box 146, Jan.–March 1948; Property Division of the Decartelization Branch, April 9, 1948, OMGUS, Records of the Economics Division, Decartelization Office, Box 130, Decartelization, IG Farben, 1948.

48. "Report of the Committee Appointed to Review the Decartelization Program in Germany," [April 1949].

49. Eisenberg, *Drawing the Line*, pp. 335–38, 450–53.

50. Lucius Clay, "Ferguson Committee Report," April 24, 1949, in Lucius D. Clay, *The Papers of General Lucius D. Clay*, ed. Jean Edward Smith (Bloomington: Indiana University Press, 1974), p. 1129.

51. Eisenberg, *Drawing the Line*, pp. 211–21.

52. Gillen, "Deconcentration and Decartelization in West Germany, 1945–1953," p. 25.

53. Ordinance No. 78, FO 1039/290; Law No. 56, FO 1036/111.

54. "Report of the Committee Appointed to Review the Decartelization Program in Germany," [April 1949].

55. Gillen, "Deconcentration and Decartelization in West Germany, 1945–1953," p. 65.

56. Volker R. Berghahn, *The Americanization of West German Industry, 1945–1973* (Cambridge: Cambridge University Press, 1986), p. 102.

57. Ordinance No. 78; Law No. 56.

58. "Report of the Committee Appointed to Review the Decartelization Program in Germany," [April 1949], p. 104.

59. Quoted in Gillen, "Deconcentration and Decartelization in West Germany, 1945–1953," pp. 35–40; "Report on Progress of Decartelization Branch since Feb. 12, 1947," June 14, 1947, OMGUS, Records of the Economics Division, Decartelization Branch, Box 142, Progress Report.

60. Quoted in Gillen, "Deconcentration and Decartelization in West Germany, 1945–1953," pp. 35–40; "Report on Progress of Decartelization Branch since Feb. 12, 1947," June 14, 1947.

61. "Authorized Visit to Berlin to Coordinate Justice and Decartelization Investigation," December 23, 1947, OMGUS, Records of the Economics Division, Decartelization Branch, Box 146, Nov.–Dec. 1947. For the U.S. government's ball bearing case, see chapter 4.

62. George Marshall, "Problems of European Revival and German and Austrian Peace Settlements," November 18, 1947, in Department of State, *Germany, 1947–49*, p. 12.

63. "Revised Plan for Level of Industry," August 1947, OMGUS, Records of the Economics Division, Decartelization Branch, Farben Control, Box 63, Policy File.

64. "Comparative Readings in Basic U.S. Policy Directives on Germany," June 15, 1947, OMGUS, Records of the Economics Division, Decartelization Branch, Farben Control, Box 64, Policy Directives.

65. Martin, *All Honorable Men*, pp. 226–33.

66. Quoted in Gillen, "Decartelization and Deconcentration in West Germany, 1945–1953," p. 49.

67. Memorandum, James Martin to the Screening Commission, December 21, 1946, OMGUS, Records of the Economics Division, Decartelization Branch, Box 145, Nov.–Dec. 1946.

68. Quoted in Gillen, "Deconcentration and Decartelization in Germany, 1945–1953," p. 48.

69. "Decartelization and Deconcentration, Background Information," March 1950, FO 1036/176.

70. "Deconcentration and Decartelization," September 4, 1950, FO 1036/176.

71. Donald Gainer to Ivone Kirkpatrick, July 15, 1950, FO 1036/176.

72. "Implementation of Allied Decartelization Laws," May 27, 1952, FO 1036/178.

73. All four powers shared authority over Berlin, which made it doubtful that Britain and the United States could act on their own against a firm headquartered there.

74. Clay, "Ferguson Committee Report."

75. Memorandum to Richardson Bronson re Anti-Friction Bearing Industry, May 5, 1948, OMGUS, Records of the Economics Division, Decartelization Branch, Box 146, April–June 1948.

76. Lucius D. Clay, *Decision in Germany* (Garden City, N.Y.: Doubleday, 1950), p. 334.

77. Kenneth Myers to Leland Spencer, October 25, 1948, OMGUS, Records of the Economics Division, Decartelization Branch, Box 146, Oct.–Dec. 1948.

78. Clay, "Ferguson Committee Report."

79. Gillen, "Decartelization and Deconcentration in West Germany, 1945–1953," p. 63.

80. Clay, *Decision in Germany*, p. 325.

81. Lucius Clay, "Achievements of Military Government in 1948," January 1949, in Department of State, *Germany, 1947–49*, p. 15.

82. Clay, "Ferguson Committee Report."

83. Memorandum, State Department to Willard Thorp, May 5, 1948, Clayton-Thorp Papers, Box 15, Reading Files, Memoranda, January–December 1948, Harry S. Truman Library, Independence, Mo.

84. Gillen, "Decartelization and Deconcentration in West Germany, 1945–1953," p. 62.

85. Johnston Avery et al. to Lucius Clay, March 13, 1948, O'Mahoney Papers, Box 246, Resources File, 1948, Deconcentration in Germany.

86. Quoted in Martin, *All Honorable Men*, p. 277.

87. Eisenberg, *Drawing the Line*, p. 378.

88. Clay, *Decision in Germany*, p. 331.

89. Jean Edward Smith, *Lucius D. Clay: An American Life* (New York: Holt, 1990), p. 244.

90. Clay, *Decision in Germany*, p. 331.

91. Gillen, "Decartelization and Deconcentration in West Germany, 1945–1953," pp. 55–58.

92. James Stewart Martin to Joseph C. O'Mahoney, May 4, 1948, O'Mahoney Papers, Box 246, Resources File, 1948, Decartelization in Germany. In 1948, Martin was busy organizing the presidential campaign of former vice president Henry Wallace in Maryland. Apparently, his taste for lost causes was infinite.

93. *New York Times*, July 25, 1948, p. 28.

94. *New York Times*, December 3, 1948, p. 3.

95. *New York Times*, December 10, 1948, p. 20.

96. Clay, "Ferguson Committee Report."

97. Gillen, "Decartelization and Deconcentration in West Germany, 1945–1953," p. 72.

98. Memorandum of conversation, "Decartelization Policy in Germany," February 10, 1950, HICOG, Decartelization Division, Box 5, Decartelization.

99. Ibid.

100. *New York Times*, August 13, 1949, p. 3.

101. Gillen, "Deconcentration and Decartelization in West Germany, 1945–1953," p. 73.

102. Memorandum, "Recommended Revisions of the Prohibited and Limited Industries Agreement," October 23, 1950, HICOG, Decartelization Division, Box 7, Industries Agreement.

103. See chapter 4.

104. *New York Times*, May 1, 1949, pp. 1, 7.

105. *New York Times*, May 7, 1949, p. 7.

106. "Decartelization and Deconcentration," June 6, 1951, HICOG, Decartelization Division, Box 3, Conference (Brussels).

107. *New York Times*, December 25, 1949, p. 14.

108. Report of speech by Fritz Berg, December 11, 1953, HICOG, Decartelization Division, Box 5, Decartelization.

109. Memorandum, HICOG Bonn to Department of State, Washington, February 13, 1953, HICOG, Decartelization Division, Box 5, Decartelization.

110. Thomas Alan Schwartz, *America's Germany: John J. McCloy and the Federal Republic of Germany* (Cambridge, Mass.: Harvard University Press, 1991), p. 205.

111. Berghahn, *Americanization of West German Industry*, pp. 168–69.

112. Ibid., p. 181.

113. Memorandum, F. H. Clopstock to L. M. Pumphrey, February 2, 1950, HI-COG, Decartelization Division, Box 1, Banking '49–'50.

114. Ibid.

115. "Draft Law on the Regional Scope of Credit Institutions and Their Branches," November 15, 1950, HICOG, Decartelization Division, Box 1, Banking '49–'50.

116. Hawkins to McCloy, July 29, 1949.

117. "Have the Admittedly Divergent Views of the Allies Concerning the Treatment of IG Farben Led to Different Treatment in the Various Zones?" [1950], FO 1036/180.

118. Ibid.

119. Hawkins to McCloy, July 29, 1949.

120. For Farben's management problems, see Hayes, *Industry and Ideology.*

121. "Have the Admittedly Divergent Views of the Allies."

122. "The Deconcentration of IG Farbenindustrie AG," April 16, 1952, FO 1036/184. The spin-offs were Cassella Farbwerke Mainkur AG; Chemiewerk Homburg AG; Dr. Alexander Wacker, GmbH; Duisburger Kupferhutte; Chemische Werke Huls, GmbH; Dynamit AG; and Wasag Chemie AG.

123. Memorandum from German government, [1951], translation, FO 1036/180.

124. Ibid.

125. "Have the Admittedly Divergent Views."

126. Memorandum, [1951], FO 1036/181.

127. For the suit, see chapter 4.

128. Memorandum, [1951]; memorandum from German government, [1951].

129. C. C. Oxborrow to Economic Adviser, June 5, 1951, FO 1036/181.

130. Hermann Gross, "Second Supplement to Further Facts and Figures Relating to the Deconcentration of the I.G. Farbenindustrie," December 1950, FO 1036/180.

131. Allied High Commission for Germany, press release no. 394, January 15, 1952, FO 1036/182.

132. "Terms of Licenses under I.G. Farben Patents," January 25, 1952, HICOG, Subject Files, TRIFCOG, Box 29, Press Reports.

133. Schwartz, *America's Germany*, p. 62.

134. Military Government Law No. 75, [November 1948], HICOG, Decartelization Division, Box 5, Decartelization Main File; Allied High Commission Law, February 22, 1950, FO 1036/167; Eisenberg, *Drawing the Line*, p. 452.

135. Eisenberg, *Drawing the Line*, pp. 452–54.

136. Schwartz, *America's Germany*, pp. 186–88.

137. Ibid.; Bipartite Board, Ordinance No. 112, November 17, 1947, HICOG, Decartelization Division, Box 2, Cartels: Coal.

138. "Meeting Between the Allied High Commissioners and Representatives of the German Coal Mining Industry," April 14, 1950, FO 1036/168.

139. Memorandum, R. G. Wayland to Mr. Willner, November 1, 1951, HICOG, Decartelization Division, Box 2, Cartels: Coal; Schwartz, *America's Germany*, pp. 94–95.

140. "The DKLB Plan of 15 September 1950," HICOG, Decartelization Branch, Box 2, Cartels: Coal; Schwartz, *America's Germany*, pp. 190–91.

141. Dean Acheson to Certain American Diplomatic Officers, November 18, 1949, and June 8, 1950, HICOG, Decartelization Division, Box 15, Steel Industry, Formation of Unit Companies. The course of these talks is not clear.

142. François Duchene, *Jean Monnet: The First Statesman of Interdependence* (New York: Norton, 1994), p. 214.

143. Corwin Edwards, *Control of Cartels and Monopolies: An International Comparison* (Dobbs Ferry, N.Y.: Oceana, 1967), p. 246.

144. Clay, *Decision in Germany*, p. 334.

145. Schaller, *American Occupation of Japan*, pp. 29–30.

146. "History of the Nonmilitary Activities of the Occupation of Japan: Volume X, Reform of Business Enterprise; Part D, Promotion of Fair Trade Practices," p. 8, National Archives Microfilm, Supreme Command for the Allied Powers (SCAP), Box 8476, Public Relations, Record Group 331, National Archives.

147. Quoted in J. W. Dower, *Empire and Aftermath: Yoshida Shigeru and the Japanese Experience, 1878–1954* (Cambridge, Mass.: Harvard University Press, 1979), p. 344.

148. For the TNEC, see chapter 2.

149. "Interpreter's Notes on a Talk Given by Dr. E. C. Welsh," March 13, 1948, SCAP, Box 8476, Public Relations.

150. E. C. Welsh, "Economic Deconcentration?" December 5, 1947, SCAP, Box 8476, Public Relations.

151. Unfortunately for the Zaibatsu families, severe inflation during the late 1940s eroded most of the value of the bonds they received in compensation for their property.

152. "History of the Nonmilitary Activities of the Occupation of Japan: Volume X, Reform of Business Enterprise; Part A, Elimination of Zaibatsu Control," pp. 37–40, National Archives Microfilm, SCAP.

153. Quoted in Schonberger, *Aftermath of War*, p. 64.

154. "History of the Nonmilitary Activities of the Occupation of Japan: Elimination of Zaibatsu Control," pp. 31–32. For the recommendations themselves, see appendix 4, "Edwards Mission Report, Summary of Recommendations," May 26, 1946; Schaller, *American Occupation of Japan*, pp. 40–41.

155. "History of the Nonmilitary Activities of the Occupation of Japan: Elimination of Zaibatsu Control," appendix 4, p. 49.

156. "History of the Nonmilitary Activities of the Occupation of Japan: Elimination of Zaibatsu Control," pp. 87, 122–25, 133–34.

157. Ibid., pp. 68–71, 214–15.

158. Memorandum for Chief, ESS, "First Year's Occupation of Japan," SCAP, Box 8468, History ESS/FTD.

159. Proposed Trade Association Law, October 28, 1947, SCAP, Box 8476, Antimonopoly and Trade Association Laws.

160. Antitrust Legislation, April 1947, SCAP, Box 8476, Antimonopoly and Trade Association Laws.

161. Elimination of Concentration of Excessive Economic Power Law, [1947], Tom Clark Papers, Attorney General Files, Box 45, AG Correspondence, 1945–49, Hutchinson, Walter R., Truman Library.

162. "History of the Nonmilitary Activities of the Occupation of Japan: Volume X, Reform of Business Enterprise; Part C, Deconcentration of Economic Power," p. 17, National Archives Microfilm, SCAP.

163. George Kennan, *Memoirs, 1925–1950* (New York: Pantheon Books, 1967), p. 388.

164. "Acting Political Adviser in Japan to Secretary of State," March 23, 1948, in Department of State, *Foreign Relations of the United States, 1948*, vol. 6, *The Far East and Australasia* (Washington, D.C.: Government Printing Office, 1974), p. 689; Schaller, *American Occupation of Japan*, p. 113.

165. Memorandum for the Record, F. W. Marquat to Edward Welsh, April 18, 1948, SCAP, Box 8458, Deconcentration Review.

166. Unsigned memorandum, April 1, 1948, SCAP, Box 8476, Public Relations.

167. E. C. Welsh, "Assessment of Deconcentration Situation," November 29, 1948, SCAP, Box 8468, History ESS/FTP.

168. Welsh, "Economic Deconcentration?"

169. Edward Welsh to Wright Patman, April 1, 1949, SCAP, Box 8467, Public Relations.

170. Welsh, "Assessment of Deconcentration Situation."

171. Quoted in Dower, *Empire and Aftermath*, p. 344.

172. *Newsweek*, December 1, 1947, p. 368.

173. *Congressional Record*, December 19, 1947, pp. 11686–90; January 19, 1948, pp. 298–300.

174. Schaller, *American Occupation of Japan*, pp. 112–18; Schonberger, *Aftermath of War*, pp. 134–60.

175. Royal to Roy Stuart Campbell, February 25, 1948, and O. Freile to General Marquat, March 26, 1948, both in SCAP, Box 8458, Deconcentration Review.

176. Joseph Robinson to R. S. Campbell, March 7, 1949, SCAP, Box 8458, Letters.

177. Walter R. Hutchinson to Tom Clark, September 15, 1948, Clark Papers, Attorney General Files, Box 45, AG Correspondence, 1945–49, Hutchinson, Walter R.

178. Hadley, *Antitrust in Japan*, pp. 114–15.

179. Memorandum, F. W. Marquat to Deconcentration Review Board, June 5, 1948, and memorandum, Deconcentration Review Board to Supreme Commander

for Allied Powers, July 2, 1948, both in SCAP, Box 8458, Reorganization of Banks.

180. Memorandum, "Policy Basis for Deconcentration–anti-monopoly–anti-Zaibatsu Program," [1948], SCAP, Box 8468, General Program.

181. Hadley, *Antitrust in Japan*, pp. 114–15, 174.

182. E. C. Welsh, "Sale of Securities through SCLC," October 1, 1947, SCAP, Box 8468, Deconcentration—General; press release, November 6, 1948, SCAP, Box 8470, SCAPIN Memos.

183. ER&R Law, May 4, 1950, SCAP, Box 8470, Correspondence—General; "History of the Nonmilitary Activities of the Occupation of Japan: Elimination of Zaibatsu Control," p. 160.

184. Antitrust and Cartels Division, "1949 Historical Report from EES/FTP," January 20, 1950, SCAP, Box 8468, ESS/FTP.

185. "Acting Political Adviser in Japan to Secretary of State," March 23, 1948.

186. " History of the Nonmilitary Activities of the Occupation of Japan: Deconcentration of Economic Power," pp. 81, 84–85, 89–91, 98–99, 105–8, 111–13.

187. These companies avoided the prohibition on holding companies by investing only a minority of their capital in securities.

188. William S. Broder provides a good history of the economic problems faced by Japan as well as the various measures taken to alleviate them in *The Pacific Alliance: United States Foreign Economic Policy and Japanese Trade Recovery, 1947–1955* (Madison: University of Wisconsin Press, 1984).

Chapter 6. The New Order in Practice: The Cases of Oil and Steel

1. For the relationship between Farben and Standard, see chapter 3.

2. Henrietta M. Larson, Evelyn H. Knowleton, and Charles S. Popple, *New Horizons: History of Standard Oil Company (New Jersey), 1927–1950* (New York: Harper & Row, 1971), pp. 98–99.

3. "Pool Association," September 17, 1928, in U.S. Senate, Subcommittee on Multinational Corporations of the Committee on Foreign Relations, *Multinational Corporations and United States Foreign Policy, Part 8*, 93rd Cong., 2nd sess., 1974, p. 35.

4. U.S. Senate, Subcommittee on Multinational Corporations of the Committee on Foreign Relations, *Multinational Corporations and United States Foreign Policy, Part 6*, 93rd Cong., 2nd sess., 1974, p. 49.

5. Federal Trade Commission, *The International Petroleum Cartel* (Washington, D.C.: Government Printing Office, 1952), p. 225.

6. Larson, Knowleton, and Popple, *New Horizons*, pp. 52–58; U.S. Senate, Subcommittee on Multinational Corporations of the Committee on Foreign Relations, *Multinational Corporations and United States Foreign Policy, Part 7*, 93rd Cong., 2nd sess., 1974, pp. 21–25.

7. "Heads of Agreement for Distribution," December 15, 1932, in U.S. Senate, *Multinational Corporations and United States Foreign Policy, Part 8*, pp. 21–25.

8. FTC, *International Petroleum Cartel*, pp. 236–40.

9. "East of Suez" refers to any point usually reached from Europe via the Suez Canal.

10. Larson, Knowleton, and Popple, *New Horizons*, pp. 306–8, 315–18; U.S. Senate, *Multinational Corporations and United States Foreign Policy, Part 7*, pp. 57–59; Daniel Yergin, *The Prize: The Epic Quest for Oil, Money, and Power* (New York: Touchstone Books, 1991), p. 268.

11. FTC, *International Petroleum Cartel*, pp. 163–93; Larson, Knowleton, and Popple, *New Horizons*, pp. 58, 138.

12. Larson, Knowleton, and Popple, *New Horizons*, pp. 98–99.

13. Ibid., p. 95.

14. Ibid., p. 333; Yergin, *Prize*, p. 268.

15. Harold Ickes to Editor of the *New Republic*, August 6, 1945, Ralph K. Davies Papers, Box 15, Confidential Correspondence, 1940–48, Harry S. Truman Library, Independence, Mo.

16. U.S. Senate, *Multinational Corporations and United States Foreign Policy, Part 7*, p. 29; Yergin, *Prize*, pp. 403–5.

17. "Agreement on Petroleum Between the Government of the United States of America and the Government of the United Kingdom of Great Britain and Northern Ireland," [August 1944], OFF 5588, Box 1, Franklin D. Roosevelt Library, Hyde Park, N.Y.

18. Harold Ickes to Franklin Roosevelt, [August 16, 1944], OFF 5588, Box 1, Roosevelt Library.

19. Quoted in Yergin, *Prize*, p. 402.

20. For a list of those behind the agreement, all of whom save Ickes were associated with the State, War, and Navy Departments, see Harold Ickes et al. to Franklin Roosevelt, August 7, 1944, OFF 5588, Box 1, Roosevelt Library.

21. "Overseas News Agency Report," September 6, 1944, Wendell Berge Papers, Box 43, Antitrust (General) (Subject File), Library of Congress, Washington, D.C.

22. *The Nation*, August 19, 1944, p. 201.

23. J. Howard Pew, statement, October 25, 1944, Joseph O'Mahoney Papers, Box 228, Legislation 1945, Cartels no. 2, American Heritage Center, University of Wyoming, Laramie. Emphasis in original.

24. Yergin, *Prize*, p. 403; George W. Stocking, "Economic Change and the Sherman Act: Some Reflections on 'Workable Competition,'" in Robert F. Himmelberg, ed., *Antitrust and Business Regulation in the Postwar Era, 1946–1964* (New York: Garland, 1994), p. 342.

25. The two managed to break the contract that had created the Iraq Oil Company, which had prohibited them from joining such a venture in Saudi Arabia.

26. U.S. Senate, *Multinational Corporations and United States Foreign Policy, Part 7*, pp. 64–66.

27. Ibid., pp. 32–35; Larson, Knowleton, and Popple, *New Horizons*, pp. 737–40.

28. FTC, *International Petroleum Cartel*, pp. 29, 160, 162.

29. Burton I. Kaufman, "Oil and Antitrust: The Oil Cartel Case and the Cold War," in Himmelberg, ed., *Antitrust and Business Regulation in the Postwar Era*, pp. 114–15.

30. For the origins of these studies, see chapter 4.

31. U.S. Senate, *Multinational Corporations and United States Foreign Policy, Part 7*, pp. 15–20.

32. See chapter 4.

33. "Report by the Departments of State, Defense and the Interior on Security and International Issues Arising from the Current Situation in Petroleum," [1952], in U.S. Senate, *Multinational Corporations and United States Foreign Policy, Part 8*, pp. 4, 7.

34. Ibid., p. 6; Corwin Edwards, *Control of Cartels and Monopolies: An International Comparison* (Dobbs Ferry, N.Y.: Oceana, 1967), pp. 357–58. Anglo-Iranian was a British firm, whereas British stockholders owned 40 percent of Royal Dutch/Shell, the balance belonging to investors in the Netherlands.

35. Anglo-Iranian, which controlled all of Iran's output, had absolutely refused to increase the relatively low royalty it paid Tehran for oil even while American firms—with Washington's encouragement—were cutting more generous deals with other countries.

36. Anglo-Iranian claimed that it rightfully owned Iran's oil fields and therefore that any oil from there was stolen from it.

37. "Report by the Department of Justice on the Grand Jury Investigation of the International Oil Cartel," [1952], in U.S. Senate, *Multinational Corporations and United States Foreign Policy, Part 8*, p. 12.

38. Yergin, *Prize*, p. 474.

39. U.S. Senate, *Multinational Corporations and United States Foreign Policy, Part 7*, p. 289.

40. U.S. Senate, Subcommittee on Multinational Corporations of the Committee on Foreign Relations, *Multinational Corporations and United States Foreign Policy, Part 9*, 93rd Cong., 2nd sess., 1974, p. 46; Yergin, *Prize*, pp. 477–78.

41. The Iranian consortium included the seven sisters, the leading French company, and a handful of American independents. British Petroleum had 40 percent; Royal Dutch/Shell, 14 percent; each of the leading American firms, 7 percent; the French, 6 percent; and the independents, 5 percent. Technically,

Iran retained ownership of its petroleum industry, but the consortium managed the oil fields and refineries.

42. U.S. Senate, *Multinational Corporations and United States Foreign Policy, Part 9*, p. 46.

43. Ibid., pp. 73–74.

44. "Memorandum from the Special Assistant to the President," November 22, 1955, in Department of State, *Foreign Relations of the United States, 1955–57*, vol. 4, *Western European Security and Integration* (Washington, D.C.: Government Printing Office, 1986), p. 352.

45. Robert Eisenberg on Steel Export Price Agreement, September 11, 1953, HI-COG, Decartelization Division, Box 15, Steel Industry Reorganization, Record Group 466, National Archives, Washington, D.C.

46. "Memorandum from the Special Assistant to the President," p. 352.

47. Memorandum of Meeting Held 19 December, 1950, HICOG, Decartelization Division, Box 2, Coal & Steel Community.

48. François Duchene, *Jean Monnet: The First Statesman of Interdependence* (New York: Norton, 1994), pp. 246–47; Thomas Alan Schwartz, *America's Germany: John J. McCloy and the Federal Republic of Germany* (Cambridge, Mass.: Harvard University Press, 1991), p. 201.

49. Duchene, *Jean Monnet*, p. 249.

50. "Report by the Foreign Operations Administration," March 16, 1955, in Department of State, *Foreign Relations of the United States, 1955–57*, vol. 4, p. 272.

51. "Report by the Department of State," March 16, 1955, in Department of State, *Foreign Relations of the United States, 1955–57*, vol. 4, p. 262.

52. "Memorandum from the Assistant Secretary of State," February 14, 1955, in Department of State, *Foreign Relations of the United States, 1955–57*, vol. 4, pp. 262–63.

53. "Letter from the President of the High Authority," March 17, 1955; "Memorandum of a Conversation," April 20, 1955; "Memorandum of a Conversation," April 20, 1955, all in Department of State, *Foreign Relations of the United States, 1955–57*, vol. 4, pp. 275–76, 283–89.

54. "Report by the Department of State," March 16, 1955.

55. "Report by the Foreign Operations Administration," March 16, 1955.

56. "Report by the Department of State," October 28, 1955, in Department of State, *Foreign Relations of the United States, 1955–1957*, vol. 4, pp. 342–43.

57. "Minutes of the 34th Meeting of the Council on Foreign Economic Policy," December 20, 1955, in Department of State, *Foreign Relations of the United States, 1955–57*, vol. 4, p. 373.

58. Memorandum, Miss Dennison to Mr. Humelsine, May 11, 1948, and R. E. Freer to Harry Truman, April 29, 1948, both in White House Central Files,

Confidential Files, Box 39, State Department Correspondence, 1948–49 (2 of 6), Harry S. Truman Library, Independence, Mo. Agreements granting aid contained provisions requiring "appropriate measures . . . to prevent, on the part of private or public commercial enterprises, business practices or business arrangements affecting international trade which have the effect of . . . interfering with the achievement of the joint program of European Recovery."

59. Charles S. Maier, *In Search of Stability: Explorations in Historical Political Economy* (Cambridge: Cambridge University Press), 1987.

60. "Report by the Foreign Operations Administration," March 16, 1955.

61. Edwards, *Control of Cartels and Monopolies*, pp. 337–69.

62. Tony Freyer, *Regulating Big Business: Antitrust in Great Britain and America, 1880–1990* (Cambridge: Cambridge University Press, 1992), pp. 295–98.

63. James Atwood and Kingman Brewster, *Antitrust and American Business Abroad*, 2nd ed. (Colorado Springs: McGraw-Hill, 1981), vol. 1, p. 4.

Conclusions

1. Richard Hofstadter, "What Happened to the Antitrust Movement?" in *The Paranoid Style in American Politics and Other Essays* (New York: Vintage Books, 1967), p. 188.

2. Antitrust Division, "Cartels and General Post-War Policy," Thurman Arnold Papers, Box 29, Correspondence, November 1942, American Heritage Center, University of Wyoming, Laramie.

3. Memorandum of Conversation with Baron Boel, February 23, 1945, Jasper E. Crane Papers, Box 832, Correspondence, Foreign Relations Department, 1940–45, Hagley Museum and Library, Wilmington, Del.

4. Alan S. Milward, *The Reconstruction of Western Europe, 1945–1951* (London: Routledge, 1984), pp. 362–420.

5. Harm Schröter, "Small European Nations: Cooperative Capitalism in the Twentieth Century," in Alfred Chandler, Franco Amatori, and Takashi Hinkino, eds., *Big Business and the Wealth of Nations* (Cambridge: Cambridge University Press, 1997), pp. 201–2.

6. Ibid.

7. Alfred Chandler, Jr., *Scale and Scope: The Dynamics of Industrial Capitalism* (Cambridge, Mass.: Belknap Press, 1990).

8. Steven Tolliday tells the sad story of British steel in *Business, Banking, and Politics: The Case of British Steel, 1918–1939* (Cambridge, Mass.: Belknap Press, 1987).

9. Susan K. Sell discusses these issues in *Power and Ideas: North–South Politics of Intellectual Property and Antitrust* (Albany: State University of New York Press, 1998).

Essay on Sources

Sources on antitrust and the creation of the postwar world are numerous but widely scattered. Scholars have examined various facets of the matter in the course of studying other subjects such as the creation of the European Coal and Steel Community, the postwar reconstruction of Japan, and the histories of various firms. No one, however, has examined the story as a whole.

The press did cover many aspects of the process. The *New York Times*, the *Wall Street Journal*, *Time*, *Newsweek*, *The Nation*, the *New Republic*, and *Business Week* all contain informative articles. The Wendell Berge Papers in the Library of Congress in Washington, D.C., contain a large collection of press clippings from regional papers on the subject.

Chapter 1. The Cartel Ideal

In the 1930s and 1940s, many scholars published general studies of cartels, including Ervin Hexner, *International Cartels* (Chapel Hill: University of North Carolina Press, 1946); Kenneth L. Mayall, *International Cartels: Economic and Political Aspects* (Rutland, Vt.: Tuttle, 1948); Robert Liefmann, *Cartels, Concerns and Trusts* (London: Methuen, 1932); Karl Pribam, *Cartel Problems: An Analysis of Collective Monopolies in Europe with American Application* (Buffalo, N.Y.: Hein, 1937); and George W. Stocking and Myron W. Watkins, *Cartels in Action: Case Studies in International Business Diplomacy* (New York: Twentieth Century Fund, 1946), and *Cartels or Competition: The Economics of International Controls by Business and Government* (New York: Twentieth Century Fund, 1948). Narrower examinations of various aspects of the subject include the League of Nations World Economic

Conference, *Final Report* (C.E.I. 44), June 3, 1927; Leisa G. Bronson, *Cartels and International Patent Agreements* (Washington, D.C.: Library of Congress Reference Service, 1944); Edouard Herriot, *The United States of Europe* (New York: Viking Press, 1930); and William Oualid, *International Raw Materials Cartels* (Paris: International Institute of Intellectual Cooperation, League of Nations, 1938).

Since 1950, such studies have become rarer, but good ones do exist. They include Kingman Brewster, *Antitrust and American Business Abroad* (New York: McGraw-Hill, 1958); Tony Freyer, *Regulating Big Business: Antitrust in Great Britain and America, 1880–1990* (Cambridge: Cambridge University Press, 1992); Akira Kudo and Terushi Hara, eds., *International Cartels in Business History: International Conference of Business History 18, Proceedings of the Fuji Conference* (Tokyo: University of Tokyo Press, 1992); Debora Spar, *The Cooperative Edge: The Internal Politics of International Cartels* (Ithaca, N.Y.: Cornell University Press, 1994); and Wilfried Feldenkirchen, "Big Business in Interwar Germany: Organizational Innovations at Vereinigte Stahlwerke, IG Farben, and Siemens," *Business History Review* 61 (1987): 417–51. William A. Brock and Jose A. Scheinkman, "Price Setting Supergames with Capacity Constraints," *Review of Economic Studies* 52 (1985): 371–82; D. K. Osborne, "Cartel Problems," *American Economic Review* 66 (1976): 835–44; and George J. Stigler, "A Theory of Oligopoly," *Journal of Political Economy* 72 (1964): 44–61, examine the economics of cartels. Alfred D. Chandler, Jr., *Scale and Scope: The Dynamics of Industrial Capitalism* (Cambridge, Mass.: Belknap Press, 1990), and Alfred Chandler, Franco Amatori, and Takashi Hikino, eds., *Big Business and the Wealth of Nations* (Cambridge: Cambridge University Press, 1997), place cartels in a broader context.

Ervin Hexner, *The International Steel Cartel* (Chapel Hill: University of North Carolina Press, 1943); Richard A. Lauderbaugh, *American Steel Makers and the Coming of the Second World War* (Ann Arbor, Mich.: UMI Research Press, 1980); and Daniel Barbezat, "Comptoir Sidérurgique de France, 1930–1939," *Business History Review* 70 (1996): 517–40, all chronicle the activities of the international steel cartel. For electrical equipment, see Federal Trade Commission, *Report on International Electrical Equipment Cartels* (Washington, D.C.: Government Printing Office, 1948); U.S. Congress, Temporary National Economic Committee, *Investigation of Concentration of Economic Power: Monograph No. 31, Patents and Free Enterprise*, 76th Cong., 3rd sess., 1940; Arthur A. Bright, *The Electric-Lamp Industry: Technological Change and Economic Development from 1800 to 1947* (New York: Macmillan, 1949); and Leonard S. Reich, "Lighting the Path to Profit: GE's Control of the Electric Lamp Industry, 1892–1941," *Business History Review* 66 (1992): 305–34. Of particular value are court decisions in the antitrust cases involving General Electric, which discuss matters of fact as well as of law. These include *United States* v. *General Electric Company et al.*, 272 U.S. 476; *United States* v. *General Electric Co. et al.*, 80 F. Supp. 989; and *United States* v. *General Electric Co. et al.*, 82 F. Supp. 753.

Stocking and Watkins, *Cartels in Action*, and Hexner, *International Cartels*, contain information on the rubber cartel.

Chapter 2. The Context of Antitrust

Alfred D. Chandler, Jr., *The Visible Hand: The Managerial Revolution in American Business* (Cambridge, Mass.: Belknap Press, 1977), and Robert H. Wiebe, *The Search for Order, 1877–1920* (New York: Hill and Wang, 1967), give overviews of the economic and social transformation of American society in the late nineteenth and early twentieth centuries. Thomas McCraw, *Prophets of Regulation: Charles Francis Adams, Louis D. Brandeis, James M. Landis, Alfred E. Kahn* (Cambridge, Mass.: Belknap Press, 1984), and "Rethinking the Trust Question," in Thomas McCraw, ed., *Regulation in Perspective* (Cambridge, Mass.: Harvard University Press, 1981), examine attitudes toward big business during this period. Freyer, *Regulating Big Business*, and A. D. Neale, *The Antitrust Laws of the United States of America: A Study of Competition Enforced by Law* (Cambridge: Cambridge University Press, 1960), trace the evolution of antitrust laws. Louis D. Brandeis, *Other People's Money; and How the Bankers Use It* (Fairfield, Conn.: Kelly, 1986), and *The Curse of Bigness* (New York: Viking Press, 1935); Herbert Croly, *The Promise of American Life* (New York: Macmillan, 1909); Theodore Roosevelt, *The New Nationalism* (New York: Outlook, 1911); and Woodrow Wilson, *The New Freedom: A Call for the Emancipations of the Generous Energies of a People* (Englewood Cliffs, N.J.: Prentice-Hall, 1961), all elucidate Progressive Era attitudes toward big business. Ellis Hawley, ed., *Herbert Hoover as Secretary of Commerce: Studies in New Era Thought and Practice* (Iowa City: University of Iowa Press, 1981); Ellis Hawley, *The New Deal and the Problem of Monopoly: A Study in Economic Ambivalence* (Princeton, N.J.: Princeton University Press, 1966); and Robert F. Himmelberg, *The Origins of the National Recovery Administration: Business, Government, and the Trade Association Issue, 1921–1933* (New York: Fordham University Press, 1993), bring the story of antitrust up through the 1930s. Otis Graham provides an interesting perspective on intellectual developments in "The Planning Ideal and American Reality: The 1930s," in Stanley Elkins and Erik McKitrick, eds., *The Hofstadter Aegis: A Memorial* (New York: Knopf, 1974). Gerard Swope, "The Swope Plan—Details," in J. George Frederick, ed., *The Swope Plan: Details, Criticisms, Analysis* (New York: Business Bourse, 1931), constitutes the chief American defense of cartels.

For the antitrust drive in Roosevelt's second administration, see Hawley, *New Deal and the Problem of Monopoly*; Alan Brinkley, *The End of Reform: New Deal Liberalism in Recession and War* (New York: Vintage Books, 1995); and the publications of the Temporary National Economic Committee, particularly its final report, *In-*

vestigation of Concentrations of Economic Power, 77th Cong., 1st sess., 1941. Of particular value are the papers of the chair of the TNEC, Senator Joseph O'Mahoney, in the American Heritage Center at the University of Wyoming, Laramie. O'Mahoney collected papers from bureaus throughout the government, as well as some from outside it, and there are few aspects of the drive to make the world safe for competition on which this collection does not touch.

The first source on Thurman Arnold is his own papers in the American Heritage Center. See also the collection of his letters edited by Gene M. Gressley, *Voltaire and the Cowboy: The Letters of Thurman Arnold* (Boulder: Colorado Associated University Press, 1977), as well as Arnold's own books: *Folklore of Capitalism* (New Haven, Conn.: Yale University Press, 1937), *The Bottlenecks of Business* (New York: Reynal & Hitchcock, 1940), *Democracy & Free Enterprise* (Norman: University of Oklahoma Press, 1942), and *Fair Fights and Foul: A Dissenting Lawyer's Life* (New York: Harcourt, Brace & World, 1969). Alan Brinkley provides a scholarly assessment of Arnold's career in "The Antimonopoly Ideal and the Liberal State: The Case of Thurman Arnold," *Journal of American History* 80 (1993): 565–90.

Chapter 3. Reform versus Mobilization

Good histories of the American experience in World War II include John Morton Blum, *V Was for Victory: Politics and American Culture During World War II* (New York: Harvest Books, 1976); Brinkley, *End of Reform*; Bruce Catton, *The War Lords of Washington* (New York: Harcourt, Brace, 1948); William L. O'Neill, *A Democracy at War: America's Fight at Home and Abroad in World War II* (New York: Free Press, 1993); and Richard Polenberg, *War and Society: The United States, 1941–45* (New York: Lippincott, 1972).

For the development of chemical cartels before 1939, as well as their wartime experience, see the DuPont Records at the Hagley Museum and Library in Wilmington, Delaware, in particular the Walter S. Carpenter Papers, the Jasper E. Crane Papers, and the files of DuPont's Foreign Relations Committee. Thurman Arnold's papers also contain much material on the subject. Useful books include Peter Hayes, *Industry and Ideology: IG Farben in the Nazi Era* (Cambridge: Cambridge University Press, 1987); Henrietta Larson, Evelyn H. Knowleton, and Charles S. Popple, *New Horizons: History of Standard Oil Company (New Jersey), 1927–1950* (New York: Harper & Row, 1971); W. J. Reader, *Imperial Chemical Industries: A History*, vol. 1, *The Forerunners, 1870–1926*; vol. 2, *The First Quarter-Century, 1926–1952* (London: Oxford University Press, 1975); and Graham D. Taylor and Patricia E. Sudnik, *DuPont and the International Chemical Cartels* (Boston: Twayne, 1984). U.S. Senate, Special Committee Investigating the National Defense Program, *Investigation of the National Defense Program: Part 11, Rubber*, 77th Cong., 1st sess., 1942, outlines the agreements between Standard Oil and IG Farben. The papers in the Roy A. Pewitt Files in the National Archives in Washington, D.C., Record Group 122, contain much of the information compiled during the war by the Federal Trade Commission on international cartels.

Arnold's papers contain much information on the Antitrust Division's offensive against international cartels in 1940 and 1941, as do those of Wendell Berge. George Edward Smith, *From Monopoly to Competition: The Transformation of Alcoa* (Cambridge: Cambridge University Press, 1988), chronicles Alcoa's encounters with the antitrust laws. Several congressional hearings contain valuable information as well: U.S. House, Committee on Patents, *Preventing Publication of Inventions and Prohibiting Injunctions on Patents*, 77th Cong., 2nd sess., 1941; U.S. Senate, Committee on Patents, *Patents*, 77th Cong., 2nd sess., 1942; and U.S. Senate, Subcommittee on Scientific and Technical Mobilization of the Committee on Technical Mobilization, *Scientific and Technical Mobilization*, 78th Cong., 1st sess., 1943, and 78th Cong., 2nd sess., 1944. *Ethyl Gasoline Corporation et al.* v. *United States*, 309 U.S. 453, is the chief decision that the Antitrust Division secured against patent cartels during this period.

Department of State, *Foreign Relations of the United States, Diplomatic Papers, 1943*, vol. 1, *General* (Washington, D.C.: Government Printing Office, 1963), and *Foreign Relations of the United States, Diplomatic Papers, 1944*, vol. 2, *General: Economic and Social Matters* (Washington, D.C.: Government Printing Office, 1967), contain information on wartime commodity accords, as do the O'Mahoney Papers. The chief sources for the rubber case are the Senate hearings *Investigation of the National Defense Program: Part 11, Rubber*, and Larson, Knowleton, and Popple, *New Horizons*. Papers of Harry S. Truman in the Senatorial File at the Truman Presidential Library in Independence, Missouri, also contain a good deal of information, including some unpublished hearings. The Franklin D. Roosevelt Library at Hyde Park, New York, has much information on antitrust during the war, particularly in the Office Files, Personal Secretary's Files, Secretary's Files, and Francis Biddle Papers. The Senate hearings *Scientific and Technical Mobilization* contain discussion of patent reform, but O'Mahoney's papers are the chief source on congressional action (or inaction) on cartels. The DuPont Records as well as the National Association of Manufacturers (NAM) Papers at the Hagley Museum and Library give industry's views on cartel legislation.

Chapter 4. Making the World Safe for Competition

Polemical works during and immediately after World War II dealing with cartels are numerous. They include United Nations, Department of Economic Affairs, *International Cartels: A League of Nations Memorandum* (New York: United Nations

Publications, 1947) (drafted by Corwin Edwards); U.S. Senate, Subcommittee on War Mobilization of the Committee on Military Affairs, *Economic and Political Aspects of International Cartels*, 78th Cong., 2nd sess., 1944 (also by Edwards); U.S. Senate, Subcommittee on War Mobilization to the Committee on Military Affairs, *Cartels and National Security*, 79th Cong., 2nd sess., 1944; Howard Watson Ambruster, *Treason's Peace: German Dyes & American Dupes* (New York: Beechhurst, 1947); Wendell Berge, *Cartels: Challenge to a Free World* (Washington, D.C.: Public Affairs Press, 1944); Joseph Borkin and Charles A. Welsh, *Germany's Master Plan: The Story of Industrial Offensive* (New York: Duell, Sloan and Pearce, 1943); Robert A. Brady, *The Spirit and Structure of German Fascism* (London: Gollancz, 1937); Bronson, *Cartels and International Patent Agreements*; Josiah E. Dubois, *The Devil's Chemists: 24 Conspirators of the International Farben Cartel Who Manufacture Wars* (Boston: Beacon Press, 1952); Franz Neuman, *Behemoth: The Structure and Practice of National Socialism* (London: Gollancz, 1942); Guenter Reimann, *Patents for Hitler* (London: Gollancz, 1945); and Charles R. Whittelsey, *National Interests and International Cartels* (New York: Macmillan, 1946). Joseph Borkin's *The Crime and Punishment of IG Farben* (New York: Free Press, 1978) constitutes a more scholarly update on the evils of cartels and German business in general.

The NAM Papers are an excellent source for business opinion on cartels. NAM summed up its position on the subject in *NAM Looks at Cartels: Positions Formulated by the Committee on International Economic Relations and Approved by the Board of Directors Together with an Analysis of the Economic Aspects of Cartels Prepared by the Research Department* (New York: National Association of Manufacturers, 1946). Anton de Haas provided one of the few American defenses of cartels in *International Cartels in the Postwar World* (Washington, D.C.: American Enterprise Association, 1945). Evidence of British opinion is to be found in the DuPont Records, in the Berge and O'Mahoney Papers, in the Clayton-Thorp Papers at the Truman Library, as well as in the Records of the State Department and in the Harley Notter Papers, both Record Group 59 in the National Archives. The best source, however, is probably the Foreign Office Records in the Public Records Office in Kew, England.

Berge's papers as well as the Office Files, Personal Secretary's Files, Secretary's Files, and Biddle Papers at the Roosevelt Library all contain information on the revival of antitrust after 1944. The Pewitt Files also offer a good deal of information, particularly on the alkali case. Charles W. Cheape, *Strictly Business: Walter Carpenter at DuPont and General Motors* (Baltimore: Johns Hopkins University Press, 1995), provides the perspective of a leading corporate executive on these events. Reader, *Imperial Chemical Industries*, and Taylor and Sudnik, *DuPont and the International Chemical Cartel*, are useful sources as well. The Dupont Records are valuable for both DuPont's and ICI's reaction to antitrust prosecutions.

The Notter Papers contain all the memos and minutes of the Cartel Committee, and Harley Notter's *Postwar Foreign Policy Preparation, 1939–1945*, General Foreign Policy Series, no. 15 (Washington, D.C.: Department of State, 1949), deals extensively with the subject as well. The British Foreign Office Records include information on negotiations between Washington and London on cartels and on the development of the ITO. Other sources on efforts to restructure the international economy during and after the war include Department of State, *Foreign Relations of the United States, Diplomatic Papers, 1942*, vol. 1, *General: The British Commonwealth; The Far East* (Washington, D.C.: Government Printing Office, 1960); *Foreign Relations of the United States, Diplomatic Papers, 1945*, vol. 6, *The British Commonwealth; The Far East* (Washington, D.C.: Government Printing Office, 1969); *Foreign Relations of the United States, 1945*, vol. 2, *General: Political and Economic Matters* (Washington, D.C.: Government Printing Office, 1967); *Foreign Relations of the United States, 1946*, vol. 1, *General: The United Nations* (Washington, D.C.: Government Printing Office, 1972); *Foreign Relations of the United States, 1947*, vol. 1, *General: The United Nations* (Washington, D.C.: Government Printing Office, 1973); and *Foreign Relations of the United States, 1948*, vol. 1, *General: The United Nations* (Washington, D.C.: Government Printing Office, 1974); Susan Aaronson, *Trade and the American Dream: A Social History of Postwar Trade Policy* (Lexington: University Press of Kentucky, 1996); Richard N. Gardner, *Sterling–Dollar Diplomacy: The Origins and the Prospects of Our International Economic Order* (New York: McGraw-Hill, 1969); and R. F. Harrod, *The Life of John Maynard Keynes* (New York: Discus Books, 1951). Information on the fate of the ITO comes from the Clayton-Thorp Papers, the Tom Clark Papers, the White House Central Files, and the William L. Clayton Papers, all in the Truman Library.

Court decisions in the antitrust cases, which address questions of fact as well as of law, are among the best sources on the cases themselves. They include *Timken Roller Bearing Co. v. United States*, 341 U.S. 593; *United States v. General Electric Company et al.*, 272 U.S. 476; *United States v. General Electric Co. et al.*, 80 F. Supp. 989; *United States v. General Electric Co. et al.*, 82 F. Supp. 753; *United States v. Imperial Chemical Industries Limited et al.*, 100 F. Supp. 504; *United States v. Imperial Chemical Industries Limited et al.*, 105 F. Supp. 215; *United States v. Line Material Co. et al.*, 333 U.S. 287; *United States v. Minnesota Mining & Manufacturing Co. et al.*, 92 F. Supp. 947; *United States v. National Lead Co. et al.*, 63 F. Supp. 513; *United States v. National Lead Co. et al.*, 333 U.S. 364; *United States v. National Lead Co. et al.*, 333 U.S. 319; *United States v. Timken Roller Bearing Co.*, 83 F. Supp. 284; *United States v. United States Alkali Export Association, Inc., et al.*, 86 F. Supp. 59; and *United States v. United States Gypsum Co. et al.*, 333 U.S. 364. Mira Wilkins, *The Maturing of Multinational Enterprise: American Business Abroad from 1914 to 1970* (Cambridge, Mass.: Harvard University Press, 1974), contains valuable information on the response of American firms to the changing legal atmosphere.

Chapter 5. Among Unbelievers: Antitrust in Germany and Japan

John Lewis Gaddis, *The United States and the Origins of the Cold War, 1941–1947* (New York: Columbia University Press, 1972), discusses postwar planning. The Notter Papers contains information on plans for decartelization and deconcentration in both Germany and Japan, as does Notter's book, *Postwar Policy Preparation*. Hearings by the U.S. Senate, *Cartels and National Security*, provide a view from the legislative branch.

The chief sources on the occupation of Germany are the Records of the Office of Military Government and the Records of the Office of the High Commissioner, Record Group 260 and 446, respectively, in the National Archives, as well as the British government's Foreign Office Files. Other primary sources include Lucius D. Clay, *The Papers of General Lucius D. Clay*, ed. Jean Edward Smith (Bloomington: Indiana University Press, 1974), and Department of State, *Germany, 1947–1949: The Story in Documents* (Washington, D.C.: Government Printing Office, 1950). Lucius Clay's memoirs, *Decision in Germany* (Garden City, N.Y.: Doubleday, 1950), are useful, as are those of James Stewart Martin, *All Honorable Men* (Boston: Little, Brown, 1950). Secondary sources include Volker R. Berghahn, *The Americanization of West German Industry, 1945–1973* (Cambridge: Cambridge University Press, 1986); Carolyn Woods Eisenberg, *Drawing the Line: The American Decision to Divide Germany, 1944–1949* (Cambridge: Cambridge University Press, 1996); Gregory A. Fossedal, *Our Finest Hour: Will Clayton, the Marshall Plan, and the Triumph of Democracy* (Stanford, Calif.: Hoover Institution Press, 1993); John Gimbel, *The American Occupation of Germany: Politics and the Military, 1945–49* (Stanford, Calif.: Stanford University Press, 1968); Martin F. Parnell, *The German Tradition of Organized Capitalism* (Oxford: Clarendon Press, 1994); Thomas Alan Schwartz, *America's Germany: John J. McCloy and the Federal Republic of Germany* (Cambridge, Mass.: Harvard University Press, 1991); and Jean Edward Smith, *Lucius D. Clay: An American Life* (New York: Holt, 1990). François Duchene, *Jean Monnet: The First Statesman of Interdependence* (New York: Norton, 1994), chronicles the creation of the European Coal and Steel Community.

The chief source on occupied Japan is the Records of the Supreme Command for the Allied Powers, Record Group 331, in the National Archives. The microfilms of the "History of the Nonmilitary Activities of the Occupation of Japan," Supreme Command for the Allied Powers, in the National Archives, is quite valuable as well. Also useful are Department of State, *Foreign Relations of the United States, Diplomatic Papers, 1945*, vol. 6, *The British Commonwealth; The Far East* (Washington, D.C.: Government Printing Office, 1969); *Foreign Relations of the United States, 1947*, vol. 6, *The Far East* (Washington, D.C.: Government Printing Office, 1972); and *Foreign Relations of the United States, 1948*, vol. 6, *The Far East and Australasia* (Washington: Government Printing Office, 1974). George Kennan's *Memoirs, 1925–1950* (New York: Pantheon Books, 1967), contains information on key decisions.

Studies of postwar Japan include William S. Borden, *The Pacific Alliance: United States Economic Policy and Japanese Trade Recovery, 1947–1955* (Madison: University of Wisconsin Press, 1984); J. W. Dower, *Empire and Aftermath: Yoshida Shigeru and the Japanese Experience, 1878–1954* (Cambridge, Mass.: Harvard University Press, 1979); Eleanor M. Hadley, *Antitrust in Japan* (Princeton, N.J.: Princeton University Press, 1970); Michael Shaller, *The American Occupation of Japan: The Origins of the Cold War in Asia* (New York: Oxford University Press, 1985); and Howard B. Schonberger, *Aftermath of War: Americans and the Remaking of Japan, 1945–1952* (Kent, Ohio: Kent State University Press, 1989).

Chapter 6. The New Order in Practice: The Cases of Oil and Steel

Daniel Yergin's classic, *The Prize: The Epic Quest for Oil, Money, and Power* (New York: Touchstone Books, 1991), provides an excellent history of the petroleum industry. Equally valuable for cartels are U.S. Senate, Subcommittee on Multinational Corporations of the Committee on Foreign Relations, *Multinational Corporations and United States Foreign Policy*, 93rd Cong., 2nd sess., 1974, and Federal Trade Commission, *The International Petroleum Cartel* (Washington, D.C.: Government Printing Office, 1952). Larson, Knowleton, and Popple, *New Horizons*, deals extensively with the activities of the petroleum cartels, as do chapters in Robert F. Himmelberg, ed., *Antitrust and Business Regulation in the Postwar Era, 1946–1964* (New York: Garland, 1994). The Office Files, Personal Secretary's Files, and Secretary's Files at the Roosevelt Library contain information on the Anglo-American Oil Accord, and the files in the Ralph K. Davies Papers in the Truman Library have documents relating to these negotiations as well as to the postwar petroleum cartel.

Department of State, *Foreign Relations of the United States, 1955–57*, vol. 4, *Western European Security and Integration* (Washington, D.C.: Government Printing Office, 1986), chronicles American policy toward the European Coal and Steel Community. Books on the spread of antitrust worldwide include Corwin Edwards, *Control of Cartels and Monopolies: An International Comparison* (Dobbs Ferry, N.Y.: Oceana, 1967); Charles S. Maier, *In Search of Stability: Explorations in Historical Political Economy* (Cambridge: Cambridge University Press, 1987); Helen Mercer, *Constructing a Competitive Order: The Hidden History of British Antitrust Policies* (Cambridge: Cambridge University Press, 1995); Freyer, *Regulating Big Business*; and Brewster, *Antitrust and American Business Abroad*.

Index